Global Perspectives on E-Learning

*To my parents, Dr. and Mrs. Richard D. Carr, who taught me to question,
and
my husband, Davin Carr-Chellman, who helps me find answers.*

Global Perspectives on E-LEARNING

Rhetoric and Reality

Editor
Alison A. Carr-Chellman
Pennsylvania State University

SAGE Publications
Thousand Oaks ■ London ■ New Delhi

Copyright © 2005 by Sage Publications, Inc.

All rights reserved. No part of this book may be reproduced or utilized in any form or by any means, electronic or mechanical, including photocopying, recording, or by any information storage and retrieval system, without permission in writing from the publisher.

For information:

Sage Publications, Inc.
2455 Teller Road
Thousand Oaks, California 91320
E-mail: order@sagepub.com

Sage Publications Ltd.
1 Oliver's Yard
55 City Road
London EC1Y 1SP
United Kingdom

Sage Publications India Pvt. Ltd.
B-42, Panchsheel Enclave
Post Box 4109
New Delhi 110 017 India

Printed in the United States of America

Library of Congress Cataloging-in-Publication Data

Global perspectives on e-learning: Rhetoric and reality / edited by Alison A. Carr-Chellman.
   p. cm.
Includes bibliographical references and index.
ISBN 1-4129-0488-9 (cloth) — ISBN 1-4129-0489-7 (pbk.)
  1. Distance education. 2. Education—Effect of technological innovations on. 3. Educational technology—Social aspects.
I. Carr-Chellman, Alison A.
LC5800.G56 2005
371.35′8—dc22
                                     2004016442

This book is printed on acid-free paper.

04 05 06 07 08 10 9 8 7 6 5 4 3 2 1

Acquisitions Editor:	Diane McDaniel
Editorial Assistant:	Margo Beth Crouppen
Production Editor:	Julia Parnell/Diana E. Axelsen
Typesetter:	C&M Digitals (P) Ltd.
Indexer:	Jeanne Busemeyer
Cover Designer:	Janet Foulger

CONTENTS

Acknowledgments	vii
Introduction	1
Alison A. Carr-Chellman	
Matrix of Case Studies	14

**Part I: Online Education in Asia:
An Analysis of China, Taiwan, and India**   **17**

1. China's Online Education: Rhetoric and Realities   21
   Ke Zhang

2. The Gap Between E-Learning Availability and
   E-Learning Industry Development in Taiwan   33
   Jiang Jia Qi

3. Distance Education and Online Technologies in India   52
   Priya Sharma

**Part II: Online Education in Europe: An Analysis of Ireland,
the United Kingdom, Turkey, and International Study Circles**   **67**

4. Online Learning and Differential Participation
   in a Democratic Society: Ireland as a Case Study   71
   Sarah FitzPatrick and Paul Conway

5. E-Learning, Democracy, and Social
   Exclusion: Issues of Access and Retention in the United Kingdom   89
   Ormond Simpson

6. International Study Circles   101
   Ben Salt

7. A Critical Look at Distance Education in Turkey   115
   Husra Gursoy

**Part III: Online Education in North America:
An Analysis of the U.S. and Canadian Contributions** 127

  8. Canada's SchoolNet: Wiring Up Schools? 131
     Leslie R. Shade and Diane Y. Dechief

  9. The New Frontier: Web-Based Education in U.S. Culture 145
     Alison A. Carr-Chellman

**Part IV: Online Education Down Under:
An Analysis of Aotearoa/New Zealand and Australia** 161

  10. New Zealand: Is Online Education a Highway to the Future? 163
     Bill Anderson

  11. Towards Borderless Virtual Learning in Higher Education 179
     Colin Latchem

**Part V: Online Education in Africa:
An Analysis of Namibia and Sub-Saharan Africa** 199

  12. Development and Democracy in Namibia: The Contribution
     of Information and Communication Technologies (ICTs) 205
     R. Kavena Shalyefu and Hilda Nakakuwa

  13. Can You Lead From Behind? Critical Reflections
     on the Rhetoric of E-Learning, Open Distance Learning,
     and ICTs for Development in Sub-Saharan Africa (SSA) 222
     Wayne Mackintosh

  14. Stalled: E-Learning as Thwarted Innovation 241
     Robert Zemsky and William F. Massy

Conclusion 257
     Alison A. Carr-Chellman

Index 261

About the Editor 275

About the Contributors 277

ACKNOWLEDGMENTS

I would like to acknowledge the help of many people who have assisted in the preparation of this book including all of the authors whose hard work made this critique of e-learning possible. I am deeply appreciative of the assistance of Diane McDaniel and everyone at Sage who helped me through this first book project. I am grateful for the help of my colleagues at Penn State who have read and reviewed this work at various stages in its development and have helped me to formulate a much stronger critique as a result of their feedback. I also acknowledge the assistance of the following reviewers, who were invaluable in their help to improve this work:

Roberto Muffoletto, Appalachian State University
Paul Gathercoal, California Lutheran University
Chris Zirkle, Ohio State University
Don Ely, Syracuse University
Mike Hannafin, University of Georgia

Finally, I would also very much like to thank Brain Loader and the people at *Information, Communication & Society* journal who helped us get started on this project by publishing earlier versions of the chapters on the United States, China, Ireland, and International Study Circles in 2000. I am deeply grateful for their early assistance in this important work.

INTRODUCTION

Alison A. Carr-Chellman

The goal of shaping information technology to democratize education is highly appealing, but there are, at present, no strong well-organized forces promoting that end.

—L. Winner, 1998

Online education has been heralded as the next democratizing force in education, particularly in higher education (Daniel, 1996; Jones, 1997). By opening access to populations which have not had access either because of geographical location, job status, or physical handicap, the rhetoric of online education suggests that this new technology will democratize education, breaking down the elitist walls of the ivory tower. However, it is not at all clear that the reality of implementing distance learning solutions have in fact any potential, much less actual value for democratizing higher education. Much the opposite, founded on the myth of the meritocracy, online education has the potential to exacerbate already intractable views of individual achievement through education as rectifying failures to meet the needs of disadvantaged populations. This text presents several cases of international online education and the rhetoric that surrounds its introduction.

It has been many decades since higher education has seen a true democratic revolution. Perhaps the last great opening of the university gates in the United States was due to the G.I. bill, which brought many service people who otherwise could not have afforded higher education into residential university life. Since that time, the debate over the extent to which the higher education system serves as a democratizing force or an elitist institution has waxed and waned.

Online education, particularly online degree programs, promise to be the next force for democratizing higher education. And very few have critiqued this movement. David Noble (1998) is perhaps one of the first, and most outspoken critics, offering a historical perspective linking correspondence education with online learning. Most critiques were focused on the degradation of quality inherent in distance education schemes. But advocates point to open access as the most compelling reason to formulate public policy and public budgets which favor online technologies for delivering higher education, not only in the United States, but globally. This book examines the rhetoric of democracy that surrounds the call for online higher education in general and the ways that rhetoric meets with reality.

THE CASE FOR DEMOCRACY

There is no question that online education is the fastest growing market segment of adult education. Although this area only amounted to somewhere around $550 million of the adult education market in 1998, the growth expectations are phenomenal. Some have suggested that adults will be spending upwards of $9.3 billion by 2003 (Beer, 1999). It is clear that online education is a potential gold mine, but in general, the profit motive is not what is most often cited as the rationale for expanding online higher education programs globally. When politicians speak about distance education and allocating public funds for technologies to support online degree programs, they prefer open access and democracy to crass profit as a supporting justification. But the views on the democratizing effects of online higher education vary from full support accompanied by cries of elitism, to full rejection accompanied by cries of Luddite.

Issues of Open Access

For most of us, the idea of open access—the elimination of elitism as a function of place and prestige—holds the promise of equity. The basic premise of the rhetoric of democracy in online education is that if we can make education available to those who currently must work to earn a living and cannot attend residential programs because of geography or family obligations, then we are making these opportunities available more equitably. In making the case for convergence of means as opposed to convocation of location as a founding principle for organizing the university, Hall (1995) points out the inherently exclusive nature of university life:

> In fact, all of the university's traditions and practices assume that scarcity is the controlling condition of educational opportunity. As a result, the opportunity for students to pursue a university education must be rationed, parceled out, limited to those most qualified to benefit from it. To a remarkable extent, this sense of scarcity drives the assumption and understandings about what university learning is and should be, fostering a sense of exclusivity among those who guard the gate. (p. 5)

The premise has substance. As Gubernick and Ebeling (1997) suggest,

> Modern technology brings education to the students rather than forcing students to subsidize fancy campuses and featherbedding faculties. Not coincidentally, it makes it possible for all students—not just those at the fanciest colleges—to have access to the best lecturers and the best teachers. . . . Online education makes it possible for students all over the world to study at prestigious U.S. schools without leaving their homes. (p. 85)

Indeed, the promise of online education is to bring institutions that have been deeply entrenched in elitist notions of prestige and privilege into an era of open access. At a recent meeting of faculty most interested in the future of online education (Winner, 1998), Phil Agre called for the collapse of the "long presupposed distance between the educated person and the rest of society." He suggested that online learning may be a way to shorten that distance, "The model of liberal education depended on a kind of leisure that our students mostly don't have and do not expect to have and can't identify with." Instead, there is hope, Agre suggests, for "a positive democratic vision of what a liberal education is, one that would draw upon the power of digital technologies as an occasion for progressive social change" (Winner, 1998, p. 8).

In addition to open access as a way to move us beyond elitism, online education has the potential benefit of increased anonymity among participants. Although some would argue that this could be a deficit, increasing the problematics of building strong community, others (Hiltz & Wellman, 1997) suggest that this anonymity can create strong bonds among socially diverse groups: "The lack of traditional spatial and group constraints means that virtual communities are often heterogeneous in social characteristics, such as lifecycle, gender, ethnicity, and socioeconomic status" (p. 45). While this may be true, there is nothing inherent in the characteristics of the online media itself, which forces any sense of confrontation or contact with this diversity. There is no need in a completely anonymous space to share details about oneself, particularly should one be concerned that those details might be judged negatively by others in the online community. For instance, how likely is it that someone would suggest they are of a low class in an online education experience? And without this information, which may be ascertained in face-to-face contacts through various other nonverbal, nontextual information, how likely is it that those involved in the online education experience will realize that they are involved in a diverse learning group? It is central to the construction of a viable democracy that diversity is recognized and celebrated rather than concealed. It is not inherent in online education to advance either of these agendas, but rather the media lends itself more to concealment than to revelation.

Finally, some theorists are concerned that while the rhetoric of open access appears to generate movement toward democratic goals, there is no evidence that this is likely within capitalist societies:

> The Internet has opened up very important space for progressive and democratic communication, especially for activists hamstrung by traditional commercial media. This alone has made the Internet an extremely positive development. Some have argued that the Internet will eventually break up the vise-like grip of the global media monopoly and provide the basis for a golden age of free, uncensored, democratic communication. Yet whether one can extrapolate from activist use of the Internet to seeing the Internet become a democratic medium for society writ large is another matter. The notion that the Internet will permit humanity to leapfrog over capitalism and corporate communication is in sharp contrast to the present rapid commercialization of the Internet. (McChesney, 1998, p. 21)

Thus, the concept of open access carries with it some substantive *possibility* toward a democratization of higher education. However, there are also many corresponding concerns that are justifiably voiced in association with online education approaches. As shall be shown in some of the cases of international distance education, the reality of open access can be far more complex than advocates and politicians may lead us to believe.

In general, one of the fundamental justifications for the need for open access of higher education is that it will allow those who cannot afford to attend traditional, residential colleges the opportunity to pursue higher education goals—and consequently to pursue advancement in their own careers. Deeply rooted in these arguments is the underlying assumption that the primary benefits of higher education are *vocational*. Clearly the benefits of a liberal education seem to be increasingly in question (Berube, 1998), and this trend is seen as a threat to the democratic goals of public higher education. As Van Dusen (1998) points out,

> In between, the ideal of public education, championed by Jefferson, Webster, and others, posited public citizenship and private virtue as culture's progress. Some of our literature continues to espouse these values. However, along the way, possibly following well-publicized critiques of public education, these traditional values became overshadowed—if not supplanted—by ones that are nakedly economic/utilitarian. (p. 67)

This theme is so strong in the online education community that it is rare to see any courses on Shakespeare, Kant, or impressionist painters offered online. Instead, cyberspace is flooded with courses on webmastery, business administration, educational leadership, and almost any sort of information technology/computer literacy one can imagine. It is certainly an admirable goal to help adult learners to gain vocational advantages via continued education. And it is a goal that has been well filled by many community colleges, university continuing education arms, and universities specializing in distance education, such as University of Phoenix, Walden, and Nova Southeastern University. This raises the question, is it truly a democratic goal which drives institutions such as University of Maryland, New York University, UCLA and even my own Penn State to offer primarily vocationally oriented degree programs online? What are the alternative explanations? It could be a move to try to offer more prestigious brand names to those who have traditionally had only the options listed above, which do not command high enough respect and corresponding salaries to make the learning effort worth many vocationally oriented students' while. Or it could be that administrators within higher-prestige institutions, pressured by decreases in governmental funding to higher education are seeking (and finding) new, very profitable markets.

The open access justification for online education programs is based on the concept that everyone can gain equitable access to those resources which are offered online. However, as many of our cases in this text will show, this is often not the case. While images of poor, rural South American farmers gaining access to new streams of revenue through Web design skills or e-commerce may be appealing, they are far from viable. The poorest adults, particularly in international contexts, may have no access to electricity or telephones, much less high-speed internet connections to institutions of higher education. The concept of "anywhere anytime" education on demand works only for those who already have access to technology in their homes and the funds to pay for online access charges. For the rest, they either don't have access or have to *travel* to gain access—creating the same problem that residential instruction presents. Hills (1998) points out the effects of the information superhighway to favor multinational corporations and the wealthy:

> In general, the restructuring of world telecommunications reflects the resurgence of the North and particularly the United States. Its domestic and international structure mirrors the increasing disparity between rich and poor. Despite the promise of cheaper technologies, the potential for their use to create greater democracy and equality, and the technological utopias such as the information superhighway—proselytized by the North as of benefit to the South—the reality of liberalization and privatization has been to benefit multinational companies and Northern mercantilist states. (p. 119)

With respect to the impacts of online education in the emerging global economy, the reality of public policies that favor the haves correspondingly punish the have-nots. It is important for those who wish to see the advance of democratization via international online education to pay close attention to the types of public policies and public budgets that are constructed. Careful analysis of the impacts of such policies and public financial decisions should focus on whom they truly benefit and whom they disadvantage.

Online education may widen the gap between haves and have-nots and produce a two-tiered educational system. As Winner (1998) points out, this split in educational institutions aligned with vocational goals may cause increased elitism rather than a breaking of the elitist monopoly on higher education,

> In the coming decade, higher education seems likely to split into two distinctly different sectors: (1) two hundred or so institutions that deliver high quality, face-to-face teaching for those slated to become social elites; and (2) several thousand semi-campus, semi-cyberspace, hybrid organizations—colleges, universities and business firms—ready to pump instruction and credentials to a flexible global workforce. (p. 9)

Throughout this text, you will see that it is strongly suggested that this widening gap between haves and have-nots is not so much about economies as it is about power.

If everyone has access to learning opportunities, have we created a more democratic system? Or is a system of higher education that somehow seeks to subvert dominant *power* dynamics a more democratic solution? In perhaps one of the most important statements of the relationship between democracy and the new technologies, Hirschkop (1998) clearly states that the inequitable distribution of information itself is not at the core of an undemocratic life. While acknowledging that the pursuit of knowledge is a noble act, he asserts that information has been widely available for some time and this alone will not alter the capitalist political structure of power currently in place:

> It was not a momentary loss of judgment (or the need for a savior in a dark age) that led so many on the left to delude themselves about the democratic possibilities of the new media. Belief in what technology could do depended on a fundamental misreading of the nature of liberal-capitalist states and of political power in the late 20th century. (p. 215)

Hirschkop further explicates what he means by the "nature of liberal-capitalist states" by exploring the attraction of the hope of technology as the undoing of the multinational corporation:

> Who can resist the poetic justice of corporate power selling its gravedigger to the masses, in inexpensive, high-tech form? But the attraction of poetic justice has always been that, unlike the real kind, one can sit and observe its progress. When the very structure of a society depends upon a lack of democracy, however, democracy will depend upon a fight, and upon social forces with the interests, will, and intelligence to struggle for it. Technology will doubtless have a role in this struggle, but it offers no shortcuts; one cannot buy democracy off a shelf or download it from a Web site. It demands courage, fortitude, and political organization, and, as far as we can see, Microsoft has yet to design software that can deliver these. (p. 217)

Indeed, the open access of information and learning opportunities hold the *promise* of democracy, moving information into the hands of the masses, but as long as the fundamental roots of power are not addressed, the struggle is not likely to commence. According to Dawson and Foster (1998), however, in such a wide and fast moving system as the Internet, there is hope and possibility for revolution:

> The worst fear of capital in the new information environment is that citizens will become informed and interactive in ways that go against plans for a commercialized I-way, and that challenges the entire political-economic universe as it is now constituted. They are right to be scared. For the powers to change society radically will continue to reside with the currently marginalized

majority. The rule of capital is rooted as much in the capacity to gain the consent of the governed—to obtain their collaboration in their own marginalization and exploitation—as it is in the actual material means of control. If virtual capitalism—the dream of Bill Gates—is an inverted world in which all of human culture increasingly serves the market, the mere possibility of resistance holds out the hope that it can be set right-side-up again, or better yet, transcended altogether. (pp. 64–65)

It is my view that it is not likely that this revolution will produce a "going against" of the main plans for commercialization and vocationalization of higher education online without an intentional effort to subvert the capitalist paradigm of profit and efficiency above all. It is possible that forces may collude to produce just such a revolution, but it will require a struggle against narrow definitions of educational market needs and a conscious effort to create more access opportunities to forcibly close the gap between haves and have-nots. The current online education movement includes little of this spirit and even less in the reality of implementation. In some cases, the rhetoric lines up with these goals, but the reality doesn't meet it. In other cases, the rhetoric itself is completely bereft of concern for social justice within online learning. Ultimately, the international cases in this book share a variety of stories that illuminate the ways in which this democratic goal may or may not be actualized in international contexts.

Issues of Individualization, Customization, and Globalization

One of the main criticisms of globalization is the underlying tendency to colonialize and import dominant paradigms into contexts that are either unfriendly to those paradigms or that can be harmed by those solutions. Approaches such as Rogers' (2003) diffusion of innovations to solving international problems do not respect the indigenous knowledge present in any given context and tend to view Western solutions as superior regardless of the systemic implications of those solutions in different cultures. This concern certainly does extend to online education. First, inherent within what is often perceived as a value-neutral tool (the computer technology necessary for online learning) are a number of culturally biased amplifications which reinforce "cultural patterns of thinking that have their roots in the Industrial Revolution" (Bowers, 1998, p. 51). Included among these amplifications according to Bowers are (1) context-free forms of knowledge; (2) conduit view of language; (3) Western view of autonomous individuals; (4) Western ways of experiencing time; (5) Western value of anthropocentrism; and (6) subjectively determined moral values.

Second, in order to fulfill the dreams of efficiency that make online education appealing to legislators and university administrators, customization and cultural sensitivity cannot be given adequate attention. Making a single course that is available around the world for anyone interested in it is efficient, but culturally and contextually bankrupt. Clark (1987) presents the argument that in globalizing any product, there is a certain amount of homogenizing that has to occur. In fact, given the market forces, it is imperative that the product is palatable to the largest majority of potential buyers. Thus in order to make something truly marketable globally, it is necessary to homogenize it:

> The people who fell asleep throughout this entire controversy were of course the 1.8 billion consumers on whom the controversy [of globalized marketplaces] allegedly centered. There was certainly no reason for them to know that they were all being herded into one global village where the process of homogenization could be more easily accomplished. (p. 30)

Canadian theorists Barlow & Robertson (1996) concerned with the impact of NAFTA as it applies to educational "products" clearly voice a concern for the cultural implications of homogenized educational products:

> The conscious recognition of the role of foreign corporations in the transformation of Canada may provoke the question, How will a Canadian public system, serving our needs and transmitting our culture and social commitment, survive? To remodel a society, it is essential to influence the hearts and minds of the young. At its most basic level, the assault on Canada's education system is an attack on the history, culture, and values of the nation itself. (p. 70)

How much more substantive is this concern when the cultures are more varied? How can American professors, instructional designers, and Web educators realistically be expected to anticipate the cultural needs and contextual sensitivities necessary to create a course deliverable worldwide? Or will we focus instead on creating completely homogenized courses that will not offend anyone from Kazakhstan to California? Can education *be* homogenized? What real-world examples will be acceptable to use in a global course on, say, the basics of business ethics? Isn't learning necessarily contextualized in our own cultures and contexts? This is one of many questions this book takes up seriously in an attempt to shed light on a number of different cases of online learning internationally.

Issues of Public Funding and Public Policy

Wiring the world is not a cheap proposition. And the politicians would have us believe that investing in technology (at the expense of other more traditional spending) is necessary and unstoppable—and most important, it will benefit everyone, it will be a public good. Noam Chomsky (1998) suggests our faith in this assumption may be misplaced:

> Its particularly harmful to democracy when media systems are in the hands of private tyrannies ... Here's this huge system, built at public expense. Most media analysts with their heads screwed on see, and even report, that it's very likely going to end up in the hands of a half-dozen megacorporations internationally. (p. 188)

Naturally, these megacorporations may be willing to pay for part of the expenditure, although this is not entirely clear. Much as our sports stadiums are being built with a sponsor's name prominently displayed when the public has paid for a larger proportion of the building expenses than has the corporation, politicians are billing these expenditures as "good for our community" or in the case of online education "advancing the goals of democracy through open access." However, to the extent that corporations are willing to pick up the tab, it will be because they perceive a profit payoff. As, Hirschkop (1998) puts it:

> The relatively low cost of PCs and modems disguises the enormous costs of computing research and development as well as the laying down and maintenance of a network infrastructure. The money has to come from somewhere, and that somewhere is going to be the federal government and those corporations (IBM and AT&T for instance) that can look upon it as an investment in future profit rather than an extension of democracy. (p. 213)

What will these corporations (and for that matter federal governments) want for their investment? Baseball stadium sponsors only want the chance to advertise—repeatedly, but where education is concerned, there may be more far-reaching demands. With the advent of corporate universities, there is no reason why a corporation underwriting the online education infrastructure couldn't demand control over the curriculum creating an even more direct link between public universities and corporate training needs. In such a marketplace of vocational education opportunities, what will happen to those courses on Shakespeare, Kant, and impressionist painters? What will happen to unpopular, unmarketable, and nonvocationally oriented ideas? Higher education has always been the bastion of unpopular ideas. As a public institution, higher education may have fallen away from making itself relevant to the public, but it has always maintained a space for even the most politically incorrect of ideas. Can this continue in the face of online education, tightening budgets, and corporate capitalism's free reign in our culture?

As Winner (1998) points out, "State legislatures would now rather invest in digital bandwidth than spend money on conventional settings for teaching and learning." (9)

This concern is more clearly laid out by Lawrence Gold, higher education director for the American Federation of Teachers, in a recent article from the *Chronicle of Higher Education* (Olsen, 1999). He states that those same legislators who are

> not interested in providing more facilities, not interested in beefing up videoconferencing programs, not especially interested in teacher salaries, and certainly not interested in replacing adjuncts with full-time faculty members are in fact very interested in spending a ton of money for something we don't know a whole lot about. (p. 3)

If we were to carefully consider how best to invest those public monies currently being spent for increasing technology and marketing online education, it might represent only a resistance to change to suggest that we revert to more support for conventional learning environments. Surely, most universities would do well to update their facilities and pay faculty competitively. However, there may be more effective means for advancing the cause of democracy, including more support for scholarships for low income residential students, financing organizing efforts to create truly democratic uses of technologies, and even culturally sensitive online education for empowering those populations who are currently oppressed by multinational corporations. *These* expenditures may advance democracy, but they are not likely to gain wide support from legislators or corporations and therefore may not be presented to the public as options.

Perhaps instead of concentrating on outreach through new educational products for new markets, the task of those who care about university outreach should be to advance the cause of higher education's mission. If we can show the importance and relevance of the university to the public, we may increase the likelihood of public support for public higher education.

THE STRUCTURE OF THIS TEXT

This text is divided into several sections based on geographic location. This approach to stratifying the contributions seemed the most logical for us and for our readers. Thus, after the introductory remarks, we explore, in order, Asia, Europe, North America, Oceania, and Africa. This organization has worked very well in terms of common themes that emerge from countries that are grouped together. For example, the theme of urban versus rural cut across many cases, but tended to clump together in certain geographical regions. The order of geographic region proceeds from wide to narrow and back to wide again. Specifically, Asian countries such as China and India have large widespread centralized systems while Europe and even more so North America have decentralized more targeted systems. The focus broadens out again as we move toward Africa, which has governmentally centralized efforts that reach far into rural areas but tend to be less coordinated with other nearby African countries. This sort of broad-zoom-broad approach follows Reigeluth's Elaboration Theory suggestions for instructional strategy.

It is important to be clear that we have certainly not exhausted all of the most interesting cases in the world for e-learning, online education, or more broadly distance education. Rather, we understand that this book is a beginning point. Clearly, there are contexts, even whole continents missing from this assessment. We attempted to be as comprehensive and inclusive as was practical and effective. We would have liked to include cases from the Middle East and Latin America as well as more from Africa than we were able to gather. However, at some point, a book concerning itself with international cases simply has to create a relatively permeable boundary around itself and move out to the rest of the world. We hope that the cases we have here are illustrative of similar experiences in other contexts and invite additional scholarship on the topic for future research.

Understanding the themes across different sections of the book is aided with the use of the Thematic Matrix (see p. 14, this volume), which displays a matrix arrangement of country by theme. The countries are listed in the order they appear in the book. The geographic organization of the book helps the readers to immerse themselves in a particular context and to remain in that mind-set for a sustained period of reading. We feel that this is essential in developing a deep understanding of globalization and internationalization of learning and distance education, which are highly context dependent. What is gained by this approach and organization is a clear opportunity to study specific regions that tend to share similar thematic elements, however, should the reader prefer to read the book thematically, this can be easily accomplished by utilizing the Thematic Matrix and focusing on a particular issue of interest.

There are many issues as highlighted in the table—from rural to urban differentiations, from class distributions to discussions of access to radio and other more traditional forms of distance learning as compared to e-learning resources. However, as the reader reviews all of these cases, it is compelling to see how many different stories are contained in this collection. Perhaps because e-learning is so completely decentralized, or because there are no governing bodies or standards at this time, or because of the relative newness of the movement, the cases show an enormous range of histories and issues associated with the implementation of e-learning across the globe. In fact, the efforts are indeed vastly different but united by certain themes (see the Thematic Matrix). Understanding these contexts, differences, and similarities as you read the book will help to frame the dialogue that *is* global e-learning.

Each section begins with a brief discussion of the theoretical grounding of the section. This is an opportunity to synthesize the individual cases that follow and draw out connections and issues that emerge among the chapters. Each chapter is similar in structure and begins with a section that introduces the major issues or themes of the chapter and suggests some issues for readers to think about as they read the chapter. We felt that this approach was superior to the traditional end of chapter questions in that this device will help establish in advance an organizer for readers as they read the chapter rather than as a wrap-up activity subsequent to reading the chapter. The final chapter in the text offers some possibilities for alternative methods of measuring effects of online learning, and the text concludes with a brief afterword. We encourage all readers to create their own meanings from and interpretation of these cases. While we recognize that we have surely not exhausted the important contexts worthy of examination, we hope that others will look at their own context and find those commonalities that may assist in moving online learning more toward real democratic practice.

Thematic Matrix

Chapter	Country	Page number	Focus	Primary Theme	Secondary Theme	Tertiary Theme(s)
1	China	21	Rural/urban divide	Equity	Workforce	Access, low-tech approaches, balance
2	Taiwan	33	E-learning availability	E-learning as export	Industry development	Digital gap, industry policy support, equity, IT literacy
3	India	52	Educational equity	Rural/urban	Class	Equity
4	Ireland	71	Innovative social practice	Equity and discourse	ICT growth, access, quality	ICT policy and promise
5	United Kingdom	89	The Internet and e-learning	Social exclusion	Access and retention	Costs and benefits
6	International	101	International study circles—labor	Power	Class	Cross-cultural communications, labor
7	Turkey	115	SchoolNet K-12	Obstacles	Access	Low-tech approaches, access, equity
8	Canada	131	SchoolNet K-12	Rural/urban	Workforce	K-12, technological determinism, public v. private, export
9	United States	145	Culture of United States	Power	Equity	Public v. private, technological determinism, export
10	New Zealand	163	Higher education	Decentralization	Social justice	Public v. private, power, access
11	Australia	179	Higher education	Cultural sensitivity	Public v. private	Power
12	Namibia	205	ICT and democratic development	Development	Risk/obstacles	Access, social justice, cultural sensitivity
13	Sub-Saharan Africa	222	E-learning for development	Innovation	Universities and development	Risk/obstacles, access, social justice, cultural sensitivity, technology for development
14	International Weather Station Project	241	Measurement alternatives	Power	Obstacles	Measurement

REFERENCES

Barlow, M., & Robertson, H. (1996). From homogenization of education. In J. Mander & E. Goldsmith (Eds.), *The case against the global economy: And for a turn toward the local* (pp. 60–70). San Francisco: Sierra Club.

Beer, M. (1999, May 16). Feeding hungry minds. *San Francisco Examiner,* p. 2.

Berube, M. (1998, March 27). Why inefficiency is good for universities. *Chronicle of Higher Education,* pp. B4–B5.

Bowers, C. A. (1998, Spring). The paradox of technology: What's gained and lost? *Thought & Action,* 49–57.

Chomsky, N. (1998). Propaganda and control of the public mind. In R. W. McChesney, E. M. Wood, & J. B. Foster (Eds.), *Capitalism and the information age: The political economy of the global communication revolution* (pp. 179–190) New York: Monthly Review Press.

Clark, H. F. (1987). Consumer and corporate values: Yet another view on global marketing. *International Journal of Advertising, 6*(1), 29–42.

Daniel, J. S. (1996). *Mega-universities and knowledge media: Technology strategies for higher education.* London: Kogan Page.

Dawson, M., & Foster, J. B. (1998). Virtual capitalism: Monopoly capital, marketing, and the information highway. In R. W. McChesney, E. M. Wood, & J. B. Foster (Eds.), *Capitalism and the information age: The political economy of the global communication revolution* (pp. 51–67). New York: Monthly Review Press.

Gubernick, L., & Ebeling, A. (1997, June 16). I got my degree through E-mail. *Forbes,* pp. 84–86, 88, 90, 92.

Hall, J. W. (1995). The revolution in electronic technology and the modern university: The convergence of means. *Educom Review, 30*(4), 1–7.

Hills, J. (1998). U.S. Rules. OK?: Telecommunications since the 1940's. In R. W. McChesney, E. M. Wood, & J. B. Foster (Eds.), *Capitalism and the information age: The political economy of the global communication revolution* (pp. 99–121). New York: Monthly Review Press.

Hiltz, S. R., & Wellman, B. (1997). Asynchronous learning networks as a virtual classroom. *Communications of the ACM, 40*(9), 44–49.

Hirschkop, K. (1998). Democracy and the new technologies. In R. W. McChesney, E. M. Wood, & J. B. Foster (Eds.), *Capitalism and the information age: The political economy of the global communication revolution* (pp. 207–217). New York: Monthly Review Press.

Jones, G. R. (1997). *Cyberschools.* Englewood, CO: Jones Digital Century.

Lyotard, J. (1984). *The postmodern condition: A report on knowledge.* Manchester: Manchester University Press.

McChesney, R. W. (1998). The political economy of global communication. In R. W. McChesney, E. M. Wood, & J. B. Foster (Eds.), *Capitalism and the information age: The political economy of the global communication revolution* (pp. 1–26). New York: Monthly Review Press.

Noble, D. (1998). Digital diploma mills: The automation of higher education. *First Monday, 3*(1). Retrieved November 7, 2004, from http://www.firstmonday.dk/issues/issue3_1/noble

Olsen, F. (1999, August 6). "Virtual" institutions challenge accreditors to devise new ways of measuring quality. *The Chronicle of Higher Education*, pp. A29–A30.

Rogers, E. (2003). *Diffusion of innovations*, 5th ed. New York: Free Press.

Sclove, R. (1995). *Democracy and technology*. New York: Guilford Press.

Simpson, L. C. (1995). *Technology time and the conversations of modernity.* New York: Routledge.

Van Dusen, G. C. (1998). Technology: Higher education's magic bullet. In R. W. McChesney, E. M. Wood, & J. B. Foster (Eds.), *Capitalism and the information age: The political economy of the global communication revolution* (pp. 59–67.) New York: Monthly Review Press.

Winner, L. (1998, June 2). Tech knowledge review. *NETFUTURE: Technology and human responsibility, 72,* 4–10.

PART I

ONLINE EDUCATION IN ASIA:

An Analysis of China, Taiwan, and India

Witness not the sages of the past,
Perceive not the wise of the future,
Reflecting on heaven and earth eternal,
Tears flowing down I lament in loneliness.

—Chen Zi'ang

Asia and all Eastern cultures are far from being the same as Western cultures. I suppose this is perhaps one of the more obvious statements made in this text. But it is worthy of emphasis. Online learning, like all education, does not happen in a vacuum. This is part of the message of this book—that we recognize that learning is not a-cultural or a-contextual, but rather is highly dependent on the culture and context in which the learning and learners are embedded.

AUTHOR'S NOTE: An earlier version of this chapter was published as Carr-Chellman, A. A., & Zhang, K. (2000). China's future with distance education: Rhetoric and realities. *Information, Communication and Society*, *3*(3), 303–312. The author wishes to thank Dr. Ali Carr-Chellman for her active initiatives in this research project and her contributions to the earlier version.

In the case of this section, we consider three very different contexts within the Eastern culture: Taiwan, China, and India. Jiang's examination of Taiwan is focused primarily on the ways in which Taiwan has focused on the industrialization of e-learning. In particular, Taiwan has focused most of its efforts on the use of e-learning in industry, but those who are more interested in e-learning for the purposes of advancing social equity are lonely voices indeed. As Jiang points out, the orientation from the government and policy makers has been to benefit those in the industrial marketplace. Yet industry's perpetual quest for higher profits should not be the goal of government policy. Taiwan wishes to create an R&D center that will serve the global Chinese community, which certainly may benefit the rural poor in Taiwan and mainland China, but the primary purpose is not to serve that population, but rather to serve the needs of industry in an effort to create a high profile for Taiwan's e-learning efforts.

Zhang's discussion of China's e-learning initiatives clarifies the complexity of the power relationships and the cultural difference from traditional Western contexts. As is the case in Taiwan and India, one of the primary motivators for governmental reach to disenfranchised populations is to create a large, educated, and skilled workforce. One of the interesting bits of rhetoric in these cases is the idea that policy makers and governmental officials are discussing the importance not only of honing a large skilled workforce, but also of transcending issues of class. This is rather a curious and complex orientation from China in particular as a traditional communist society. It is far more understandable from India, where the gap between rich and poor is notoriously enormous.

Another somewhat confusing aspect of China's case is that much of the rhetoric is centered on democracy, and access in particular, as the lived experience of democracy. Understanding that China is still a stalwart of communism, the notion that the rhetoric of democracy informs in any significant way the selling of public policy and public expenditures for the purposes of online learning seems an internal contradiction. One final interesting aspect of the Chinese case is the status that online or distance learning has traditionally held in Chinese society. As Zhang points out, there are many actual benefits for a person who chooses to remain employed while seeking a degree within Chinese society. What is most interesting is not that this performance is adequately rewarded; that would be expected given the communist nature of Chinese society. What is interesting is the idea that there is no differentiation between an online degree and one earned at a traditional bricks and mortar institution. Perhaps it should not surprise us that there should be less brand loyalty in Chinese culture; however, education abroad at specific institutions has long been prized in China. This is in stark contrast to India where, as Sharma points out, "Distance education in India has consistently been viewed as a second-rate education alternative, and traditional education is still reserved for elite, urban consumers" (p. 5, this volume).

In all three cases—Taiwan, India and China—there is a certain loneliness and silence that is apparent in the e-learning culture of these countries. Those in the rural countryside of all three nations have been left behind. In comparison to Western cultures, where class is the primary determinant of access and attrition rates among e-learners, Eastern cultures intersect class and geographic location for a double threat to equity. India offers a particularly poignant image of this threat. As the software and movie industry booms in the urban centers of India make the rich richer, those in the poor and remote villages are deprived of many of the most basic life needs, from electricity to learning. The result of this rural disconnect is truly a sense of loss and loneliness.

⁂ ONE ⁆

CHINA'S ONLINE EDUCATION:

Rhetoric and Realities

Ke Zhang

Although little is currently known of distance education in China, especially in Western educational circles, there is a long-standing well-established instructional television system of distance education that has flourished in China since the 1960s (Howells, 1989). In fact, one of the world's largest education systems is the Dianda system in China, a combined radio-television university system capable of enrolling upwards of 100,000 learners (Keegan, 1994). With the advent of online education, however, China must face a brave new world of innovation. This chapter examines the political rhetoric surrounding the allocation of funds and energies to online learning, considers the critical components of that rhetoric, and discusses the impacts on the way China adopts the new online learning technologies. As you read this chapter, please reflect upon the following questions:

- How does the political rhetoric match or mismatch the reality of online education in China?
- How does the regional economical divide impact the implementation of online education in China?

- What would you question about China's online education as envisioned in the political rhetoric?
- How does online education in China differ from that in the United States? What causes such differences?
- What are the major challenges China is facing in its endeavor with online education? What would you suggest the Chinese government do to overcome the challenges?

It is clear from recent political statements that China is prepared to leverage distance education to reach a broader audience through the Internet. The latest survey on Internet development in China (China Internet Network Information Center, 2003) shows that as of June 30, 2003, there were 25.72 million computers through which at least one person has accessed the Internet and over 68 million Internet users in mainland China. The Ministry of Education (MOE) of the People's Republic of China (PRC) anticipated more than a million Chinese being able to access distance open higher education starting in fall 1999.

The Central Committee of the Chinese Communist Party (1999) clearly emphasized the importance of the emerging educational technology in "Decisions on Furthering Educational Reform and Advancing Quality Education":

> *Part 2, item 15:* take full advantage of the modern distance education network to provide lifetime learning opportunities for all social members, to provide appropriate education needed in rural areas and outlying districts.

At the Sixteenth National Congress of the Chinese Communist Party, the national leadership (Jiang, 2002) emphasized again the strategic importance of education in national development and the strategy of using technology to leverage education at all levels. The MOE (2002b) made it clear in its Focuses for the Year of 2003:

> [Focus on] piloting the network technologies and traditional face-to-face teaching methods . . . conducting research on multimedia and network-based courseware. . . . Actively develop the web-based public service system in education, create and share quality educational resources.

INTERNET DEMOCRACIES

The Ministry of Education (2002b) made the value of open access very clear in its goal statement:

> [One of our goals is to] achieve equal access to education and fairness in education, [to ensure] everyone in the country has the opportunity to receive good education ... establish an open educational system and a human resource development system that cover the entire country, both cities and rural areas, to create multiple-leveled, multiple-formed learning opportunities for all people.

At the 16th National Congress of the Chinese Communist Party in November 2002, President Jiang (2002) again stressed the strategic importance of education in his report to the congress, and mentioned in particular the great needs for more accessible and improved education in rural China:

> We should ... promote quality-oriented education to cultivate hundreds of millions of high-quality workers, tens of millions of specialized personnel and a great number of top-notch innovative personnel.... We should continue to make nine-year compulsory education universal across the country, intensify vocational education and training, develop continued education and set up a system of life-long education. We should increase input in education, give more support to rural education, and encourage nongovernmental sectors to run schools. We should improve the state policy and system for aiding students in straitened circumstances.

Thus, distance education is seen as a way to transcend social class, and it seems relatively clear that vocational/occupational education is an important component of Jiang's vision of China's education. In a similar fashion, Wei Yu (1999), vice minister of the Ministry of Education at that time, recognized the following as one of the key elements in developing China's modern distance education:

> To provide more technologies for the peasants, to apply modern educational technology to promote education in our outlying districts, poorer areas, minority nationality regions, and less-developed areas. For those areas, the first and foremost is to promote nine-year compulsory education and to de-illiteracy, and then to improve the educational level gradually to advance economic development there.

In general, the educational level of people in rural China is significantly lower than that of the city populace, and so is the technology availability. Therefore, when the big cities are ready for Internet-leveraged distance education, the rural poor may just not have the technology or the knowledge and skills required for online learning. Precisely which areas would benefit from the advanced technologies, particularly the Internet, is not entirely clear despite the rhetoric. In a speech offered by Wei (1999), the importance of radio and television for rural areas seems clear:

> We think that, although TV, as the major distance education deliver medium, is one-way broadcasting, it costs much less, especially given the fact that TV is highly accessible—in rural areas the average ownership of TV sets is ninety-two percent in 1997. In addition, currently the costs for the computer networking systems in our country are fairly high, and (the network systems thus) have limited availability. Therefore in the near future, especially in the rural areas, satellite TV education will still be playing an important role. However, as CERNET (the Chinese Education and Research Net) and other computer networking technologies develop, distance education is developing with a trend to be multimedia and interactivity. . . . As a developing country, we must watch the trends closely, and actively conduct related research. Also we must explore a development path based on our own situations. . . . Considering the regional imbalance in economic development, the Chinese government will develop informationized education through three stages: the first is to develop educational technologies, focusing on multimedia, and to promote school applications; the second is to spread knowledge on networking systems, to learn to take advantage of online resources; and the third is to develop Modern Distance Education, to build and provide enormous online resources, so to satisfy the ever-growing needs in the society for lifetime learning.

Thus, it would seem that while radio and television will continue to be the major educational media in rural China, it is not clear if many poor areas will benefit from the Internet connections in the near future. The three-stage development plan (Wei, 1999) seems to be based on the current status of the relatively developed regions, yet in reality, there is a serious shortage of schools, teachers and other basic facilities in rural China (MOE, 2002b), and not only are computer and network technologies not widely accessible there, but also the populace is not well prepared with knowledge and skills for online learning. The State Council (2003) has re-emphasized the importance of education in rural China and has specified that the key task there is to ensure education to all school-aged children by building more schools, making facilities and teachers available, and providing financial support to the poor families. Based on the real needs in rural China, the Ministry of Finance and Ministry of Education (2002) specify the allocation of educational funds from the central government to the rural areas in the following fashion: school construction and maintenance (60%), information technology and teaching facilities (10%), purchase of desks and chairs (10%), books and fee waivers for the poor (10%), and professional development of teachers and principals (10%). Although it is envisioned that online learning will reach larger audiences and help fulfill the educational needs across China in the political rhetoric, the reality appears more controversial and challenging with the dramatic differences between the cities and the rural areas in terms of the educational needs and readiness for Internet enhanced education.

RURAL CHINA: LEFT BEHIND?

The Chinese government attempts to provide equal access to education nationwide, as clearly stated consistently in the political rhetoric (Wei, 1999; Jiang, 2002; MOE, 2002b; State Council, 2003). However, the regional economic conditions vary, drastically in many cases, and the immediate needs for education in those areas vary significantly as a result. The central government realizes the economic divide and attempts to resolve the unhealthy imbalance. The 16th National Congress has put more attention on the development of western regions, which are generally rural, remote, and poor areas. Many policies are established to help speed up the economic development in the western regions, and more money is allocated there for economical and educational development from the central government (State Council, 2003). Online education has been identified as one of the strategies to narrow the educational gap between urban and rural areas. One of the major efforts is to build a computer network system in 152 universities in the western region, with 900 million RMB Yuan (approximately US$108 million) special fund from the central government (MOE, 2003). However, it is not clear how Internet technology will serve the needs for basic or 9-year compulsory education in the rural areas, which is indeed critically needed, as the government recognizes.

China's Education and Research Network (2003) has identified three distance education models that are currently practiced in rural China: (1) educational CD display centers, (2) satellite TV learning centers, and (3) networked computer labs. Clearly the TV distance education system is, and will still be for a long time, a very important part of the distance education system in rural China, especially for the 9-year compulsory education.

In an important document titled "State Council's decision on Improving Education in Rural China," the State Council (2003) specified the educational goals in rural China, which focus on 9-year compulsory education, vocational education and adult education for the rural populace. In addition to financial investment from all levels of government and fee waivers for the poor, the government is working to establish and to continuously improve a one-to-one educational support system. This support system involves two types of collaboration between the schools and cities/counties in the eastern (developed) and the western (less developed) regions. One type of collaboration is between the eastern schools and their sister schools in the western region; another is between cities and less developed sister counties/cities in the same province.

Through the one-to-one support system, some universities in the developed cities have provided free software, hardware, courseware, and satellite technologies to universities in the western region, such as Shanghai Jiaotong University and Xi'an Jiaotong University to Tibet University (Liu, J., 2003). They have also sent over technicians to help set up the technologies. More courses from the universities in better developed regions are made available to students in the sister universities in the less-developed areas (Liu, J., 2003). At the same time, the MOE is calling for excellent courseware nationwide and will select 1500 quality courseware programs from the pool and make them available to all schools and the general public, free of charge (Feng, 2003). More schools in rural China are getting networked, by satellite or cable, to the Education and Research Network, which provides free teaching and learning resources, and they are also getting free courseware and other resources from their sister schools (Shi, 2003). In Inner Mongolia Autonomous Region alone, since the implementation of the "All Schools Connected Project," over 3,000 schools have built a distance education network system, benefiting 100,000 students in the remote areas (Shi, 2003).

Teachers in rural schools are also learning to use the Internet resources available through the distance education systems to prepare and improve teaching (Liu, W., 2003). However, the policy-driven support system seems to be limited and may not necessarily lead to long-term collaboration. It is not clear if the one-on-one support system will be evaluated or rewarded in any way, or if there are any incentives involved except for the political policies. Rural China is not attracting as much private investment in education as the developed cities are. As a self-regulating governmental behavior in the more and more market-driven economy, it is very hard to ensure or sustain such collaborations to operate effectively in the long term. More social sectors in addition to the government need to be involved in the tough campaign for equal access to education across the country, online or in person.

MEETING THE DEMAND: MOTIVES

The motives for Chinese distance education expansion and funding are quite different from those of the Western countries. While some facets of the movement are similar, the motive is strongly rooted in the ability of the government to educate adequately large masses of people (as opposed to trying to make a profit from the learners). As Gao (1991) points out:

> In a country like China, which has 1.2 billion people, the demand for education is so great that traditional education cannot be expected to meet the needs. (p. 54)

Thus, while many universities in the United States are trying to find ways to capture this huge distance learning market, it is recognized in China that traditional education cannot possibly serve the entire adult education market, and instead, alternatives must be pursued.

Such a mammoth effort at providing basic education to millions of learners requires differentiated staffing. In order to ensure excellent teaching, only the best university teaching models are offered the opportunity to instruct at a distance. Tutors are employed locally to help with interaction and guidance not provided by radio or TV broadcasts (Zhao, 1988). Web-based distance education in China will also likely rely on a differentiated staffing pattern such as this. It is an economical way to handle large, even huge, numbers of learners. In much the same way that the current U.S. system employs adjuncts and part-time instructors rather than full-time, tenure-track faculty, differentiated staffing patterns can be extremely flexible and economic.

Naturally, given the motives to educate large masses of Chinese in basic education, literacy and work skills, the orientation of this education is information presentation and skill training. The vast majority of offerings via Chinese distance education to date has been highly vocational in nature. As an example, when looking at the number of subjects offered at Central Radio and Television University (CRTVU), there are sixty-five specialties in engineering, while there is only one in Chinese language and literature (Zhao, 1988). Recent trends, particularly in online learning, are toward the "hot" topics such as information technology, computer science, management, and English language.

DEMOCRACY REVISITED: OPEN ACCESS

While the rhetoric of democracy is clear through political speeches cited previously here, the reality of implementation is likely to leave the rural poor behind. First, far more access to radio and television exists in rural China than to Internet connections, and this raises questions of open access. While reportedly more than 70,000 public schools employ computer education programs in China and more than 10 million students have mastered basic computer skills, most computer technologies are still available primarily on school grounds and most of these schools are in the cities, with not many in the rural areas. In the relatively developed regions, many schools' public libraries have Internet connections, and these resources are openly available to all in the community. There are currently four major networking systems in China, including China's Education and Research Net, which provides regional networking centers devoted to education and research. Thus, access is relatively available, but mostly in centralized locations, such as in working places, offices, and public Internet cafés. As far as individual homes are concerned, it is available mostly in the cities and very rarely in rural China.

One of the recent changes in China's distance education system can also be seen in the United States. The melding of traditionally residential, high status universities and traditionally distance universities is beginning. The official Web site of the Ministry of Education for the PRC states that the most recent distance higher education will be delivered through a cooperation of the CRTVU and several high-status, traditional universities including top schools like Tsinghua University. This move is surprising given the fact that the distance learning degrees are equivalent in the eyes of the government to traditional degrees.

The rhetoric is clearly centered on open access and social equalization. The reality of economic development for most rural poor will likely not include huge infusions of funds in the form of Internet connections, servers, and computers. The reality is that in rural China the immediate needs are to build more physical schools, to fix the classrooms in dangerous condition, to have more teachers, and to make sure that school-age children can and do go to school (Jiang, 2002;

MOE, 2003; State Council, 2003). Thus, it's clearly stated in the State Council (2003) and MOE (2003) documents that the allocated government money will be used to address the above issues, and only 10% of the special fund is allocated for information technology and teaching facilities (Ministry Of Finance and Ministry Of Education, 2002). The cities are the likely winners in this game of haves and have-nots of Internet technology. The cities are seen by many in the Chinese population and government as the place where technological innovation is most likely to serve two purposes. First, masses of the population perceived as somewhat educated (as opposed to the rural poor with more illiteracy and less education) will be able to leverage their learning via distance education. Second, placing technology in the hands of learners will create a tertiary effect in terms of technological development and economic development. It is hoped that the increase of access to high technology and the application of technology in education will stimulate the development of technological industries, such as software development, hardware manufacturing, and other technology advancement. And the development of computer technology and associated industries, in return, will push back the frontier of online education. Thus despite all the nice hope to narrow the regional gap through online education, it may on the contrary cause more severe imbalance between urban and rural China, when the rich areas benefit from more quality online education while the poor are left behind with low-tech distance education.

POWER TO THE PEOPLE

The Chinese government has assured all students involved in distance education degree seeking that the rewards for their degrees are equivalent to those earned at traditional universities:

> After graduation, in-service (distance) students are recognized as having equivalent status to that of conventional college graduates ... They receive the same salary as conventional college students ... When they are assigned a new job, they will be treated equally as conventional college graduates. (Zhao, 1988, p. 225)

Clearly, the government values distance learning outcomes (degrees, certificates, etc.) at the same level in terms of hiring and promotion. However, because learners are often employed full-time while pursuing part-time education programs, they emerge from the distance learning experience with far more work experience, which gives them an actual advantage in the job market over traditional college students.

This situation has prevailed throughout the radio and television distance learning era. There is no cause to consider that the procedures will likely change dramatically when utilizing the Web as a delivery medium. Thus, what are the likely impacts of this approach, particularly on a society that has a traditionally strong hierarchical education (and employment) system? Of particular interest here is that this system in the past has always been one in which social prestige is based on your educational level and that is based on testing very early in life which tracks learners into specific educational programs. Internet learning, like radio and television learning, can allow many more students to pursue higher education degrees, and it seems that as long as they are able to complete the requirements, they will earn equal status with traditional university graduates.

In many ways, the Chinese distance education history and future plans are relatively progressive. Not only does the government fund the establishment of the online learning centers, but other interests contribute by giving time off, benefits, and salaries to distance learners. From one perspective, this may be seen as unfair. Those in distance programs graduate in a shorter time period with work experience to back up their education, making them highly desirable on the job market. Also, they enjoy pay while they learn as well as equal status with traditional university students. Residential students in China must pay higher tuition fees, earn little or no salary during their education, and typically take more time to complete their programs even under full-time conditions. In essence, the traditional students graduate from a prominent residential Chinese university with the status of the brand name associated with their universities, and little other advantage. Some would argue that this is precisely the elimination of elitism that democratic goals of distance education seek. Perhaps it is, but has it in its current form of TV and radio broadcasts, or will it, in future Internet forms, create more power in the hands of the individuals equally?

CUSTOMIZATION AND GLOBALIZATION

Recently, many online education offerings became available in China from the United States and other overseas institutions. However, these attempts are not culturally grounded. The Chinese government values scholars with degrees from overseas universities, but in many cases, the credibility of a foreign degree via the Internet is questioned in China. Typically, learners enrolled in Internet courses with high-status Chinese universities must take exams in person at an assigned location with photo ID to prevent them from cheating. With strict test administration, the universities offering distance education via the Internet try to maintain their high status by ensuring the same high credibility of their distance degrees as well as the residential ones. Currently, most U.S. online education programs do not require similar ID checks, and many Chinese are thus skeptical about the quality and credibility of these online degrees from a foreign country.

Naturally, Chinese and English are completely different, not only in terms of language but also culturally, and not all Chinese know English well enough to take a course in English, in person or online. Thus it is very likely that if Chinese learners have the opportunity to obtain a degree from a top university in China, they will not choose a barely known Internet-based university overseas in another language. To the extent that universities with stronger brand recognition in China get into the online education game, there may be more of a market for Chinese learners.

PUBLIC FUNDING AND ALTERNATIVES

For those who are able to access distance learning opportunities, there is a great financial benefit in store. As indicated in an interview with Liu Zhipeng (1999), the associate director of the Higher Education Department within the MOE promotes the Modern Distance Education (MDE) project in order to achieve two goals: (a) to extend the scope of education so that more people can have the opportunity for higher education, and (b) to improve the quality of education with advanced technologies. In the future, the state will invest 360 million RMB yuan (equivalent to U.S. $45 million approximately) in education on the MDE project, and it will actively seek sponsorship from international organizations and domestic and overseas enterprises as well. The cost to the students, however, is extremely economical. Two traditional, high-status Chinese universities (Shanghai Foreign Language University and Shanghai Jiaotong University) have recently been offering online courses to the public at a cost of between US$1.00 and US$1.50, excluding fees for learning materials. This is perhaps one of the most progressive plans in distance learning; the burden of the system is borne primarily by the government. Also in several recent government documents, it is clearly stated and reconfirmed that the government will increase the investment in education substantially in the years to come.

Several top universities in China have been building and implementing a distance education network, including Web-based degree and non-degree programs. Hu'nan University has developed an online college through collaborative efforts. As of February 22, 2002, the MOE had approved 66 universities to pilot MDE with Internet technologies (MOE, 2002a). Traditionally, distance education in China uses satellite TV networking, simultaneous TV conference, and correspondence as the major delivery methods. And now the Internet is introduced as a powerful leverage to make education available to more audiences with more flexibility. With consistent financial investment to develop online education, the government also encourages corporations, organizations, and other social units to participate in the MDE project, with financial or technological investment or any other form of contribution.

CONCLUSION

It is clear that the distance education system employed in China, primarily radio and TV broadcasts in the past, has created a huge distance learning network. This network is being leveraged by the Internet, but its implementation is likely to occur more in the cities and among relatively educated populations. The increasing disparities are only now beginning to emerge between the haves and have-nots in Chinese society. Even with substantial government investment and supportive policies, the development of modern distance education in rural China is far more challenging than it is in the cities. Open access has not been met for online learning activities in China yet, as many individuals do not own computers or have access to the Internet connections at home. Therefore, online education has to be accessed at central locations and/or in the learning centers. In rural areas and less developed regions, the learning centers, existing and new ones, will be leveraged with the Internet, mostly through satellite technologies. The system is highly vocationally oriented, including many topics in information technology. And it is hoped that the teaching and learning of technology will promote the related technology industries, most likely in the cities. Yet in rural China, the critical need is still to secure 9-year compulsory education and to make the basic facilities available. To bridge the gap between the cities and the rural areas will be a long-term, challenging task (MOE, 2002b), and the market economy makes it even harder to achieve such a goal without heavy investment from the private businesses and industries. While the system as it is currently constructed is highly progressive, with very low cost to the learners, the global capitalism and the commercialized economy certainly challenge such an operational model. With the controversy between political rhetoric and social reality, China yet needs to figure out a system to develop a healthily balanced economy and education across all regions and classes as well.

REFERENCES

Central Committee of the Chinese Communist Party. (1999). *Decisions on furthering educational reform, and advancing quality education in an all-round way.* Retrieved September 12, 1999, from http://www.online.edu.cn/remotetech/xgzc/zy.htm

China's Education and Research Network. (2003). *Three distance education models in rural schools.* Retrieved November 3, 2003, from http://www.edu.cn/20031010/3092487.shtml

China Internet Network Information Center. (2003). *12th statistical survey on the Internet development in China.* Retrieved November 3, 2003, from http://www.cnnic.cn/develst/2003-7/

Feng, R. (2003). *MOE: 1500 excellent courseware free online: Improving course quality.* Retrieved from China's Elementary and Middle School Teachers Web site: http://www.chinatde.org/xwzx/zc0027.htm[AU: Please provide retrieval date.]

Gao, F. (1991). The challenge of distance education in China. *American Journal of Distance Education, 5*(2), 54–58.

Howells, G. (1989). Distance teaching in China. *Journal of Educational Television, 15*(2), 79–85.

Jiang, Z. (2002, November). *Report to the 16th National Congress of the Chinese Communist Party.* Retrieved November 3, 2003, from http://www.china.org.cn/english/features/49007.htm

Keegan, D. (1994). Very large distance education systems: The case of China. *ZIFF papiere 94.*[AU: Please provide page references]

Liu, J. (2003). *Shanghai Jiaotong University, Xi'an Jiaotong University collaborate with Tibet University on distance education.* Retrieved November 3, 2003, from China's Education and Research Network Web site: http://www.edu.cn/20031020/3093072.shtml

Liu, W. (2003). *Teachers in rural schools: Distance education provides opportunities.* Retrieved November 3, 2003, from China's Education and Research Network Web site: http://www.edu.cn/20030922/3091532.shtml

Liu, Z. (1999). *Important experiment of developing modern distance open education: Interview with Liu Zhipeng, Associate Director of Higher Education Department, Ministry of Education, P. R. China.* Retrieved September 13, 1999, from http://www.online.edu.cn/remoteedu/xgzc/fy.htm

Ministry of Education, P. R. China. (2002a). *MOE approval for piloting modern distance education in 21 universities.* Retrieved November 3, 2003, from the P.R. China Ministry of Education Web site: http://www.moe.edu.cn/stat/zonghe/03.htm

Ministry of Education, P. R. China. (2002b). *Studying the spirit from the 16th National Congress of the Chinese Communist Party, creating a new era of educational reform and development.* Retrieved November 3, 2003, from http://www.moe.edu.cn/news/2003_03/20.htm

Ministry of Education, P. R. China. (2003). *Computer network construction project for universities in the western region.* Retrieved November 3, 2003, from http://www.dost.moe.edu.cn/data/file/zbtb.htm

Ministry of Finance and Ministry of Education, P. R. China. (2002). *Memo on allocation and utilization of the second batch of special funds from the central government for "poor area compulsory education project."* Retrieved November 3, 2003 from http://www.moe.edu.cn/jytouru/jyjingfei/07.htm

Shi, G. (2003). *Inner Mongolia Autonomous region implements modern distance education network project: Schools in remote districts benefit from excellent resources.* Retrieved November 3, 2003, from China's Education and Research Network Web site: http://www.edu.cn/2003091/3090125.shtml

State Council, P. R. China. (2003, September 20). *State council's decision on improving education in rural China.* Retrieved November 3rd, 2003, from http://www.edu.cn/20030922/3091463.shtml

Wei, Y. (1999). China's modern distance education. Retrieved September 13, 1999, from http://www.online.edu/cn/remoteedu/ycjyz/gyycjj/zg.htm

Zhao, Y. (1988). China: Its distance higher-education system. *Prospects, 28*(2), 217–228.

TWO

THE GAP BETWEEN E-LEARNING AVAILABILITY AND E-LEARNING INDUSTRY DEVELOPMENT IN TAIWAN

Jiang Jia Qi

One of the objectives of Taiwan's National Science Council (NSC) has been to develop the country into a global R&D powerhouse of e-learning related technology. In order to upgrade Taiwan's economic competitiveness in the knowledge economy era, much effort has been put into constructing a more technology-oriented and Internet-conscious society.

At present, the central government focuses on creating domestic market demand for e-learning products both by fostering the information technology (IT) industry and by creating a sound economic environment for the e-learning businesses. The intent of this policy is that the e-learning industry will finally transform Taiwan from a manufacturer of IT hardware to a user of IT applications.

The enterprises and government have long since devoted themselves to multimedia instruction design, e-conferencing programs, online video games, digital entertainment, streaming media, video on demand, and relevant applications in developing e-learning content and supplementary services. The final goal is to catch up with more developed countries in online e-learning.

In support of these efforts, the Taiwan government enacted the Six-Year National Development Plan, Challenge 2008, thus officially launching digital industry infrastructures to serve the e-learning industry development. In essence, the plan seeks to increase market demand for e-learning by promoting its applications to other pursuits, such as on-the-job training and e-commerce of agriculture and commercial fishing.

However, the public use of e-learning facilities has not grown at the same pace as the e-learning industry development. As demonstrated above, there is commercially driven momentum behind the government's policy support for the e-learning industry, and the benefits to underprivileged groups and equity of educational resources are not high priorities in that policy. As you read this chapter, please reflect on the following questions:

- Why does the Taiwanese government commit itself to the development of the e-learning industry?
- What does the basic digital gap come from in Taiwanese society?
- Which group of people are the main beneficiaries of e-learning in Taiwan?
- What role should the government play in the development of e-learning in pursuit of educational equity?
- Who should take the most responsibility of promoting e-learning in the service of universal population? The IT industry or the government?
- How does the e-learning industry policy guide lead the development of e-learning availability in rural and urban areas?

In Taiwan, as in many other countries in the world, the innovation of the Internet and online distance learning carry a special responsibility to bridge the existing gaps and discrepancies between lower-income and rich households, rural and urban areas, elder and younger generations, females and males, low and high educational levels. Furthermore, e-learning has the potential of breaking down geographical and spatial constraints in educational opportunities. Yet the e-learning industries around the world have magnified the disparity and inequity in the educational, economic, and vocational opportunities.

In Taiwan, the digital gap is no less apparent than in any other place around the world. In an effort to counter the widening gap, government and enterprises have taken several steps to promote popular usage and access to the Internet. According to statistical data retrieved from Focus on Internet News and Data (FIND), an affiliate of the Institute of Information Industry, by the end of 2003 broadband cable (including cable modem and ADSL) users reached 2.7 million, which is a 10% growth over the last quarter in 2002—an exciting number for both government and enterprise.

Nevertheless, public access to the Internet still is not completely equal among different groups. According to data from the Ministry of Transportation and Communication (MOTC), the populations owning broadband cable concentrate in the urban areas of north and south of Taiwan, while rural areas in the east and south of Taiwan have low Internet access and usage rates. Against this backdrop, the Executive Yuan in the central government set up a plan to hook up 6 million broadband cable connections within six years for the Six-Year National Development Plan, Challenge 2008.

Aside from the access gap, there exists also the IT skill and Internet literacy gaps. Many people who have computers and access to the Internet at home do not know how to collect data and evaluate information through critical thinking and apply the technology to their benefit.

THE DIGITAL GAP AND INTERNET USAGE IN TAIWAN

A two-phased investigation conducted by the MOTC in March 2003 through the Computer Assisted Telephone Interview (CATI) yielded *The Report on The Internet Usage of The Population in Taiwan.* According to this report, the population using the Internet has grown continuously from 2001 through 2003. The first phase of the investigation targeted 6,110 inhabitants through phone interviews, and the second targeted 3,084 inhabitants above age 15 who had access to the Internet in the previous month.

It may be inferred from data in the report that the gender gap is decreasing and that the generation gap of IT literacy probably will reduce over time as successive e-generations are born in an IT-conscious society. However, a persistent digital gap appeared in low-income families, those with little or no education, and ethnic minorities (such as aboriginal Taiwanese).

The data also demonstrated that the home is becoming a popular location to get on the Internet, next to the work place and school. Surprisingly, ownership of a computer does not imply higher IT literacy and proficiency. The capacity of computer owners to use the Internet to locate, analyze, evaluate, and synthesize information thus poses another issue worth attention.

First, concerning the access format, ADSL surpassed phone dial-up in 2003; dial-up users reached a predominant 60.7% of those surveyed, which is a 52.9% growth over 2001. On the other hand, the dial-up users dropped by 49.7% from 2001 through 2003, reaching 24.6%. Most families have changed from dial-up to ADSL in recent years.

The Digital Access Index 2002 of International Telecommunication Union (ITU), taking into consideration the rate of DSL layout in each country, ranked Taiwan ninth internationally (FIND, 2003). Nevertheless, high ranking in the global Digital Index does not imply high Internet literacy or availability of Internet resources.

Second, concerning the location where users get online, out of 3,084 interviewees, 86.2% reported that they get on the Internet at "home," followed by "office or companies" (36.2%), then "school (including dormitory) and research centers" (22.2%), and "café and stores" (18.9%). Compared to the data in 2001, home as the most frequent location to get on the Internet grew by 9.5% in 2003, while "school (including dormitory) and research centers" as locations to get on the Internet dropped by 12.7% over the same time. The conclusion is that home has become the main location to get online.

The population of the Internet users at home has the following characteristics: They are mainly males between 15 and 40 years of age, especially students with education beyond high school. Overall, 75.9% of citizens have home Internet access in Taipei City, as compared to 65% in Taiwan overall, with 48.9% in the east of Taiwan and 48.1% in the south of Taiwan.

Third, concerning the economic aspect, the average cost per family to get online is NT$962. Specifically, of all the interviewed families having access to the Internet, 30.9% spend NT$1,000 to NT$1,500 per month, 19.5% spend NT$750 to NT$1,000 per month, 11.8% spend NT$250 to NT$500 dollars per month, 10.6% spend NT$500 to NT$750 dollars per month. Therefore, a total of 72.8% families spent NT$250 to NT$1,500 per month to get online. The average cost to get online is still high.

According to the statistical data from Research Development and Evaluation Commission Executive Yuan (2002), the average disposable income per household in Taiwan was NT$89,000 in 2001, which was 2.5% lower than that in 2000;

the highest family income was 6.39 times that of the lowest family in 2001. The discrepancy between the richest and the poorest further expanded in Taiwan (Research Development and Evaluation Commission Executive Yuan, 2002).

Fourth, concerning the population who never use the Internet, 36.2% are the elderly, 16.9% lack the necessary skill to get online, an additional 14.9% see no need to use the Internet, while another 11.8% lack the hardware equipment to get online. Lack of skill, education, and equipment still compose the main reasons preventing people from using the Internet. Furthermore, the use of the Internet increases along with the educational levels of the interviewees. For interviewees with no more than primary school education, Internet usage is 18.1%, which increases to 38.3% for those who have a junior high school education, 58.7% for those with a senior high school education, 80.5% and 88.5% for those with college and university educations, and 97.2% for those of graduate school educations.

Fifth, a total of 79.7% of users get online to "browse and collect information," followed by 36.9% who get online to "collect e-mail," 18.7% who go online to "play online games," 16.3% who go online to "fulfill work requirement," and 11% who go online for "e-learning and distance education." Among 6110 interviewees, 71% own personal computers at home, headed by Taipei city families 81%, followed by metropolitan Kaohsiung and northern Taiwan families in general (75.5% and 75.1% respectively), while only 56% of families in east Taiwan own personal computers at home. On average, each family in Taiwan owned 1.6 personal computers at home in 2003, which is 0.2% growth per family from 2001. One sees a large gap between Internet access and usage in economically developed metropolitan north and south Taiwan, as compared to the rural east and mid Taiwan.

Sixth, concerning the ethnic minority, the computer ownership rate for the aboriginal Taiwanese is only 35.2%, their Internet access at home is 22% and their Internet literacy is 9.3% (The Government Information Office of the Republic of China, R.O.C, Taiwan, 2003). Besides, the digital application capacity of the aboriginal ethnic is very far behind the national average of 66.9%, based on *The 2002 Investigation of the Digital Divide in Taiwan Areas* conducted by the Graduate School of Social Informatics of Yuan Ze University as commissioned by the Research Development and Evaluation Commission Executive Yuan (The Government Information Office of the Republic of China, R.O.C., 2003). Although computer ownership has increased due to the drop in computer prices and broadband handset rate has also improved due to the discount packages offered by the Internet service providers and cable companies, the coverage of owning broadband handset is not universal. The broadband cable handset is still beyond reach for people in the remote and mountainous east area and for low-income families.

The minority groups are no less eager to participate in the e-learning trend, and are even more anxious for the possible economic opportunities entailed, demonstrated by the fact that although Internet access has improved throughout the urban areas of both the north and south of Taiwan, 23.6 % of interviewees still call for further accessibility initiatives according to the National Information and Communication Initiative (NICI) statistical data.

Given the improvement of Internet access from 2001 through 2003, there were still 35.8% of interviewees who suggested that the government "lower the price of access hardware to the Internet to encourage Web usage." That was followed by 23.6% who wanted the government to "enhance the availability of the Internet in public places," 22.4% who hoped that the government would "speed up the hardware broadband infrastructure of the Internet," 18.4% who expressed the desire that the government would "reinforce the Web security control," 16.3% who wished that government would "provide free information technology skill competency and a Web-based learning program," and 15.4% who desired "classification and prohibition of pornography from the Internet."

According to the MOTC report, by 2003 over 10 million people had used the Internet in Taiwan, meaning that an average of one person out of two has been on the Internet. However, with the access divide narrowing since 2001, Taipei still leads as having the most access to the Internet (62.2%), followed by metropolitan Kaohsiung and northern Taiwan (51.5% and 51.5% respectively), east rural Taiwan (46.9%), mid-rural Taiwan (44.6%), and south-rural Taiwan (Kaohsiung City excluded) (41.7%).

E-LEARNING INDUSTRY POLICY GUIDANCE

The basic idea behind policy guidance for development of the e-learning industry is to increase market demand for e-learning corporate applications and to boost Taiwan's global economic competitiveness through the use of those applications. All national projects and initiatives serve these two goals (*National Science and Technology Program for E-Learning*, (n.d.), introduction section, para. 9).

An exception to the enterprise-driven policy is the project of the National Digital Archives Program (NDAP), which combines technology, humanity and culture. The NDAP was launched on January 1, 2002, under the auspices of the National Science and Technology Program sponsored by the NSC. The NDAP has constructed various databases, collectively called the Taiwan Digital Archives (TDA), which aimed at the digitalization of the valuable content of national museums, archives, universities, and research institutions. To name a few, there are the Academia Historical Digital Archives, National Museum History Archives, National Palace Museum Archives, National Central Library Digital Archives, and National Museum of Natural Science Digital Archives.

The National E-learning Technology Plan of the Ministry of Economy and Industry (MOEI) is meant to promulgate a learning-driven society and to enhance overall national economic competitiveness. In addition, industrial evolution and content innovation will be led by e-learning implementation and then applied to other fields of agriculture and fishing. The purpose is the creation of a self-dependent market and increased market demand for the digital learning industry, which will finally enhance Taiwan's global economy competence.

Since human resources in e-learning development play an important role in Taiwan's e-learning industries, a lot of investment has been allocated to the cultivation of human resources for information technology, as well as relevant hardware and software development. The essence of the e-learning industry development in Taiwan is a system of preferential measures, such as waiving export taxes for e-learning related products and various forms of awards and assistance to relevant academic activities. Against this backdrop, in 2003 the Executive Yuan lifted the ban on international IT talent and high-tech professionals who had working experience overseas. The lifting of the ban permits Chinese from the People's Republic of China who had working experience and advanced degrees to work in Taiwan's IT field. Moreover, to integrate present human resources in academia and research and development in industry, the National Center for High-Performance Computing is responsible for the Taiwan Advanced Research and Education Network (TWAREN) and the Knowledge Innovation National Grid (KING), which hold regular contests to nurture that manpower for e-learning content.

In Taiwan, there are the National Science and Technology Program for e-learning of the NSC and the National E-learning Technology Plan of the MOEI in the central government to promote the agenda of e-learning. The NSC takes the initiative in integrating the research and development capacities of up, mid, and down streams in the e-learning industry in Taiwan. In addition, the National Science and Technology program of e-learning brought up the idea of research and development of advanced e-learning technology through academia to ensure continuous research and development of e-learning platforms, contents and activities, and development tools. Meanwhile, through cooperation with academia, industry, and government, NSC also facilitates, encourages, and propagates e-learning inside corporations and enterprises by providing incentives and preferential measures from the government. The details can be broken down as below.

First, the National Science and Technology Program for e-learning aims at creating a "learning society" and helping Taiwan acquire competitive advantages in the global market. Thus, the goal was to provide an e-learning environment for everyone and to narrow the digital divide through the process of expansion of the e-learning market in Taiwan. However, the industry-led and enterprise benefit-driven e-learning environment does not have sufficient momentum behind it to justify e-learning exploration in the service of enhancing the equity of education, nor does it contrive to improve the overall educational structure and environment.

One goal of the program is to plan and develop e-learning tools, for example, e-school bags of multifunctional, mobile learning devices. The purpose is to enable people to access networks and learn effectively from new instructional models online. Although both goals will eventually lead to the increase of overall e-learning market demand, little research has been done regarding the efficiency of e-schoolbags. There has been no study regarding the affordability and availability of the e-school bags in remote areas and for the poor. Nor has it been fully assessed if the e-schoolbags can really replace a proficient teacher in face-to-face instruction or whether students will lose interest in the e-schoolbags over time. There is doubt about the cost to maintain, update, and repair e-schoolbags in the long term. It is certain, however, that the electronic platform for setting up the e-schoolbags database will cost more than NT$10 billion.

Second, in addition to learning devices, development tools, and promotion of new learning models on the Internet, creative content and network platforms are also necessary. Hence, the NSC brought up the concept of the Network Science Park for e-learning. The science park, which is devoted to the development of e-learning content in virtual reality, inherits the successful model of the Hsin Chu Science Park for semi-conductor manufacturers. The assumption is that the Network Science Park for e-learning can build the e-learning industry by attracting manufacturers and companies with a favorable tax rate, sound infrastructure, and excellent environment for business development.

However, cultural and educational evolution is unlike the semiconductor industry, which achieves mass production rapidly through the vertical coordination of research, production, and development within the science park. Nevertheless, cultural and educational development cannot be totally planned in advance, managed, or conducted in laboratories or factories' science parks. By and large, e-learning as an industry policy falls short in transference to educational and cultural policy.

Third, another goal set by the policy is the "fundamental research on learning and cognition in e-learning" (*National Science and Technology Program for E-learning* [n.d.], introduction section planning part). In the new instructional models on the Internet, learning is closely related to cognitive science and learning science application. However, study of the e-learning instructional systems design and how those learning models can be adapted to learner cognition is still in its preliminary stage in Taiwan. Research topics such as how to develop network-based learning design models, the impact e-learning has on children physically and psychologically, and ways to provide incentives for and eliminate barriers from underprivileged groups' participation in e-learning require further study.

BENEFICIARIES OF E-LEARNING

The customers and beneficiaries of e-learning have been identified as local enterprises, government offices and educational service providers or other companies. In other words, the main consumers of e-learning services and products are not targeted at minorities or the poor. According to the statistical data published by the Market Information Center (MIC) in June 2003 (as cited in the report of Industry Development Bureau and Ministry of Economic Affairs, [n.d.], e-learning market type can be categorized into two big chunks.

The first chunk is named "e-learning Public Network Access Solution provider market" and the second chunk is called the "instruction service provider."

The e-learning Public Network Access Solution provider market can include platform/development tools and auxiliaries (Web-based learning content management), project service (system integration and consultation service), e-learning content, and teaching kits and materials. Its targeted customers are businesses, government organizations, and educational service providers such as online instruction and traditional school and classroom instruction providers.

The Web-based/online instruction service provider includes preschool education (kindergarten education), cram school education, and technique and skill instruction for commerce and industry. Its targeted customers are individuals who can afford e-learning, including students who must pass the college entrance exam, employees who have to get a professional Microsoft diploma to get salary raises, and the unemployed who want to increase personal competitiveness in computer literacy and skill to get jobs. In urban Taiwan, teaching kits and instructional materials of e-learning concepts are popular in for-profit institutes, which are eager to be equipped with the latest computer and Internet technology to attract more potential customers.

Web-based e-learning service providers are prone to concentrate in the urban areas in the north and south of Taiwan, and they target students, corporate employees, housewives, and recreational consumers. On the other hand, the needs of nonprofit organizations and underprivileged minority groups are neglected, while rural counties without Internet access are completely excluded from opportunities to participate in e-learning. Also, economically and educationally underprivileged groups have little chance to benefit directly from development of the e-learning industry.

There are few e-learning instructional programs specifically designed for indigenous and other minority ethnic populations (let alone adequate provision of creative instructional programs suitable for a range of varying ethnicity, age, education level, economic hierarchy, and vocations) due to the limited market demand in these groups.

On the other hand, in the economically developed north and south urban areas, high Internet literacy, computer usage, and the proliferation of wireless networks and broadband handsets created an environment for sophistication with e-books (which can be connected to Internet databases) and multimedia facilities. In 2003, e-learning instruction service providers cooperated with IT-based e-learning platform/device companies, content developers, content publishers, and mobile learning vehicle manufacturers to establish the E-Learning Industry Research and Development Alliance. The alliance's aim is to get financial support from the National Science and Technology Program of E-Learning to promote the use of e-schoolbags in urban areas.

As a result, such IT innovations in software packages and e-schoolbags under the e-learning trend undoubtedly exacerbated the economic and educational gap. Urban areas in northern and southern Taiwan see the most advantage from e-learning content application and consumption, while the rural middle and east of Taiwan lag behind.

The most in need failed to benefit the most from the e-learning trend. As indicated by Cuban, the Internet has followed film, radio, broadcast TV, and the VCR and was regarded as the panacea for educational inequity. However, history tells us every 20 years or so a fresh wave of instructional technology has arrived and promised to revolutionize education with little effect (as cited in Bromley & Apple, 1998, p. 12). E-learning and the advent of the Internet does not automatically solve the gap.

E-LEARNING AVAILABILITY

Although market demand is an important indicator of e-learning industry development, the e-learning market in Taiwan is extremely limited at the present time, mainly because the poor communities are not able to use e-learning products and services, and market demand has reached a ceiling. In short, the limits of market demand have circumscribed the popularization and distribution of e-learning in Taiwan. In a word, the government policy that expected an increased market demand to promote e-learning application universally resembles a production of *Waiting for Godot*.

In Taiwanese e-learning, there are dozens of companies competing for a market worth NT$1.3 billion. By 2002, the e-learning market in Taiwan reached NT$0.768 billion, and the number expected for 2003 was NT$1.304 billion, a 69.8% growth. On the one hand, the e-learning Public Network Access Solution type of market took account of NT$0.584 billion, a growth from NT$0.424 billion. On the other hand, the e-learning instruction service type of market grew from NT$0.343 billion to NT$0.721 billion due to the SARS epidemic and the increased broadband handset rate in 2002. One can foresee fierce competition still to come.

To increase market demand, it is imperative for the e-learning industry in Taiwan to reach the global market, thus the aggression in the e-learning market in the global Chinese community. The Chinese market is just a starting point to reach the world.

Chinese society has a tradition of valuing education, even more so since the nationwide implementation of the one-child-per-family policy. In addition, the Communist Party of China has proclaimed the goal of achieving national prosperity through science and technology. Of the NT$11.32 billion market for professional software, educational software accounted for 27%. Hence, it was expected that the advent of the Internet and IT would eventually lead to educational evolution and then bridge the digital gap between the haves and have-nots in China.

In 1999, mainland China initiated the so called radical educational evolution and nation-wide promotion of quality education, (as cited in the report of the Industry Development Bureau and Ministry of Economic Affairs, 2003a, Section 3, para. 4), which aimed at elevating the educational levels of Chinese youth. An effort was made to raise the enrollment rate in higher education from 9% to 15% through long distance education (Industry Development Bureau and Ministry of Economic Affairs, 2003a, Section 3, para. 4).

As a result, a Chinese e-learning project was added to the 15 national projects to be attempted between 2002 and 2005. In October 2000, the mainland China government announced that beginning in 2001, within five to ten years, it would promote intramural connection through the Internet in K–12 level schools nationwide. The goal is that modernization of IT and communication technology will lead to an evolution in education through e-learning. Ninety percent of all private K–12 schools will have access to the Internet in order to enjoy the cornucopia of educational resources available. Schools in remote rural areas will be equipped with at least multimedia, if not full Internet.

Moreover, the magnetic effect of the market of mainland China has drawn many Taiwanese companies to make investments there. Some have even relocated their production lines and factories to China. Such emigration trends also gave rise to immense demand for new staff orientation and in-service and on-the-job training within their own firms to serve their need in provincial management. Taiwanese companies have expected to prosper from the support of the communist Chinese government in their efforts to eradicate the digital divide separating their own rural and urban areas.

However, on-the-job training and other e-learning applications are not enhancing education equity in rural areas of China; jobs created in China have concentrated in urban areas there, too. Furthermore, the tendency for manufacturers to move and send their production lines to China because of the cheaper labor costs and ample raw materials negatively affected the unemployment rate in the island. As can be seen, the increased global e-learning market demand alone does not suffice in bridging the persistent availability gap within Taiwan, therefore the availability of e-learning in the rural and mountainous area in Taiwan remains unsolved in a global market prospective.

DIGITAL GAP IN ACCESS AND SKILL COMPETENCY

The Taiwanese government has subsidized many projects to build Internet infrastructures in public places, such as libraries, schools, and community centers. However, the location where people feel most comfortable with Internet exploration and self-learning is at home.

In Taiwan, there is more public investment in wiring up libraries and schools than in wiring up homes for rural or poverty-stricken individuals. Such policy direction needs improvement. One reason is that, as demonstrated by Dotterweich in *Virtual Inequity,* home access provides ample opportunities for exploration and practice (Mossberger et al., 2003, p. 136). Moreover, "The access and skills divide seem closely linked, perhaps in a vicious cycle, meaning that 'those without skills have little need to use computers, and those without frequent availability have little chance to develop the skills that they need through trial and error and practice,'" (Mossberger et al., p. 121).

On the other hand, e-learning for everyone can be achieved through the integration of software and hardware resources by building community-based e-learning and IT service centers. Such public access to the Internet can provide both skill cultivation and information literacy courses to the community. Such public Internet-access service centers with sufficient IT support can benefit inhabitants of remote areas, low-income families, and minority groups. In urban areas like Taipei, many universities, high-speed Internet-cafés, and public libraries play the same role as the disseminator of e-learning opportunity by providing the e-learning programs and activities to all walks of citizens. In a similar manner, the underprivileged in remote areas can easily have access to diversified e-learning facilities and resources provided in the community-based IT service centers.

Local governments must take responsibility to collaborate and cooperate with businesses, academia, and professional volunteers, who can provide both technical consultation and support. Existing community centers mentioned above might have the content and free software, but they lack the necessary technology to incorporate IT into the daily lives of the citizens they serve. With such a technological capacity, community service centers can apply IT tools not only to advocate online learning, but also online organizations, community information clearinghouses, networking and online communities.

CONCLUSION

The distribution of technical skills and information literacy are important factors in the innovation of e-learning technology, as well as the future development of the knowledge economy and cultivation of high quality manpower. Therefore, the government should commit itself to achieving equity in technical support, equalized use and public access to the resources on the Internet, and promote literacy of information and computer skills through collaborating with academia, industry, and local government. As pointed out by Dotterweith, "There is an important role in supporting the acquisition of information literacy, as well as technical competence, in order to capture the social benefits of technology and promote equal chance for political and economic participation" (Dotterweith, cited in Mossberger et al., 2003, p. 133).

In the educational aspect, the government should take responsibility to improve existing deficiencies in education, cultural stimulation, and economic opportunity in the poor community, which can only be worsened in an e-learning age. It is an ideal that indigenous and creative instructional programs are available and affordable for different ethnicities, minorities, ages, education levels, economic hierarchies and vocations. As mentioned by Dotterweith, it is the government that should provide equal educational opportunity and public investment in lifelong learning through public investment and increased quality and availability (Dotterweith, cited in Mossberger et al., 2003, pp. 136–138).

Specifically, instruction on software and information literacy in the Internet should be offered regularly by the community IT centers, schools, continuing education institutes, and libraries. The government should also promote the distribution and use of free software in low-income communities as well as in nonprofit organizations by providing the minimum of network platform and computer equipment. (Chi-Hong, T., Tzi-jen, T., Ting, Ching-Chen, M., C-Q., Chao-Qei, H., et al., 2001, subtopic 2, para. 6).

Second, bridging the digital gap between the haves and have-nots should not become an excuse to benefit certain e-learning enterprises, and the government should not recklessly promote e-learning multimedia facilities such as e-schoolbags.

Third, e-learning development shouldn't be solely guided by industry. Industry-oriented policy guidance should enlist the brainpower of educational and cultural fields, and seek its cooperation (Hsih-Hwa Wu, 2001). More social, cultural, and human compassion should be emphasized in e-learning development projects.

It is an optimistic sign that the central government has subsidized and cooperated with academia in establishing the Digital Culture Development and Training Centers to provide lifelong and continuing education through e-learning content on the Internet. Take, for example, the Digital Culture Center of the National Tong Hwa University in east Taiwan. The program is manned by the Institute for Information Industry task force, which joined forces with the academia of the Dong-Hwa University in building the first Digital Culture Center in east Taiwan (National Dong-Hwa University, 2003). Additionally, the Ministry of Education has led the e-Generation Manpower Cultivation Plan and constructed the Public Network E-learning System, in an effort to develop a Web-based learning content and environment for junior high schools and primary schools (Ministry of Education, 2003).

Finally, application of the advanced information technologies in the National Digital Archives Program should not be the final word for information and knowledge propagation and distribution for the benefit of every citizen launched by the government. Aside from the managing, preservation, and dissemination of digital information over networks, a broader ambition to use e-learning for nurturing creative minds across all educational and cultural fields should be attempted. Since, after all, e-learning as an educational tool should be embedded in the culture and the people.

REFERENCES

Bromley, H., & Apple, M. W. (Eds.). (1998). *Education/technology/power: Educational computing as a social practice.* Albany, NY: State University of New York Press.

Chi-Hong, T., Tzi-jen, T., Ching-Chen, M., Chao-Qei, H., et al., (2001). *Symposium subject five: Internet literacy and digital gap.* Symposium conducted at the meeting of the IT Society and the Digital Gap, Taipei, Taiwan. Retrieved February 16,

2003, from http://www.iis.sinica.edu.tw/2001-digital-divide-workshop/discuss5.htm

E-Taiwan Project. (n.d.). Retrieved February 16, 2003, from http://www.etaiwan.nat.gov.tw/content/application/etaiwan/profile/guest-cnt-browse.php?cnt_id=99&PHPSESSID=7a8915036551744a9e311ce6284a9381

Focus on Internet News and Data (FIND). (2003, November 28). *International telecommunication union (ITU): Taiwan ranked nine in the global digital access index 2002.* Retrieved July 13, 2004, from http://www.find.org.tw/news[AU: Are corrections OK?]

Government Information Office of the Republic of China, Taiwan. (2003, June 28). *Executive Yuan's NICI Committee officially established "bridging the digital divide leading team" and drafted "Bridging the digital gap initiatives."* Retrieved January 22, 2004, from http://publish.gio.gov.tw/newsc/newsc/920628/92062802.html

HanTeng, L. (2002, October 15). The Taiwan culture research and its absence in the National Digital Archives Program. *Culture studies monthly, 2*. Retrieved February 8, 2004, from http://www.ncu.edu.tw/~eng/csa/journal/journal_park143.htm

Hsih-Hwa, W. (2001). *Information literacy and the digital gap.* Paper presented at the 2001 Symposium on IT Society and the Digital Gap. Abstract retrieved January 22, 2004, from http://www.iis.sinica.edu.tw/2001-digital-divide-workshop/discuss5.htm

Industry Development Bureau & Ministry of Economic Affairs. (2003a). *The competence evaluation of the e-learning industry in Taiwan.* Retrieved January 22, 2004, from http://www.elearn.org.tw/NR/exeres/F34350E7-D49C-40A0-A2AE-36F1700CE166.html

Industry Development Bureau & Ministry of Economic Affairs. (2003b). *2003 yearly demonstration of e-learning industry promotion and development plan.* Retrieved February 16, 2003, from http://www.elearn.org.tw/NR/exeres/F34350E7-D49C-40A0-A2AE-36F1700CE166.htm

Kao Chong, G., Deh-Tsai, L., & Fon-Ching, L. (2001). *Symposium subject six: From digital divide to the digital opportunity.* Symposium conducted at the meeting of the IT Society and the Digital Gap, Taipei, Taiwan. Retrieved January 22, 2004 from http://www.iis.sinica.edu.tw/2001-digital-divide-workshop/discuss6.htm

Kao-Hong, Y. (2003, December 24). E-learning alliance promises on-line instructional platform within two years. *Journal of China Times.* Retrieved February 16, 2003, from http://www.itnet.org.tw/ssl/html-new/library/archive_12_2003.htm#921224-4

Li, J. (2004, February 13). *Taiwan government further lowered the threshold of high technology professional overseas to work in Taiwan.* Udn news. Retrieved March 10, 2004, from http://216.239.41.104/search?q=cache:0oq7h5I4ZrsJ:www.udn.com/2004/5/7/NEWS/FINANCE/FIN5/2008371.shtml

Ministry of Education. (n.d.). Retrieved March 7, 2004, from http://140.111.1.192/secretary/e2008/2008-e2.htm

Ministry of Education. (2002, July 18). *E-generation manpower cultivation plan.* Retrieved March 7, 2004, from http://216.239.41.104/search?q=cache:nscbCojLpwgJ:www.cepd.gov.tw/2008/

Ministry of Transportation and Communication & Bureau of Statistics. (2003, May). *The report on the internet usage of the population.* Statistic Bureau: Taipei, Taiwan.

Mossberger, K., Tolbert, C. J., & Stansbury, M. (2003). *Virtual inequity: Beyond the digital divide.* Washington, DC: Georgetown University Press.

National Dong-Hwa University. (2003, August 1). *2002 achievement report on digital culture education information system.* Retrieved March 7, 2004, from http://dcc.ndhu.edu.tw/91report.pdf

National Information and Communication Initiative Committee (NICI). (2003, January 1). *NICI mid-term initiatives & plan from January 2002 to December 2007.* Retrieved March 7, 2004, from http://www.nici.nat.gov.tw/content/application/nici/general/guest-cnt-browse

National Science Council. (n.d.). *2002 introduction to the national science and technology program for e-learning.* Retrieved February 16, 2003, from http://elnp.ncu.edu.tw/startE.php

National Science and Technology Program for E-learning. (n.d.). *The national e-learning project plan.* Retrieved January 22, 2004, from http://elnp.ncu.edu.tw/startE.php

Research Development and Evaluation Commission Executive Yuan. (2002, August 16). *The discrepancy between the richest and the poorest further expanded in 2001.* Retrieved March 7, 2004, from http://www.gov.tw/todaytw/1-13-16-0.htm

Research Development and Evaluation Commission Executive Yuan. (2003, May). *2002 investigation of the digital divide in Taiwan areas.* Retrieved March 7, 2004, from http://64.233.161.104/search?q=cache:_oPvIDHO9yMJ:203.67.133.67/digital/OBJECT/BranPage/

Servon, L. J. (2002). *Bridging the digital gap: Technology, community, and public policy.* Malden, MA: Blackwell

THREE

DISTANCE EDUCATION AND ONLINE TECHNOLOGIES IN INDIA

Priya Sharma

India ventured into distance education in the early 1960s with the introduction of correspondence courses to serve rural and underserved communities. The development of distance education systems became a priority during the era of postcolonial development and independence, when basic inequalities of the educational system were highlighted and educational discourse began to revolve around the concepts of popular education, integration of vernacular schooling systems, and equitable access. Initially, distance education began as an attempt to provide broader access to learning at lower costs than a traditional university. The first open and distance education university was established in 1982 and, as of 2001, India had 10 open universities and 62 centers of distance education housed in conventional universities (Ghosh, 2001). The largest of the open universities, the Indira Gandhi National Open University (IGNOU), serves approximately 600,000 students in gaining higher education degrees in 50 different fields (Overland, 2000). Despite the seemingly high number of enrolled students, distance education in India has consistently been viewed as a second-rate education alternative, and traditional education is still reserved for elite, urban consumers. The advent of the Internet and the explosive growth of online education around the world have prompted some discussion about the possibility of integrating online components within the Indian distance education setting. My intention in this chapter is to examine the state of traditional and distance education in India, and identify the viability and importance of online education given the current social, economic, and infrastructural status quo. Here are some questions to consider as you read this chapter.

- What are the most important practical and ethical considerations in conceptualizing the application and role of online distance education in developing nations?
- What do you see as the primary concerns of the different online education stakeholders—government, industry, academia, rural, and urban populations—within the Indian context?
- What do you see as the most important comparisons between online distance education in developed and developing nations?
- What types of fruitful collaborations between educators and researchers in developing and developed nations would you recommend for addressing these types of contexts?

THE CURRENT STATE OF EDUCATION

In 2002, India's population was estimated to have crossed the one billion mark and adult illiteracy was at 44%. According to the Indian Education Ministry, the public expenditure on education in 2002 was at 3.2% of GDP and has increased an average of 0.11% per year since 1951. At the same time, the number of educational institutions has increased within the period from 1951 to 2002. The Indian Education Ministry reported that there were three times as many primary schools, about 18 times as many high schools, about 24 times as many colleges of general education, and ten times as many universities in 2002 as compared to 1951. Although this growth seems impressive in numbers, it has been insufficient to keep pace with the explosive population growth and accompanying social and cultural complexities. Money that would otherwise be channeled into education is mostly redirected into battling poverty and food shortages and providing the most basic amenities of life. Approximately 26% of the population lives below the poverty level, with approximately equal distribution in both the rural and urban areas (Ministry of Economics Survey, 2001–2002). Providing access to education has become the single most important item on the government's agenda and the Indian government has established an ambitious target of reducing illiteracy to 5% by the year 2020 (Black, 2004). To achieve this target, it is necessary for primary and basic education to be a singular focus of funding and policy for the Indian government. However, it seems that the government's priorities for education in India are evolving on two very different tracks—one is focused on basic education and the other is focused on sustaining and encouraging professional development and education. In review, the expenditure within these two areas is necessarily disparate; although basic education is barely funded by the government and occasionally supported through grassroots efforts of non-government organizations (NGOs) and nonprofit organizations (NPOs), while professional education continues to attract both private and government money.

CURRENT GOVERNMENTAL FUNDING AND PRIORITIES FOR EDUCATION

After independence, instead of focusing on providing primary education, the Indian government decided to expend its energy on increasing the availability of university education at a low cost. Because of this decision, in the 1980s, about 70% of Indian adults aged 25 years and older had no primary or secondary schooling (Dhanarajan, 1997). In direct contrast, India's nearest competitor, China, has quite consistently emphasized the development of primary and secondary education. In comparison, in 1980, the population of China's labor force with a primary education was over three times that of India's labor force (Dhanarajan, 1997).

To deal with this discrepancy, the Indian Parliament passed the 93rd Constitutional Amendment, better known as the Education Bill, in 2001. Article 21A of the bill stresses the government's emphasis on equal opportunities for primary education: "The State shall provide free and compulsory education to all children of the age of six to fourteen years in such manners as the State may, by law, determine." The government, however, has not yet defined or allocated funding for this initiative and the costs of doing so are considerable. For a large portion of rural India, the exigencies of earning a living mean that parents are often unable to send children to school. According to the National Alliance for the Fundamental Right to Education (NAFRE), by age six (the age at which the bill intends to begin compulsory education) most children in villages are already engaged in some form of employment and contributing to the upkeep of the family (Mendis, 2004). The bill also does not explicitly outline strategies for mitigating residual and adult illiteracy—addressing the plight of those individuals and areas that were overlooked in the numerous literacy campaigns that have been organized by the government since 1951.

Another important statistic is the spread of literacy in different states in India. The southern states have traditionally reported higher incidences of literacy at almost 90%, while the northern states have lagged far behind with literacy levels as low as 40%. According to a United Nations Development Program (UNDP) press report (2000), the northern states have higher population growth rates and more poverty. One educational imperative is the need to invest in physical and social infrastructure in poorer and remote regions to promote more equitable development, instead of channeling resources to the developed, urban, and richer states and districts. However, the government has identified no sustainable plan for promoting equitable educational access in different areas and for different people. Although distance education courses began to be offered in the 1960s to reach some portion of this population, a relatively quick examination further illustrates the divide between those that have access to education and those that do not.

GOVERNMENT-SPONSORED OPEN AND DISTANCE EDUCATION INITIATIVES

In 1986, the government's National Policy on Education (NPE) stated that "the future thrust will be in the direction of open and distance learning" to address learning for all. To broaden the reach of educational opportunity, the government of India established the National Open School (NOS) in 1989 to provide opportunities for alternative schooling to socioeconomically disadvantaged communities and remote and rural learners. NOS reportedly offered primary, secondary, higher secondary, vocational, and life-enrichment programs to students from ages 14 to 76 and claimed to have reached enrollments of 260,000 in the 5 years since its institution (Mukhopadhyay, 1995). The current mission statement of

NOS reinforces the role of information technologies in promoting equitable educational access:

> Simultaneous efforts have been contemplated to provide educational and training access to the disadvantaged and the differently abled, and link education/schooling to social and community development. Open schooling and basic education at a distance have got established, in the last two decades, as strong systemic intervention mechanisms to cater to the quality educational needs of millions of deprived people, with very low cost. Massive developments in information and communications technology have opened up wider possibilities of convergence of methods, media, resources and technologies to wider access and equity in educational provision. The National Policy on Education (NPE 1986) of the Government of India underlines that the future of educational delivery belongs to open and distance learning. (NOS, 2004)

This statement is useful as a conceptual framework for identifying possible roles of distance learning and online technologies, but it does not explicate the practical challenges of implementation. Despite the efforts of the NOS, the demand for education has far outstripped the availability of educational opportunities (Overland, 2000). Only 6.5% of Indian high school graduates pursue higher education degrees, as compared to 30% in developed countries, according to Abdul Waheed Khan, vice chancellor of IGNOU. Despite continual promises from the government about increased spending on higher education, the reality is that most money will probably be channeled into primary and secondary education, in direct contrast to the Indian government's focus on higher education in the 1950s and 1960s. While endorsing the potential of online technologies, Lewis Perinbam, senior adviser of Commonwealth of Learning, while acknowledging the potential of online and distance learning initiatives, clearly stresses financing and infrastructure as the two biggest challenges facing any such effort:

> The growing demands for more education, the lack of financial and, more importantly human resources, the erosion of quality in education systems, and the demands of the knowledge era for skills are propelling political leaders to crusade for educational reform—including making access to learning an easier process.
> ... Increasingly, educational institutions have taken education to their students regardless of the barriers of space, time, prior knowledge, gender and affordability. India can play a pivotal role in changing outmoded ideas because it has been a pioneer in harnessing distance and open learning to its progress and development.

> ... Distance education entities of the future will practice a variety of expanded skills and employ a range of programmes [sic] and technologies from franchises at traditional campuses serving the science, technology and business science needs of those able to pay, to the subsidised [sic], specially tailored programmes [sic] directed to learning centers [sic] during non-working hours. But they will succeed only with a political commitment to serving their nation's learning needs—the necessary financing and infrastructure (Perinbam, 1997).

Even in higher education, the development of online instruction has been relatively modest despite the hype. The slow growth is partially due to increased governmental pressure for universities to seek independent funding for their distance education initiatives. IGNOU is one of the governmental units that includes online delivery of instruction as one of its emphasis areas and offers two degrees via its virtual campus. Other premier academic institutes such as the Indian Institute of Technology and Birla Institute of Technology have also created online delivery for some of their courses and the School of Education Technology at Jadavpur University has developed several computer-assisted instruction modules as well as authoring tools. The Center for Development of Advanced Computing (a scientific society of the Department of Information Technology of the Government of India) has an ongoing research project of maintaining a national resource center for online learning. The project, titled Vidyakash (http://www.ncst.ernet.in/vidyakash/home.shtml) is aimed at developing a range of tools, knowledge bases, and training resources for online learning within the Indian context. The stated objectives of the project are to:

- develop a national knowledge base of information related to online education;
- be a nodal resource center for providing technological, managerial, and administrative expertise in on-line education;
- pursue R&D relevant to on-line learning in order to ensure appropriate application of this technology;
- interact with Indian and international agencies; and
- train the teachers in the technology and tools.

Vidyakash is also actively engaged in developing online software for designing and implementing instruction. Another initiative of the governmental National Open School is to train and prepare personnel to assume responsibilities for designing and implementing distance education courses with or without the use of technology. The school's objective is stated as follows:

> The systemic human resource development envisaged in the international certificate and diploma programmes [sic] in open schooling aim at capacity building and increasing staff competency in the areas of open schooling and open basic education for a variety of functionaries engaged in planning and management, curriculum and instructional design, self-learning material development, learner support services, and assessment and evaluation.

This training initiative is focused at trainers, instructors, and evaluators. It also appears that the training is related to traditional distance education, using very traditional methods including printed materials and audio/video materials.

In comparison to the educational needs of the democracy, the number of initiatives is miniscule. The inadequacy of the initiatives to address the needs of the general and underserved populations is aggravated by the lack of governmental funding and support. With the requirement for universities to develop and sustain online programs, it is not surprising to see that the majority of online and distance courses are geared towards serving a fraction of the population—the elite, educated, and wealthy—that is, those who are able to pay for these amenities. Thus it is unlikely that these courses will have any impact on furthering equitable access to rural and socioeconomically disadvantaged segments of the population, who do not have access to infrastructure, resources, or funding to engage in these initiatives. In addition, most online courses content revolves around an information technology (IT) curriculum, enhancing opportunities for white-collar workers who are looking for professional and career development opportunities. The initiatives in their current form continue to ignore the content around basic literacy and primary education needs of the marginalized populations.

In summary, in the past five decades since independence, India has been attempting to overcome powerful social, cultural, and economic barriers on the road to equal and equitable educational access. Stagnant illiteracy levels are exacerbated by explosive population growth and the unequal distribution of infrastructure, resources, and capital in urban and remote areas. Furthermore, the lack of an appropriate plan to encourage and sustain equal education has resulted in a furthering of the educational divide between the haves and the have-nots.

THE CONUNDRUM OF TECHNOLOGICAL DEVELOPMENT AND ACCESS

India's presence and role in the global software marketplace introduces an additional incommensurable bias in the educational divide. Despite the challenges of poverty and economy, India is rapidly emerging as the site of the fastest growing software industry. The country reportedly has about four million technology workers, including 70,000 software professionals, who are trained in about 1,700 technical institutes. The Indian software industry grew at an annual rate of approximately 60% from 1992 to 1999, at almost double the rate of the U.S. industry, generating revenues of almost $4 billion dollars (Bhatnagar, 2002). The importance of IT in sustaining development in India emerged as a key priority for the government, which has established a target of generating $50 billion in software export revenues by the year 2008 as well as increasing the density of IT and make it available to the general population. In 1998, Prime Minister Atal Behari Vajpayee established a National Task Force to produce an IT plan. The plan was developed to sustain India's competitiveness in the global IT arena, as is obvious from the preamble to the plan:

> In the history of civilisation, [sic] no work of science has so comprehensively impacted on the course of human development as Information Technology (IT). Undoubtedly, IT has been the greatest change agent of this century and promises to play this role even more dramatically in the coming decades. IT is changing every aspect of human life—communications, trade, manufacturing, services, culture, entertainment, education, research, national defense and global security. IT is breaking old barriers and building new interconnections in the emerging Global Village. IT has also become the chief determinant of the progress of nations, communities and individuals.
>
> For India, the rise of Information Technology is an opportunity to overcome historical disabilities and once again become the master of one's own national destiny. IT is a tool that will enable India to achieve the goal of becoming a strong, prosperous and self-confident nation. In doing so, IT promises to compress the time it would otherwise take for India to advance rapidly in the march of development and occupy a position of honor and pride in the comity of nations.
>
> The Government of India has recognised [sic] the potential of Information Technology for rapid and all-round national development. The National Agenda for Governance, which is the Government's policy blueprint, has taken due note of the Information and Communication Revolution that is sweeping

the globe. Accordingly, it has mandated the Government to take necessary policy and programmatic initiatives that would facilitate India's emergence as an Information Technology Superpower in the shortest possible time.

This ambitious plan focuses on the selected development and education of software professionals. A growing number of online professional development initiatives has been funded by corporations and foreign investors. Most privately offered initiatives in online learning and distance education are targeted toward the upper middle class and professionals who are seeking a career in IT and the software industry. Online courses that range from tutorials in specific test topics to software engineering institute's certification are offered by quite a few enterprises. For example, NIIT, a significant player in the IT industry, has instituted NetVarsity, which offers over 300 indigenously developed online courses and claims to have reached a student community of over 34,000. The fee for enrolling in these courses is generally quite high, but this investment is generally considered worthwhile since India exports about 60% of its software workforce to the United States and European countries (Bhatnagar, 2002).

As previously identified, these initiatives serve to reinforce the privilege and dominance of the elite population. No subsidies exist for the economically disadvantaged, either from the government or the corporations themselves. In effect, these initiatives serve only to make the corporations more powerful and the elite wealthier, while ignoring the needs of the non-elite. Afzal Mohammad, vice chancellor of Ambedkar Open University, characterizes the current focus of online courses and technology as a way to widen the gap between the rich and the poor and expresses some concern that such professional online courses could become "money-making" machines, making "a bad situation worse" (Overland, 2000). With the government's new focus on building IT capital, it is even more likely that online education will become a cash cow, serving the needs of both the industry and government for revenues.

INFRASTRUCTURAL INADEQUACIES

Although one of the imperatives of the government's IT plan is to provide access to technology and technology education for all, this is no trifling task, and nowhere is the extent of this task more apparent than in India. According to a report published in 1998 by Panos, an international organization that focuses on investigating and reporting on sustainable development issues globally, the ability to apply different technologies in developing countries is affected by four important elements: lack of adequate telecommunication infrastructure, high costs of equipment, lack of technical and design know-how, and high service costs.

The government has tried to address policy and infrastructure issues to some extent. At a national policy level, the Department of Information Technology and the Department of Telecommunications have supported an effort by the Confederation of Indian Industry to explore the viability of broadband technologies in the Indian context. While the findings of the study will be of significant interest—especially the costs that are passed on to the consumer—the fact that such explorations are being supported is some indication of the government's intent to channel money and resources into the development and proliferation of such technologies. More important will be an identification of the government's strategy in subsidizing the cost of the technologies and making it equally accessible to everyone.

Another much publicized initiative is Media Lab Asia (http://www.medialabasia.org/), a research organization that was chartered in 2001 with seed funding from the government of India and in collaboration with the Massachusetts Institute of Technology. The organization focuses on the development of technologies that address the needs of the citizens of developing nations in Asia, Africa, and Latin America. The goals of Media Lab Asia are closely tied to the use of technology for socioeconomic development:

> Media Lab Asia's charter is to pursue high-impact technology research that can improve the lives of common people in developing economies. The organization believes that new technologies, specially, ICT's (Information and Communication Technologies) offer tremendous possibilities for socioeconomic development. To cite just a few examples, speech interfaces will make information access available even to illiterates; affordable wireless technologies and hardware devices will make the Internet and computers available to a greater section of the world. The lab works proactively to harness these advances for the benefit of the masses, especially rural masses that have been untouched by ICT's.

In his speech on the anniversary of India's 55th year of independence in 2002, Prime Minister Atal Behari Vajpayee set forth a list of 15 important initiatives for reducing poverty in India. The eighth initiative points to Media

Lab Asia's work as one important factor in mitigating poverty and the digital and educational divide in the subcontinent.

> It [MediaLab Asia] would pursue high-end research in four areas germane to the needs of rural India: "World Computer" (low-cost computing devices); "Bits for All" (bringing low-cost connectivity to the doorstep of rural masses; "Tools for Tomorrow" (creation of low-cost learning tools to bring out the spirit of innovation among the rural youth); and "Digital Village" (where the above three research programmes would be demonstrated for palpable impact). Media Lab Asia has been designated as an Asian Regional Hub of the United Nations ICT Task Force for coordinating activities of academia and the private sector in the area of IT for the Masses.

For any of these initiatives to have an impact, however, the provision of basic infrastructural requirements such as electricity and phones is yet to be addressed. It was estimated that in 1999, only 86% of villages had access to electricity (statistics provided by Central Electricity Authority, Government of India). In 2002, the Ministry of Power launched an accelerated effort to complete electrification for all villages within 5 years, but until the completion of this effort, the inhabitants of approximately 82,000 villages will lack access to technology of any sort. The Ministry of Communications and Information Technology also has plans to increase India's telephone density from 4.38 to 5.61 per 100 customers by installing 13 million new telephone lines, including mobile phones. India's telephone density is currently at 5.2% in rural markets and 15% in urban markets, compared to 57% in Malaysia and 32% in China. Internet penetration in 2002 was even lower, accounting for only 0.3% of the population in comparison to 3.9% for China and 23% for South Korea.

In the face of such dismal statistics and historical records, the government's plan for improving infrastructure and technology research appears to be overly ambitious and almost impractical. Even if appropriate funding was available to be channeled in this sector, it is questionable whether the poor and rural communities would be appropriately served for it would be a very steep slope to climb from complete illiteracy to computer literacy.

As the government continues to explore large-scale initiatives, some NGOs and private corporations are attempting to address change at the grassroots level. One private initiative worth noting is the "hole-in-the-wall experiment" conducted by Dr. Sugata Mitra, the head of Research and Development at NIIT. Mitra installed an Internet-enabled computer in the wall adjoining the slums of New Delhi and tracked the activity near the computer using a video camera hidden in a nearby tree. Children approached the computer immediately and started to play with it. Within an hour, they had learned to use the mouse and navigate the Web, and within a week, they had learned to download games and music, despite the lack of English language knowledge and lack of prior education. Mitra, who is very much in favor of computer-based education, especially for the poor, calls this approach "minimally invasive education" and believes that this is the quickest way for poor children to teach themselves computer literacy. He provides a quick estimate of the cost of providing such educational opportunities for slum children:

> One kiosk, which taught some 160 children, cost 150,000 rupees (pounds2,343) to build plus the same again for the dedicated internet connection and maintenance. If we built 100,000 kiosks it would cost U.S.$2bn (pounds1.4bn) to keep them running for five years. In that time, assuming 200 children learn from each kiosk each year, 100 million children would become computer literate. The 13 year-olds of today would be 18. They would vote. I think we would have irreversible social change in India. (Mitra, quoted in Cohen, 2000)

Although an interesting experiment, it is yet to be seen if such an effort could be implemented and if it would bridge the gap between the high tech towers and the slums (Cohen, 2000). The lack of adequate funds makes it unlikely that the Indian government could absorb the $2 billion it would take to establish the kiosks. Even more important is the need to funnel money into areas where it can do the most good—such as providing basic education and amenities for these very communities of slums.

A second initiative worth noting is Schools Online (SOL), a global organization that provides access to the Internet and computers to underserved schools. SOL's network covers 56 schools in different Indian cities (Banerjee, 2003), although the network has yet to penetrate into the villages and remote areas of the subcontinent. Although many of the more elite private schools offer access to computers and teach students about IT topics, it will be a formidable challenge to introduce such amenities in public schools.

BRIDGING THE GAP: CONCLUDING THOUGHTS

We must acknowledge, however, that distance learning is not a panacea for all the ills facing education. Nor can we ignore that it has not always worked. Sometimes the human and technological infrastructure necessary for its success was not present. It requires both trained personnel and technology that is appropriate, affordable, and accessible. Conventional and distance education must work together and harness their respective capabilities. For they can do together what they cannot achieve working separately. (Perinbam, 1997) India, as a land, has thrived on contradictions. The country is the second largest producer of movies, yet not all villages have electricity. The most popular means of entertainment is a TV, yet not all families own a TV. The country produces one of the largest numbers of software engineers who are "exported" all over the world, yet more than half its population has little, if any, access to basic education. While there is certainly evidence of some effort to bridge the educational and digital divide in India, too many details remain unresolved. Infrastructure is probably the primary hurdle. For many households in India, basic amenities such as electricity and running water remain unobtainable luxuries. From that perspective, equipping households with computers and Internet connections seems almost impossible in the near future.

Education in India is fraught with difficulty for another reason—22 different spoken languages and dialects exist within a few hundred miles of each other. While a small percentage of the population is comfortable communicating in English, a vast majority is not. This issue becomes important, especially for localization of content delivery, which in turn has implications for development costs and resources. The design of online instruction requires significant effort in any context, and development of instruction within India's cultural and educational context is still to be explored. Traditionally, distance education courses have been viewed as poor alternatives to a regular university education. Overcoming this perspective will be a significant challenge in itself, apart from convincing educational establishments that distance education is a viable and useful dimension of education (Perinbam, 1997).

India also has a long way to go to before being able to provide equitable access to education, let alone online education. While online initiatives have increased access to postsecondary educational alternatives, they continue to serve the same elite populations and to ignore the marginalized communities. According to Gandhe (1999), of the 50 or 60 providers of open and distance learning in India, none made a significant impact on marginalized populations—the rural poor, women, and historically underprivileged communities. Instead, as he stringently commented, in most of them the initiatives had become "sub-servers to conventional providers due in part to a mindset that considered higher education a part of urban culture or worst still, as a cash cow to buttress cash strapped universities, affordable by only those living in cities" (Gandhe, as cited in Dhanarajan, 1997).

In summary, providing equitable education will require overcoming significant barriers and concerted effort on the part of India's government, corporations, and citizens. The most important imperative for the government is to equalize the social and physical infrastructure to provide equal access to basic amenities of life, including education. A second important step is the creation of a sustainable plan for ameliorating residual adult illiteracy and access to primary education. Only after achieving these goals can India begin to explore the magnitude of the digital divide and address methods of bridging the continuously widening chasm.

REFERENCES

Banerjee, K. (2003). Bridging the digital divide: Schools Online is helping equip one school at a time. *India Currents, 17,* 28.

Bhatnagar, M. (2002). *The reverse flow has begun in IT sector.* Retrieved January 17, 2004, from http://www.domain-b.com/infotech/itnews/200204apr/20020408_reverse.html

Black, R. (2004). *India tackles adult literacy.* Retrieved January 10, 2004, from http://news.bbc.co.uk/2/hi/uk_news/education/3365465.stm

Cohen, D. (2000, Oct 17). Hole in the wall has a whole new meaning in New Delhi. *The Guardian,* p. 12.

Dhanarajan, G. (1997). Face to Face with Distance Education. *Indian Journal of Open Learning, 6*(1–2), 1–10.

Ghosh, S. B. (2001). *Reaching the unreached for library and information science education: A perspective for developing countries. India.*

Mendis, I. D. (2004). *Operation blackboard—myth or reality?* Retrieved January 10, 2004, from http://www.the-south-asian.com/Jan%202004/education_for_all_in_india.htm

Ministry of Finance, Government of India. (2002). *Economic survey, 2001–2002.* Retrieved January 9, 2004, from http://indiabudget.nic.in/es2001-02welcome.html

Mukhopadhyay, M. (1995). Multichannel learning: The case of National Open School, India. In S. Anzalone (Ed.), *Multichannel learning: Connecting all to education* (pp. 93–105). Washington, DC: Education Development Center.

National Institute of Open Schooling. (2004). *Training courses in open schooling.* Retrieved January 22, 2004, from http://www.nios.ac.in/ictos.htm

Overland, M. A. (2000). India uses distance education to meet huge demand for degrees. *The Chronicle of Higher Education, 46,* A48–49.

Panos. (1998). *The Internet and poverty* (Briefing No. 28). London: Author.

Perinbam, L. (November 12, 1997). *A time for vision.* Paper presented at the World Conference on Education India: The next millennium, New Delhi, India.

United Nations Development Programme. (2000). *Effective devolution of power to Panchayats a must for sustainable human development, says the United Nations System.* Retrieved January 24, 2004, from http://www.undp.org.in/NEWS/PRESS/press168.htm

PART II

ONLINE EDUCATION IN EUROPE:

An Analysis of Ireland, the United Kingdom, Turkey, and International Study Circles

We make out of the quarrel with others, rhetoric,
but of the quarrel with ourselves, poetry.

—W. B. Yeats

To the western mind, Europe is full of history, steadfastness, diligence. It is an old place. It's where we come from, but less often where we are going to. It is seen more as a place of poetry, literature, and art than as a place of innovation. It is somehow fitting, then, that one of the main themes in Simpson's chapter on e-learning in the United Kingdom is retention. For the Europeans, online learning is not just about the innovation; it's not even mostly about the innovation. It's about how to make it work in the long run, how to make it history, how to pass it on to generations as yet unborn. He points to the lack of motivation on the part of e-learning proponents to admit to their high dropout rates. And he effectively makes the case that socially marginalized populations are much more likely to drop out.

In Europe, we don't speak so much about the widening gap or the digital divide. Instead we look at social exclusion. Sometimes, the language used to describe the online learning debate makes me feel like I ought to be at a cricket club. As Salt says, "The danger that computers create new elites is real" (xx). What is perhaps far more interesting about the rhetoric surrounding information and communication technology (ICT) and e-learning in Europe is the tendency to completely ignore issues of social justice and social equity. Our authors for this text aside, we find very little concern for the marginalized in the language that describes new initiatives in Europe generally. An examination of the European Web site, "Information Society Technologies" lists news and events dating back to 2002. What is most fascinating is that there are virtually no listings here that describe any sort of research study, seminar, conference, or publication dealing with social inequities in online services in Europe. Instead, below are several typical descriptions:

9 December 2003

eInfrastructures (Internet and Grids)—The new foundation for knowledge-based societies

Following an event which took place earlier this year under the Greek Presidency of the EU addressing the issue of harmonisation of policies on the access and use of IT-infrastructures for Research in Europe. Part of the activity during the event will also be the definition of a high-level committee of representatives from Networking and Grid national authorities in Europe (eInfrastructure Reflection Group). This group will aim at monitoring and supporting on a policy advisory level the creation and use of the eInfrastructure in Europe, as well as the strengthening of relations with the US Cyber-Infrastructure and other similar initiatives around the world.

25 September 2003

E-Science: the Technical Infrastructures

One of the main objectives of the Conference is to encourage debate among the public, beyond the circles of experts, on new forms of doing science.

7 September 2003

Advanced Networking Workshop "Policy Issues for NRENs in South East Europe"

The workshop aims to establish a dialogue at the level of policy developments for research and education networking and to provide inputs to the agenda of national governments and funding bodies in South East Europe.

15 July 2003

Research Networking testbeds Information Day

. . . is a public event aimed at bringing together the major players from all over Europe who have an interest in integrating and validating, in the context of user-driven large scale testbeds, the state-of-the-art networking technology that is essential for preparing the future upgrades in the information and communication infrastructure deployed across Europe.

Thus, the language used to describe initiatives in Europe invokes harmonization of policies, public debate about new forms of science and technology infrastructure, policy dialogue around advances in educational networking, and the like. This is a significant departure from our authors who sincerely engage the issues associated with socially excluded populations. It is not surprising that Simpson points to the lack of evidence that "e-learning will help solve the problems of social exclusion in either developed or developing countries." (xx). This lack of evidence is in part due to the initiatives that *are* being pursued, and they tend *not* to be concerned with the socially marginalized.

Language is actually an issue in more than one way. Not only is there concern over the rhetoric used to describe the disenfranchised and their invisibility in the rhetoric associated with future agendas in Europe, but also there is question of how we deal with native language comes into play in Europe. There are so many different languages being spoken today in Europe, and there is a deep and abiding honor given to those languages. Language becomes a representative proxy of culture, and thus asking any one culture to cede to others is particularly problematic. This, as Salt points out, is another way that participants may become marginalized. And while this may seem to be a less pressing issue than those which deal with connectivity or access, in fact, there are some deep-seated power issues that are impacted by sociolinguistic choice and agenda setting. Salt has done a particularly strong job of examining these power issues and others that arise as we collaborate across borders in Europe. As he says, "The power of neoliberal globalization to dictate the working rhythms of employees to a large extent determines which voices are heard" (p. 110, this volume).

But the language issue aside, the message from these authors is the same as Asia's rural poor, New Zealand's Maori population, and the homeless in America. Can we utilize online learning to overcome the exclusion of large masses of our population? Simpson pushes this discourse beyond merely gaining access to learning opportunities to examine issues associated with long-term impacts: "Even if e-learning was found to be successful in promoting access to education, would it have an effect on those students who had participated?" (Simpson, p. 93, this volume). Simpson is wisely pointing us toward retention and impact. These are issues worth consideration by those countries that are mostly taken up with access issues and statistics. Gursoy's description of Turkey is equally compelling as it lays out the case for countries with limited resources and high demand for extending educational opportunities. In my view, while the chapter tends to draw a bleak picture of the current situation, these problems are shared by many countries that are implementing distance education, especially developing countries. In this way, it is an incredibly illustrative contribution.

It is perhaps the luxury of Europe and other western civilizations to consider issues beyond access. When developed nations boast upwards of 50% connectivity, the issues are starkly different from Africa or rural Asia. While we are still concerned about gaining open access for those remaining 50%, we also start to worry about impacts, effects, and long-term involvement. However, this is not universally the case. As Fitzpatrick and Conway point out, access is particularly problematic for the traveling peoples and rural populations of Ireland. Through vignettes and a careful explication of innovative versus social practice discourses, Fitzpatrick and Conway highlight "the potential exacerbation of societal inequities" that are brought about by Irish implementation of ICTs. For Europe, then, the poetry of e-learning is about language—sociolinguistic as well as rhetorical language—access, and, even more so, retention.

※ FOUR ※

ONLINE LEARNING AND DIFFERENTIAL PARTICIPATION IN A DEMOCRATIC SOCIETY:

Ireland as a Case Study

Sarah FitzPatrick

Paul Conway

Information society developments have a particular significance for Ireland as a small open economy in an increasingly networked global economy, where knowledge-based innovation is becoming the key source of sustainable competitive advantage (Information Society Commission [ISC], 2004).

Situated at the edge of Western Europe, Ireland's location has traditionally circumscribed its struggle for social and economic development. Emerging from its traditional, poor, conservative, and colonial past, Ireland has recently proven itself immensely attractive to multinational capital investment. In the late 1990s, Ireland experienced unprecedented economic growth and even during the economic downturn at the beginning of the 2000s maintained a higher growth rate than its European peers (Industrial Development Authority, 2004).

In contrast with some countries where the education system is viewed as being periodically or constantly in a state of crisis, Ireland's education system is generally perceived by politicians and the public alike as having provided the basis for immense economic and social development over the last decade (Fitzgerald, 2002). It has served the majority well. However, results of literacy surveys are of concern with approximately one-fifth of adults identified as having severe literacy difficulties. In addition, and despite Ireland's very good overall performance in the Programme for International Student Assessment (PISA), approximately 10% of Irish 15-year olds scored at the lowest level of literacy in the recent PISA survey of reading literacy (Shiel, 2002).

Not surprisingly, the inclusion of disadvantaged people and regions in the information society has become one cornerstone of recent government policies; information and communication technology (ICT) offers Ireland's educationally disadvantaged the possibility of more fully participating in the information society, or the knowledge society (knowing what, knowing why and knowing how) (ISC, 2002, p. 2). This chapter focuses on the potential and promise of ICTs in the context of online education and differential participation in the Republic of Ireland in the 21st century.

The following questions are provided to prompt your engagement with the key issues in this chapter:

- In the context of discourses on technological innovation, how is language used to describe, justify, and critique the role of ICTs in education?
- What are the implications of Bruce's (1993) framework for understanding recent developments in ICT in education and society?
- What are the critical conditions that determine the discourse used to frame ICT innovations?

CONCEPTUAL FRAMEWORK

We use Bruce's (1993) description of innovative and social practice discourses as "conflicting discourses on innovation and social change" to frame policy developments in ICT in Irish education and society (p. 10). According to Bruce, *innovative discourse* "talks of changes in social systems brought about by an innovation. Within this discourse these changes are seen as positive" (p. 10). Bruce notes that *social practice discourse,* on the other hand

Table 4.1 Characteristics of Innovative and Social Practice Discourses (adapted from Conway, 2001)

	Innovative discourse	Social practice discourse
Mechanisms that drive change	Technological innovations leverage social, cultural, and political transformation in society	Technological innovations are mediated by existing social, cultural, and political forces
Descriptions of change	Significant, positive, and revolutionary	Difficult if it happens and even then evolutionary; piecemeal and often inequitable
Outcomes	Improvement in work, communication, education, etc.	Replication of existing social, cultural, and political structures and practices

"emphasizes the underlying social, cultural, economic and political processes that undermine innovations, resulting in negative outcomes or, more often, precluding any change at all" (p. 10). Each of these discourses focus on different issues and criticizes the other's viewpoint on innovation and educational change. (See Table 4.1.)

Innovation discourse is future oriented and visionary. It avoids talk about constraints either in artifacts or the social system, and it uses the language of *will* and endless possibility. Social-practice discourse, alternatively, is more cautious. It uses the language of doubt, talks about affordances and constraints, and often adopts a critical stance toward the status quo. For example, Cohen's (1989) argument that teaching as a practice of human improvement is inherently conservative (and thereby presents numerous problems and dilemmas to practitioners) is consistent with a social practice discourse.

The next section explores ICT in primary and post-primary schools and third-level colleges and universities in Ireland. Ireland's primary and post-primary sector comprises 8 years of primary education and an additional 5 to 6 years of post-primary or secondary education. Ireland's higher education sector consists of universities, institutes of technology, and colleges of education (primary teachers only). In each sector, ICT use is briefly explicated vis-à-vis growth, access, and quality. Two vignettes are presented within each sector and examined using the discourse of innovation and/or social change.

ONLINE EDUCATION IN THE IRISH EDUCATION SYSTEM

Primary and Post-Primary Sector

Growth

In 1997, the Irish government launched its first national policy for ICT in primary and post-primary schools, *Schools IT2000* (Department of Education and Science [DES], 1997). Under this 3-year policy, public investment in ICT (over 50 million, 1998–2001) targeted ICT infrastructure, teacher professional development, and integration of ICT in the curriculum. The National Centre for Technology in Education (NCTE) was established in 1998 as the government agency responsible for implementing this policy. The government's second ICT policy, *A Blueprint for the Future of ICT in Irish Education* (DES, 2001), reinforced and extended the priorities identified in *Schools IT2000*. This second policy also targeted development of the networking infrastructure required to enable broadband access to the Internet in all schools. The Government's third ICT policy (awaiting publication) is directed toward advancing online learning by developing a national broadband network for schools, learning networks within and among schools, and digital content for learning.

To determine the effect of these national ICT policies in Irish schools, three nationwide school surveys were conducted in 1998, 2000, and 2002. The most recent survey, *ICT School Census* (NCTE, 2004) was designed to assess the impact of the first two government policies for ICT in education. A key finding on this third survey (hereafter referred to as *the census*) was the relative success of both policies with regard to improving pupil-computer ratios, which have been most significant for Irish pupils in primary schools (37:1 in 1998, 18:1 in 2000, 11.8:1 in 2002). With regard to teacher professional development, the census noted that more than 75% of all Irish teachers have availed of ICT courses through the NCTE's Teaching Skill's Initiative (TSI). It also showed that teachers in primary schools integrate ICT in the curriculum much more frequently than their post-primary counterparts. Factors mediating the integration of ICT into the curriculum, cited in the census, included the design of the school day, the location of ICT equipment within the school and the examination-driven nature of post-primary education.

Access

While the two most recent ICT surveys indicated significant improvements in computer-pupil ratios, teachers' ICT skills, and integration of ICT in the curriculum between the years 1998, 2000, and 2002, they also highlighted limitations regarding access to online learning for those in primary, post-primary, and special schools. With regard to providing school access to the Internet, the second national survey indicated that the implementation of the first ICT policy was highly successful:

> Almost all schools (98%) are now connected to the Internet. Similarly, the vast majority (97%) of post-primary pupils and over three quarters (79%) of primary pupils have access to the Internet. (National Policy Advisory and Development Committee [NPADC], 2001, p. 1)

Despite this increase in numbers of (Internet-accessible) computers in schools, the census revealed that only a proportion of these computers had access to the Internet: primary schools, 39%; post-primary schools, 66%; special schools, 33%. Furthermore, analysis of the type of connectivity afforded to schools—one determinant of the quality of the online learning experience—revealed that only a minority of schools had broadband connectivity (mainly Asymmetric Digital Subscriber Line [ADSL] & satellite) with the majority of users in post-primary schools using narrow bandwidth (Public Switched Telephone Network [PSTN] line or Integrated Services Digital Network [ISDN] line) to access the Internet. While post-primary schools were shown to offer the most advanced connectivity, only 6% of these schools provided broadband access, compared with 1% of primary schools and 2% of special schools. In primary schools, the census showed that Internet access was typically provided through a standard telephone, thus limiting users to having one computer online at a time.

While teachers (particularly in primary schools) reported using the Internet to find teaching resources, pupils' access to the Internet was still limited with only one-third of primary and post-primary schools and 14% of special schools, providing access to pupils to search the Internet. Access to school computers outside class time was shown to increase with age until pupils reached the middle of their post-primary education; the census noted that the two final years of post-primary education were marked by a decline in the percentage of pupils having access to school computers outside class time.

Quality

It is important to note that these surveys are limited to providing national statistics—which more often than not fail to capture descriptions of ICT use at the local level. For example, the NCTE's Schools Integration Project (SIP) designed to support the innovative use of ICTs in teaching and learning in schools has generated a rich tapestry of exemplary practice with ICT and on-line learning (www.sip.ie). Two SIPs, briefly described as vignettes below, address the quality of ICT and online use in primary and post-primary schools.

Vignette 1 (V1): Startech–Learning Together:
Videoconferencing in geographically remote areas

Tapping the potential of online learning to connect primary school children in geographically remote areas was the focus of the SIP Startech–Learning Together Project. Participants in this SIP included a number of primary schools representing differential size, location, and socioeconomic background. Project activities utilizing videoconferencing included literacy, science, music, problem solving in maths, visual arts, and learning support. The use of online learning for the literacy project enabled children in different locations to share their responses to different books, while its use in the learning-support project enabled a teacher from the mainland at Baltimore N.S. to provide one-to-one learning-support to a pupil on Oileán Chléire–a 'remote' island of the south coast of Ireland. The project participants have identified a number of positive impacts of this SIP, which included stimulating teaching and learning, developing a growing body of expertise, increasing self-esteem, and furthering collaboration and collegiality. In the final analysis, the project leader noted,

> At its simplest, we have succeeded in finding a focus for using ICT so that it is no longer about equipment for which some use must be found. We have used technology as a tool to motivate and 'network pupils and teachers and it has given children reasons-and a new means–to learn, which appeals irresistibly to them. (Crowley, 2002, p. 45)

Vignette 2 (V2): Using ICT in the
Leaving Certificate Applied (LCA) Programme

This SIP project was designed to explore the use of ICT to teach general subjects to an LCA class. The LCA is a 2-year, alternative-leaving certificate program (for students' in their final 2 years of post-primary education) that has a strong vocational core and emphasizes preparing students for the world of work. The project leader explained,

> Our school has a long tradition of having a particular regard for education relating to social equality. Consequently, over the years we have enthusiastically taken on board programs such as . . . the LCA. In general many [students] who opt for the LCA would be non- academically motivated and/or have a negative attitude to school and learning. (Whelan, 2002, p. 137).

Given that many of the students who participated in this project did not have access to ICT outside of school hours, the project team's first task was to purchase student laptops (and equipment) to support mobile learning. The project team developed and delivered introductory ICT courses free-of-charge to students' parents and adult siblings. To provide further support and motivation early in the project, teachers and students visited a 'second chance' college located in an unemployment black spot in Wales. This college was selected for a site visit because of its innovative use of ICT to retrain adults and provide second-level courses to post-primary students. Positive outcomes of the project identified by participants included the development of digital content by/for teachers involved in the LCA, increased mobility of students who benefited from anytime-anywhere access to online and off-line resources and increased responsibility and enhanced personal organization skills for LCA students. The project leader attested to the legacy of the success of this SIP when he noted that "the most radical impact of our SIP must be the decision to become over the next few years, Ireland's first laptop-equipped school" (Whelan, 2002, p. 141).

University Sector

Growth

The Higher Education Authority (www.heanet.ie) has responsibility for providing broadband Internet services to Ireland's universities, institutes of technology, and colleges of education and researchers (40 institutions in all). Online education in the university sector is facilitated by one of three main providers: existing publicly funded distance learning-oriented institutions (Oscail—The National Distance Education Centre, based at Dublin City University); existing traditional universities; and private, for-profit, wholly online institutions that provide degree courses across a variety of disciplines. This third type of provision includes a controversial online postgraduate teacher training course for prospective primary school teachers. Growth in online education in this sector must be framed within a set of simultaneous and interrelated on-going policy developments in Ireland and Europe directed toward exploiting the potential of ICT in fostering knowledge societies.

The emergence of online learning has challenged the "lecture + seminar" delivery format of existing traditional universities. As such, the advent of virtual learning environments (VLEs) has turned the Web into a potentially highly efficient educational tool offering both the possibility of developing and disseminating a wide range of interactive multimedia-based learning materials and discussion tools for exchange of ideas between learners and teachers and among learners themselves. In the European context, Ireland was somewhat late in opening up higher education to the open university model. As Bang (2000) has observed, "Dedicated open universities are a rather new phenomenon beginning with the creation of the Open University in the UK in 1969" (p. 5). Other European countries followed suit. For example, the United Kingdom's Open University was followed by the opening of UNED in Spain (1972), FernUniversität in Germany (1975), the Open Universiteit in the Netherlands (1982), and Universitate Aberta in Portugal (1988). The "primary contribution" of the "open university model" was in offering "second chances to people that didn't have the opportunity to achieve a university degree in their youth or as their first education" (Bang, 2000, p. 5). In the context of Bang's observations in 2000, the current drive toward introducing and using VLEs across the third-level sector in Ireland, not just in distance learning institutions, reflects a transition period in European higher education with "several on-going developments in play at the same" (p. 5). As Bang noted, these include the merging of campus-based teaching and open distance learning (ODL); the shift of the ODL mission from second chance provision to further education; and market competition versus collaboration.

Bang (2000) has observed that universities in many countries across Europe are grappling with whether to adopt a *dual* or *mixed* model in relation to ODL. That is,

> The difference between dual mode and mixed mode is a rather sophisticated one with 'dual mode' referring to institutions offering campus based education and ODL in totally separate programmes, while 'mixed mode' refers to an educational setting in which ODL is mixed with a certain amount of face-to-face seminars. (p. 5)

With several ongoing developments at play at once in relation to institutional roles and course provision, there is also an emerging reorientation of the qualifications framework within Ireland reflecting European efforts (Bologna Agreement, 1999) towards recognition of qualifications across borders and credit accumulation through modularized online coursework.

The new National Qualifications Framework, developed under the auspices of the National Qualifications Authority, has adopted lifelong learning as its guiding principle in relation to teaching and learning. The development of a lifelong-learning focus and subsequent press for more flexible modularized learning opportunities has converged with the emergence of online learning opportunities in the past 5 years. Furthermore, government policy in relation to the role of ICT in society has called for a review of the role of ICT in lifelong learning (Government of Ireland, 2003b). Taken together the convergence of the EU initiative for a common higher education model across Europe and the appeal of VLEs as a viable online format for course provision have led to a change in the way in which traditional university and other third-level education is being delivered. For example, a conference held in conjunction with Ireland's presidency of the European Union (January to June 2004) titled 'Learning in the Europe of Knowledge' focused on the rich potential of new online technologies to reshape learning experiences and knowledge construction in third-level institutions.

Access

The HEAnet provides high-speed access to 40 institutions encompassing the third-level sector and research organizations. These institutions are linked in a wide area network (WAN) spanning the country. "HEAnet provides connections to networks in Europe by means of its 155Mbps link with the GEANT backbone" (http://www.heanet.ie/Heanet/history.html). Thus, at the level of the institution, the third-level sector has robust and high-quality connectivity. In terms of students' access to computers and access to online learning, various local institutional factors have played a critical role.

First, while all the universities and some of the institutes of technology have bought off-the-shelf VLEs (e.g., most have bought Blackboard.com, although one has bought WebCT), students' access to on-campus computing in some institutions may differ depending on the students' faculty, i.e. whether they are arts, science, or medicine students (Conway, 2003). Second, since online learning facilitates the possibility of off-campus access, whether students have a home computer or not is critical importance (Conway, 2003). Finally, the cultural and material barriers to third-level access by educationally disadvantaged students may be exacerbated rather than ameliorated as a result of online learning and access to ICT becoming new forms of cultural capital.

Quality

Generative descriptions of two vignettes, are used to address the quality of online learning in the university sector.

Vignette 3 (V3): Wireless computing at university: The "scholarship of teaching" as an enabling context

This case illustrates the potential of ICTs to redefine space and open up new conversations across faculty and departmental boundaries, partly, but not exclusively as a result of the advent of wireless mobile learning technologies. In University College Cork (Lyons, 2003) improving teaching and learning is driven largely by two factors: a push for quality assurance across the Irish university sector and the influence of a new discourse on teaching in higher education, namely, Boyer's 'Scholarship Reconsidered' (1990–1997). In seeking to move away from the teaching versus research debate, Boyer asserts that university faculty ought to think of their work as falling into some combination of the scholarship of discovery; the scholarship of integration; the scholarship of application; and the scholarship of teaching. In the context, of reconsidering teaching and learning in the university, a conversation has begun about many aspects of teaching and funding has been made available to advance, for example, the use of wireless and mobile learning technologies. An outgrowth of the almost weekly seminars, open to faculty across the university, is that conversations about ICT access, lecturers' deeply held beliefs about of teaching and learning are being discussed in a way that has help some staff to move beyond what Shulman has called "pedagogical solitude" (see Shulman, 1998).

Vignette 4 (V4): New private online teacher education course stirs controversy. "Hibernia's lucrative deal stirs controversy" is a headline from the *Irish Times* (7th October 2003) pointing to what some might see as the surprising impact of a new third-level college offering a new accredited postgraduate course to prepare graduates to become primary/elementary teachers. However, the controversy cannot be understood without situating it within the history of primary-teacher education culturally and historically. Historically, primary-teacher education has been privately managed by religious trustees and publicly funded by the state. The advent of profit, commercial, and non-denominational colleges such as Hibernia was seen possibly by some as breaching this long-standing collaboration between Church and State dating back to denominational structure of primary teaching, an outgrowth of 19th-century compromises and strategizing by both Church and State. Culturally, teacher education colleges have prided themselves on both the academic challenge of their course work and, at least as important, the quality of interaction between faculty and students in relation to the educational formation of beginning teachers as well as the neophytes' initial professional socialization that occurs in small, mainly residential colleges of education. Furthermore, the advent of Hibernia seemed to solve a problem, namely the shortage of trained teachers. However, as one journalist noted, "On the weekend of the August Bank Holiday this year, a sort of revolution took place in teacher training in the State" (*Irish Times,* October 7, 2003). Rather than being heralded as yet another example of the power of ICTs, the advent of online teacher education was viewed by many as a frontal assault on hard-fought-for values in relation to teachers' professional status and teacher education.

In the next section, we discuss the vignettes under three headings: discourse, rhetoric, and reality of ICTs in education, access to ICTs in education, and evidence base for ICTs in education.

DISCUSSION OF ISSUES

Discourse

We use the conceptual framework regarding discourses on technological innovation outlined at the beginning of this chapter to analyze the four vignettes presented. Each vignette describes the use of novel technologies to address a given educational problem. Thus, ICTs can provide certain solutions to actual identifiable local problems. In each case, the potential of ICT has been buttressed, to varying degrees, by current conditions. In this sense, the change is as much in the extent to which these conditions are enabling (V1, V2, V3) or impeding (V3, V4) as it is in the actual flexibility of online, wireless, and mobile learning technologies themselves. Technological innovations are mediated by existing social, cultural, and political forces, and they must be interpreted in these contexts. Where there is dissonance between the existing culture and the proposed uses of ICTs, the innovative discourse becomes a foreign language rather than an adopted one (V4). Furthermore, V4 suggests that the so-called revolutionary potential of ICT must be situated in an understanding of the history and purposes of teaching and learning in a particular cultural setting. In V4, the key affordances of online learning were presented in rhetorically powerful ways by Hibernia and its supporters in positions of power. The flexibility, access, high-quality, anytime-anywhere potential of the new program was offered very effectively against the so-called Luddite critics of Hibernia's online teacher-training course.

To the extent that these vignettes portray successful use of ICT to provide anywhere-anytime access for traditionally disadvantaged learners, they exemplify the promise of innovative discourse: technological innovation transcends social and geographical barriers. In such cases, the ICTs used address a local problem and represent a good "fit" within the current culture. However, inasmuch as these vignettes portray isolated pockets of innovation, they exemplify, or lend credence to, social practice discourse regarding technological change; technological innovation is often piecemeal and inequitable. In cases where uptake and integration of the technological change is constrained (e.g., due to cost or availability), ICT use resonates with the potential perpetuation of inequities at the heart of social practice discourse.

RHETORIC AND REALITY OF ICT IN EDUCATION

Ireland is not alone in the global drive to integrate ICTs into its education system in the emerging global knowledge order (Conway and Zhao, 2003b). Many countries are involved in this technological derby. Like other countries, Ireland's ICT initiatives at the level of policy and practice share key rhetorical features with ICT policies internationally; most adopt an innovative discourse (Zhao and Conway, 2001).

By way of summary, in relation to the discourses used to frame this paper, there are a number of noteworthy points: First, much of the policy literature resonates with an innovative discourse. Second, to the extent that it does, issues addressed by social practice discourse may not be fully thought through in the context of technological innovation. Third, consistent with a social practice discourse, the significant resistance to Hibernia's online teacher education course, for example, reminds us that despite the "rhetoric" about ICTs in education, core issues focus on the purpose and nature of education rather than the boundless potential of ICT to transform the educational landscape.

ACCESS TO ICT IN EDUCATION

Charged with contributing to the policy formulation process for ICT in the information/knowledge society, Ireland's Information Society Commission (ISC) exists at the interface between innovative discourse and social practice discourse. The ISC's remit is both to envision a future for ICT in Ireland's information society and to identify relevant issues by monitoring current progress. Issues regarding access to ICT are at the heart of the ISC's work.

In fulfilling its monitoring remit, the ISC has noted that despite the very recent availability of "flat-rate narrowband Internet access services" in Ireland, almost 40% of Irish homes currently have Internet access (ISC, 2003, p. 31). Regarding the quality of Internet access (speed, always-on, cost), however, Ireland currently ranks second last in the European Union (EU) for broadband penetration. The difficulties for businesses and individuals wishing to access broadband services are manifold:

> Not only is it extremely difficult to access very high speed broadband services, but . . . depending on location, the cost can be 20 times higher than the comparative cost in Dublin. The prohibitive cost of leased lines in particular, means that satellite is often the only realistic option. . . . This imbalance of access to broadband services, along with price differentiation, puts rural areas at a disadvantage, exacerbates the digital divide, and puts an additional cost burden on Irish companies, affecting adversely their ability to compete internationally, while inhibiting their expansion plans. (ISC, 2003, p. 7)

Thus, while Ireland's growth in connectivity levels in the last 6 months is above the EU average, the ISC has projected a maximum broadband penetration of just 12% by 2005. "To achieve this target Ireland will need over 450,000 broadband users—an almost fifty-fold increase from current levels" (ISC, 2003, p. 51).

Since the publication of the ISC's report, access to broadband connectivity to support and enable online teaching and learning has been identified as a government priority. The government's third policy for ICT in education asserts that if Ireland is to remain internationally competitive in the global knowledge economy, educational institutions must have access to high bandwidth connectivity and all students must have every opportunity to develop a keen interest and competence in using ICT. To achieve this, every school is to be equipped with a high-speed broadband connection, and a centrally managed school

Table 4.2 Rationales for Inclusion of ICT in Education

Rationale	Potential
Economic rationale	The school's potential to prepare children to meet the perceived needs of the economy—present and future
Social rationale	The potential of individuals to develop ICT competence as an essential "life skill"
Pedagogic rationale	The potential of ICT to increase the breadth and richness of teaching and learning

network is to be developed to support and underpin broadband rollout to schools. This action should begin to redress the dearth of online educational resources currently available to educators and learners (Department of Education and Science, 2001, p. 9) and result in the ready-availability of high-quality, authentic resources through a national portal for education.

Exploring the critical dimensions of access in the Irish context, reveals both an innovative and social practice discourse driving ICT policy and underscores significant challenges facing the government in achieving the promise and potential of ICT for all in the knowledge society. In the context of the massive investment in ICT internationally and the search for evidence to support such an investment, we turn next to the evidence base for ICT in education.

EVIDENCE BASE FOR ICT IN EDUCATION

The OECD report *Learning to Change: ICT in Schools* (2001) presented three key rationales for the inclusion of ICT in education. These are outlined in Table 4.2.

The economic and social rationales for ICT in education have been explicated throughout this paper. However, the pedagogical rationale for ICT in education remains largely uninformed by research regarding current practice. While Ireland's investment in ICT continues, investment in research regarding the pedagogic rationale for ICT and its online affordances has been limited. This trend is an international rather than an Irish one (Conway and Zhao, 2003a). For example, in the United States, less than 1% of the total investment in ICT in schools has been used to determine what technologies actually work and to find ways to improve them (Shaw, 2000). The promise of ICT and of online learning to improve the educational experience remains largely untested.

Claims for the potential benefits of ICT for the student have included gains in achievement, increased motivation, improved problem-solving skills, and the development of collaborative skills (White, Ringstaff, & Kellett, 2002). Researchers have concluded that ICT has the potential to positively impact teaching and learning under certain circumstances, and for certain purposes. However, our understanding of the extent to which the daily lives of learners and teachers are being affected or changed by ICT remains limited (Cuban, 2001). In the Irish context, given the ongoing and significant investment in developing a broadband network, our need to visualize the roles and functions of ICT and online learning has never been greater.

Evaluating and disseminating the results and outcomes of technology integration in Irish primary and post-primary schools is the current focus of the NCTE's Special Integration Projects (SIPs). Since its inception in 1998, SIP has supported almost 90 highly diverse school-level projects, each designed to test out or develop ICT applications, pedagogies and/or resources that may have particular relevance in the Irish context. Over 400 schools have taken part in SIP projects. To ensure that nonparticipating schools can also benefit from SIP, the project Web site explains that "the outcomes of these projects will set standards for best practice in ICT in Irish schools" (SIP). Deriving models of research-based best practice from SIPs and disseminating these models to all schools has the potential to make ICT-enhanced/transformed educational experiences a reality for all students in Irish primary and post-primary schools.

The project evaluator has noted that "if the lessons, practices, and materials emerging from the projects are to be spread effectively throughout the system as a whole, the SIP experience must be characterized by on-going systematic recording, collating, and analysis of information" (Galvin, 2002, p. 13). It is this focus on evaluating ICT projects for the purpose of extrapolating models of best practice and scaling-up ICT integration throughout Ireland's schools that must inform continued planning for that and investment in ICT in Irish education.

The critique of Hibernia College's online teacher education program by the heads of Ireland's colleges of education, which probed the *equivalence* of the online course with the existing university-accredited full-time program, represents a further call for evidence regarding the potential of ICT to deliver on established educational outcomes. Questions regarding the "fit" of online learning, in reference to our expectations and assumptions regarding what constitutes a valid or good learning experience, are at the heart of this critique, and of the collective call for evidence regarding the potential and power of ICT in the knowledge society.

CONCLUSION

This chapter has exploited and harnessed the binary relationship between innovative discourse and social practice discourse, as a tool for understanding the complexity of technological change. While each discourse has conceptual power and appeal, subscribing to just one would be naive. Alone, neither discourse adequately communicates the social, pedagogic, and economic relevance of ICT in a democratic society.

The potential of innovative ICTs, such as online learning, to widen access to and participation in education and to increase civic engagement is evident in the many recent government documents, identified in this chapter, concerning Ireland's participation in the knowledge society. A coordinated national strategy, which harmonizes the discord between innovative and social practice discourse, is vital to securing this future for Ireland's people.

The potential exacerbation of societal inequities as novel ICTs become increasingly integral to education, presents serious challenges for society in general (Bromley, 1997; Sutton, 1991), and no less so in the Irish context. As Dertouzous (2002) has observed in relation to the role of ICTs in the developing world "The potential of the Information Age seems overshadowed at every turn by the ancient forces that separate the rich from the poor" (p. 204). Clearly, the scale of the challenge is different in developed countries, but it is no less important as ICT literacy emerges as a new form of cultural capital in Ireland's Republic.

REFERENCES

Bang, J. (2000). Open and distance learning in higher education–educational perspectives. In Higher Education Authority, *Report on Symposium on Open and Distance Learning.* Dublin: Higher Education Authority. Retrieved November 1, 2004 from http://www.heanet.ie

Boyer, E. (1990/1997). *Scholarship reconsidered: Priorities of the professoriate.* San Francisco: Jossey Bass.

Bromley, H. (1997). Thinking about computers and schools: A sceptical view. In P. E. Agre & D. Schuler (Eds.), *Re-inventing technology, rediscovering community: Critical explorations of computing as a social practice* (pp. 107–126). Greenwich, CN: Ablex.

Bruce, B. C. (1993). Innovation and social change. In B. C. Bertram, J. Peyton, & T. Batson (Eds.), *Network-based classrooms: Promises and realities* (pp. 33–49). New York: Cambridge University Press.

Cohen, D. K. (1989). Teaching practice: Plus ça change. In P. W. Jackson (Ed.), *Contributing to educational change: Perspectives on research on practice* (pp. 27–84). Berkeley, CA: McCutchan.

Conway, P. F. (2001). Schools information technology (IT) 2000: Technological innovation and educational change. *Irish Educational Studies, 19,* 227–244

Conway, P. F. (2003, May). *Web-based learning as the royal road to transforming teaching and learning?* Paper presented at the Scholarship of Teaching Conference, University College Cork, Ireland.

Conway, P. F., & Zhao, Y. (2003a). From Luditess to designers: Images of teachers in political documents. In Y. Zhao (Ed.), *What should teachers know about technology? Perspectives and practices* (pp. 15–30). Greenwich, CT: Information Age Press.

Conway, P. F., & Zhao, Y. (2003b, July). *The global reach of ICT planning.* Paper presented at the conference of the International Study Association on Teachers and Teaching (ISATT), Leiden, the Netherlands, July.

Crowley, M. (2002). Startech–learning together: Video-conferencing in geographically remote areas. In C. Galvin (Ed.), *Sharing innovative practice: The NCTE's schools integration project (1998–2000)* (pp. 42–46). Dublin City University, Ireland: National Centre for Technology in Education.

Cuban, L. (2001). *Oversold and underused: Computers in the classroom.* Cambridge: Harvard University Press.

Department of Education and Science. (1997). *Schools IT2000: A policy framework for the new millennium.* Dublin, Ireland: Government Publications Office.

Department of Education and Science. (2001). *A blueprint for the future of ICT in Irish education.* Dublin, Ireland: Government Publications Office.

Department of Education and Science. (2004). *Meeting the challenge: A strategy for e-learning in schools 2004–2006.* Dublin, Ireland: Government Publications Office.

Dertouzos, M. (2001). *The unfinished revolution: How to make technology work for us instead of the other way around.* New York: Harper Collins.

Drucker, P. (2001). *The new workforce.* Retrieved November 1, 2004, from http://economist.com/surveys/displayStory.cfm?Story_id=770847

European Commission. (1994). *Europe and the global information society: Recommendations to the European Council* (Bangemann Report). Brussels: Author. Retrieved from http://www.ispo.cec.be/infosoc/backg/bangeman.html

European Commission. (1995). *Teaching and learning: Towards a learning society: White paper on education and training.* Brussels: Author. Retrieved November 1, 2004, from http://europa.eu.int/en/record/white/edu9511/index.htm

Fitzgerald, G. (2002). *Reflections on the Irish state: Ireland since independence.* Dublin: Irish Academic Press.

Galvin, C. (2002). Moving education ICT beyond schools IT 2000. In C. Galvin (Ed.), *Sharing innovative practice: The NCTE's schools integration project (1998–2000)* (pp. 137–142). Dublin City University, Ireland: National Centre for Technology in Education.

Government of Ireland. (2003a). *New connections: A strategy to realise the potential of the information society*. Dublin, Ireland: Government Publications Office.

Government of Ireland. (2003b). *The progress report on the new connections action plan*. Dublin, Ireland: Government Publications Office.

Industrial Development Authority (IDA). (2004). Retrieved from the IDA Web site: http://www.idaireland.com

Information Society Commission. (2002). *Building the knowledge society: Report to Government*. Dublin, Ireland: Government Publications Office.

Information Society Commission. (2003). *Ireland's broadband future*. Dublin, Ireland: Government Publications Office.

Information Society Commission. (2004). *Information communication society Web page*. Retrieved November 1, 2004, from http://www.isc.ie Lyons, N. (2003). Advancing the scholarship of teaching and learning: Reflective portfolio inquiry in higher education: A case study of one institution. *Irish Educational Studies, 22*(1), 69–88.

National Centre for Technology in Education (NCTE). (2004). *2002 ICT school census: Statistical report*. Dublin, Ireland: National Centre for Technology in Education.

National Policy Advisory and Development Committee. (2001). *The impact of schools IT2000: Summary*. Dublin, Ireland: NPADC/ National Centre for Technology in Education.

Organisation for Economic Co-operation and Development (OECD). (2001). *Learning to change: ICT in schools*.

Shaw, D. (2000, September 8). *K-12 education: Acting on ignorance. Web-based education commission report*. Retrieved May 21, 2001, from http://www.hpcnet.org/cgi-bin/global/a_bus_card.cgi?SiteID=179532

Shiel, G. (2002). Literacy standards and factors affecting literacy: What national and international assessments tell us. In G. Reid & J. Wearmouth (Eds.), *Dyslexia and literacy: Theory and practice* (pp. 131–145). Chichester: Wiley.

Shulman, L. (1998). Course anatomy: The dissection and analysis of knowledge through teaching. In P. Hutchings (Ed.), *The course portfolio*. Washington, DC: American Association for Higher Education.

Sutton, R. (1991). Equity and computers in the schools: A decade of research. *Review of Research in Education 61*(4), 475–503.

Whelan, D. (2002). Using ICT in the leaving certificate applied programme. In C. Galvin (Ed.), *Sharing innovative practice: The NCTE's schools integration project (1998–2000)* (pp. 137–142). DCU, Ireland: National Centre for Technology in Education.

White, N., Ringstaff C., & Kellett, L. (2002). *Knowledge brief: Getting the most from technology in schools*. WestEd.

Zhao, Y., & Conway, P. F. (2001). "What's in, what's out?": An analysis of state technology plans. *Teachers College Record*. Retrieved November 17, 2004, from http://lsc-net.terc.edu/do.cfm/paper/8380/show/use_set-teh_int

❊ FIVE ❊

E-LEARNING, DEMOCRACY, AND SOCIAL EXCLUSION:

Issues of Access and Retention in the United Kingdom

Ormond Simpson

I was at the Mathematical School, where the Master taught his pupils after a Method scarce imaginable to us in Europe. *The Proposition and Demonstration were written on a thin Wafer, with Ink composed of a Cephalick Tincture. This the student was to swallow upon a fasting Stomach, and for three Days after eat nothing but Bread and Water. As the Wafer digested, the Tincture amounted to his Brain, bearing the proposition along with it. But the success hath not hitherto been answerable, partly by some error in the* Quantum *or* Composition, *and partly by the Perverseness of Lads, to whom the Bolus is so Nauseous, that they generally steal aside and discharge it upwards before it can operate; neither have they yet been persuaded to us so long as Abstinence as the Prescription requires.*

—Jonathan Swift
Gulliver's Travels, quoted in Simpson (2002)

The search for new methods of learning to reach disadvantaged groups clearly has a long history. Some older—much older—readers of this chapter may remember the "teaching machines" of the mid 1960s. These were clunky electro-mechanical devices that displayed text and questions and took the user along various branches in response to particular answers. These machines were going to revolutionize learning but had disappeared without a trace by the end of the 1960s.

A similar revolution was going to be initiated by educational television—ETV—on which millions in various currencies were spent in various countries but to little eventual effect (Tiffin & Single Rajasingham, 2003).

Of course the internet will be different . . . While reading this chapter you might like to ask yourself the following questions:

- How far is it legitimate or feasible for governments to attempt to use the Internet as an instrument of increasing social justice?
- In particular, how successful might e-learning be in helping overcome "social exclusion" in society? Might it be more effective than conventional educational methods?
- If e-learning is effective in initially helping the educationally disadvantaged to access education, will it also be effective in retaining them in learning? Or will an apparently open door really be a revolving door?
- Will it be possible to make e-learning effective in both access and retention at a cost that maintains its supposed advantages over conventional learning?

E-LEARNING IN THE UNITED KINGDOM

As in the United States, there is much interest in the United Kingdom in online or e-learning (I shall use the term e-learning to embrace both networked and non-networked computer use). Indeed the two countries share a very common level of Web access—55% of the population having Internet access in the United Kingdom as against 57% in the United States.

The interest in the United Kingdom arises in part from the expectation among higher education institutions that e-learning will both increase efficiency by bringing down costs while enhancing students' learning experiences. These assumptions are particularly prevalent in distance education institutions. The biggest distance education provider in the United Kingdom—the United Kingdom Open University with 175,000 part-time students—will require all its students to be online by the beginning of 2005.

However, it is not clear how quickly the interest in e-learning is being translated into practice as data are hard to come by. There are even signs that the "dot-edu" bubble is deflating with the imminent winding down of the British e-university, the U.K.eU, which was launched in 2000 with £60 million ($100 million) of government money but only succeeded in attracting around 900 students. A few other U.K. universities have been more successful, but it seems unlikely that the total number of students studying at degree level online is more than a few score thousand. At lower levels, enrollment data are equally hard to come by; the U.K.'s biggest e-learning provider, the government sponsored "LearnDirect" offers 400 courses (many of just a few hours' duration) and claims more than a million enrollments since April 2000. But revealingly, the total number of online tests taken between April 2003 and April 2004 is only about 13,000, which may suggest that many learners are only lightly engaged with the operation.

The "Widening Participation" Agenda

But interest in e-learning is also driven by the U.K. government's objectives to increase efficiency and reduce costs as well as widen participation in U.K. higher education to close to U.S. levels. The declared target is that 50% of the U.K. population should have some kind of higher education experience by 2010 (compared with 60% currently in the United States). This target is set in part by economic considerations; as conventional industries disappear or are transferred to the developing world the U.K.'s future is seen as lying in a better trained workforce working in high-tech industries. In addition, the current Labour government retains enough of its social democratic origins to want to address a "social justice" target and e-learning is seen as an important resource for achieving that target.

In its consultation document "Towards a Unified E-learning Strategy" (2003) the government stated that e-learning had the "potential to revolutionize the way we teach and learn." The document claimed that e-learning could contribute towards the Government's objectives for education: raising standards, improving quality, removing barriers to learning and participation in learning, preparing for employment, upskilling in the workplace, and ensuring that all learners achieve their full potential. Underlying these aims is the often unspecified but important objective of reducing the costs of education.

Overcoming Social Exclusion

Widening participation can only be achieved by increasing the number of students coming forward from underrepresented groups. The U.K. government recognizes that there are groups in the population which are excluded to a greater or lesser extent from participating fully in society and gaining benefits from it. Such groups are typically the poor, the educationally disadvantaged, the physically and mentally disabled, immigrants, single-parent families, the unemployed, some ethnic minorities and so on. There is much overlap between those groups, and as yet, no clear definition of the blanket term used to describe them—the "socially excluded."

Indicators of social exclusion relate to economic activity, employment, housing, health, and other factors. Health is a particularly important factor as there is evidence that socially excluded groups not only have poorer health but also get less healthcare than better-off groups. This is referred to by some writers as "the inverse care law" of health care. It has been argued that a similar "law" applies to education, and certainly in the United Kingdom, the middle classes are substantially overrepresented in higher education. (This phenomenon is used by the government in its argument for the introduction of higher university tuition fees in 2006. It is suggested that it is no longer fair for middle-class students to benefit from education that in effect is subsidized through taxation from working class people who do not benefit to nearly the same extent).

E-Learning and Social Exclusion

The development of online services and the trend toward the "information society" will leave groups without access to the Internet even further excluded from the ability to exercise democratic rights and claim the full benefits of that society.

Clearly, if the Internet has potential to increase democracy, then it must enable socially excluded groups to access society's benefits to a much fairer level. In particular, it must allow them to access education as the key to the other benefits. Thus the consultation document suggested that e-learning could overcome geographical isolation and remove barriers to learning imposed by characteristics such as disability, previous negative educational experience, or monolingualism in minority languages.

However there is as yet very little evidence to support the contention that e-learning will help overcome social exclusion or widen participation. In 2003 the U.K. government funded a project to research this issue "Overcoming Social Exclusion through Online Learning" run jointly by the UKOU and the National Institute for Adult Continuing Education (NIACE). It is too soon for any results to have emerged, but an international literature survey conducted by the project found very little material that addressed the issue directly or at any depth. Much published work was found to be either very abstract or focused on very specific initiatives and did not explore wider issues of how e-learning might promote social inclusion (McGerty, 2003).

The Financial Benefits of Distance Learning

Even if e-learning was found to be successful in promoting access to education, would it have an effect on those students who had participated? There is some evidence of the financial benefits of traditional distance education to students. Woodley and Simpson (2001) surveyed the earnings of a number of UKOU graduates before and after graduation. They found an average increase of about 7% in earnings. Although this may seem small, the overall benefit to graduates over a working lifetime is considerable. Using Woodley and Simpson's figures, I calculated that the return on the investment in their course fees for students could be up to 2,000% over their lifetime. Further calculations suggested that the comparable figure for conventional graduates was much lower—around 350%—largely because of the loss of earnings during study that conventional graduates experience compared with distance education graduates who are generally able to continue with their employment while studying.

More important, Woodley and Simpson (2001) found that the growth in the earnings of distance education students was greatest for those who had entered the university with the lowest qualifications—that is, those most likely to have been drawn from the socially excluded. Thus there is some evidence that distance education can overcome social exclusion, but this evidence does not yet extend to e-learning.

ACCESS AND RETENTION IN E-LEARNING

In addition to social exclusion issues, there are two closely related topics that are critical to the development of e-learning—access and retention. Without access to e-learning, there will be no disadvantaged students to retain. Without retention the open door offered to disadvantaged students will be a revolving door that ushers them out as fast as they come in.

Access to E-Learning in the United Kingdom

Clearly access to online learning requires a reasonable level of both physical and psychological access to a computer with Internet facilities.

Physical Access

Until now, physical access suggests a computer linked to the Internet via a fixed phone line, although the advent of Wireless Application Protocol (WAP) links by which the Internet can be accessed via a wireless link from particular locations has changed that. It is not yet clear what effects such access might have.

The 55% of U.K. households with access to the Internet tend to be in higher socioeconomic groups. In addition, the growth of the number of households with computers appears to have slowed recently and might even have peaked. Recognizing this, government strategy has been to increase access to online facilities in various ways, particularly through the development of "Learning Centers" or "People's Network" centers in libraries. These are public locations where free access to networked computers is available and there are now more than 7,000 such centers over the United Kingdom. Together with facilities via libraries and educational establishments it means that even quite remote communities have some kind of Internet access. Resources at such centers vary, but most offer the opportunity to surf the Internet, use e-mail, and undertake various courses offered from various sources, such as "LearnDirect" mentioned above.

To some extent, therefore, physical access to ICT is available via such centers to most of the U.K. population. However the simple statistics do not take into account difficulties experienced in accessing such centers such as transport and child care costs together with the need to be well organized to book facilities where necessary for the length of time needed. This latter constraint can be significant—it may be possible to study for short periods and take short (1- to 5-hour courses) at a center; it can be much more difficult to study longer courses. In a recent study in the UKOU (Driver, 2001), a small group of students without computer access were enrolled to study an online course through a learning center. The course required them to be online for 7 to 8 hours a week for 30 weeks. This proved to require levels of organization beyond the abilities of students who had to try to fit their own availability around that of the opening hours of the center. In addition, there were firewall problems. In any event, none of the students completed the course.

Of course well-organized centers will overcome some of the technical difficulties experienced by learners by having IT support available, although this will be at a cost. Additionally, most courses offered at centers are much shorter than the example above so that such constraints are less important. However, the cost of developing such courses are high; it appears that for LearnDirect courses the costs can be as much as 30% higher than conventional distance education packages of correspondence materials. Research by Hulsmann (2000) also suggests that e-learning is no cheaper for institutions than conventional distance education, which vitiates some of the motivation for developing it in the first place.

Psychological Access

By "psychological access," I mean the need for potential students to be motivated to access the technology and to overcome possible anxieties about using it. Clarke (2002) in a survey of online learning and social exclusion found that many socially disadvantaged adults in the United Kingdom neither used the technology nor were interested in it. Their previous poor experiences of education left them unconvinced of the value of education to their lives, a feeling that was compounded their major doubts about the value of ICT to them together with a fear (or at least a profound lack of confidence) in using the technology. It can be argued that this is a diminishing problem and that as children who are exposed to computers at school or have used computer games mature, this technophobia will vanish. This may be true to an extent, although it is not clear how far familiarity with online chat rooms and games will enable would-be students to tackle e-learning. In any case, it will be some years before the generation familiar with computers from school form the majority of the population.

Access to E-Learning Internationally

The position in the United Kingdom of low access among underprivileged groups is replicated worldwide. Indeed the differentials in access in the developed world are small compared with those between the developed and developing world. In a recent survey reported in the *Guardian* newspaper (November 27, 2003) the International Telecommunications Union (the UN communications agency) ranked 178 countries on their ability to exploit the digital revolution based on infrastructure, education levels, Internet users, and other criteria. The top of the rankings is dominated by Scandinavian countries—Sweden is highest with a ranking of 0.85—but with Far Eastern countries rising fast; Korea is fourth. English-speaking countries have slipped since 1998–the United Kingdom has fallen three places and the U.S. five. However these changes are trivial compared with the position of African countries—for instance, Burkina Faso with a rating of 0.08 and Niger bottom at 0.04. Thus the international distribution of IT resource follows that of wealth, and it is hard to see changes in that resource in the near or middle future. Such countries will be excluded from the wealth-building activities that are occurring in countries with better IT resources such as India (0.32) and China (0.43), where IT work outsourced from developed countries is a growing source of income.

Retention in E-Learning

As suggested earlier there is little point in widening access to educational courses of any kind if the subsequent retention on that course is so low that most of the students fail or withdraw.

This will also be true of e-learning, and yet it is surprisingly difficult to get reliable data on dropout from e-learning courses. This may be one of the consequences of the higher level of competition in Web-based education; providers are no more likely to admit to high dropout rates on their products than automobile manufacturers are to admit to low reliability in theirs. And in any case, there can be difficulties in comparing retention rates for institutions with different policies and structures. For example, one well-known online university has a policy of de-registering those students (without any fee refund) who fail to log onto the university's Web site a specified number of times per week. Another university has a "flagship" online course that was recently press-released as having a more than 90% success rate. This it turned out was the percentage of active students who passed the final assessment and did not take into account the large number of students (up to 60%) who had withdrawn before that point.

What evidence is available about retention rates in e-learning suggests that the rates are often lower than in conventional distance education. Some of this evidence comes from the United States where online learning has been around longer and is more widespread. In a recent survey (2002) of 4,100 online learners the Corporate University Xchange Inc. found a dropout rate of 71% ("Open Learning Today," June 2002, quoted in Simpson, 2003).

Other evidence tends to be anecdotal—informal conversations with colleagues in the field in the United Kingdom suggests that dropout rates of up to 90% from some e-learning courses are not unheard of. An Australian colleague in a recent e-mail also notes that online learning in his institution has a higher dropout rate than conventional distance education and so on.

Given that there is little evidence available about dropout in e-learning it is not surprising that there is also little evidence for higher dropout amongst educationally disadvantaged students. But as in conventional distance education there are clear links between dropout and low previous educational qualifications (Simpson 2003) it would be very surprising if that were not also true for e-learning. Clarke (2002) suggests that dropout rates in distance education tend to be associated with factors such as lack of confidence, fear of failure, underdeveloped learning skills and isolation. Since all these factors are most likely to be associated with educational disadvantage it would be reasonable to assume that such students dropout at a much faster rate than students from better backgrounds.

Causes of Lower Retention Rates in e-learning

Once again there does not appear to be much research into the reasons for low retention on e-learning courses as distinct from conventional distance education. Clearly, many of the reasons will be similar, but if dropouts from e-learning are higher, then characteristics of the technology must be involved.

In situations like these it is not a bad idea to listen to the customer. The following is adapted from comments made by an online student writing in Australia but they could apply to e-learners anywhere:

Advice for web-based educators:
- "take a web-based course yourself"
- "warn students they have to be good typists as well as computer users"

- "don't overload—in my experience it takes one and a half times as long to cover material online as in a hard copy"
- "costs are not negligible: amortised purchase costs can come to $1000 a year if you are paying them all yourself"
- "asynchronous discussions can be boring—delays between postings can kill the spark. And joining an online conference can be disheartening—too early and you don't want to be first to post, too late and it feels like butting in"
- "technical problems are always possible—breakdowns, viruses and updates can create problems"
- "and software is not completely reliable—crashes in conventional software are still common and uploading specialist software and using it can be fraught with difficulties" (Bishop, 2002)

In addition, I have just received an e-mail from a student who writes, "If you sit at a pc all day at work then doing it in the evening as well can not only be very fatiguing but positively harmful." I have also just been speaking to a student at my own institution who enrolled for an online Spanish course that involves a sophisticated system in which synchronous phone conversations and illustrations on a computer screen are possible. She told me with some frustration that she had now spent 5 hours on the course, roughly half an hour of which she had spent speaking Spanish. The other four and a half hours had been spent trying to get the software to work.

Of course, it's unwise to draw too many conclusions from such informal and casual material. Yet most dropping out from distance education courses is very heavily "front-loaded"—it occurs at the very beginning of a course. If the usual barriers of entering learning are compounded with extra hurdles of skills requirements, software familiarization, and technical problems, then the initial dropout rate is likely to be higher.

There is of course the supposition that many of these problems will disappear as software becomes more reliable and a generation that is familiar with computers from school moves into adulthood. Neither of these suppositions is completely convincing; it seems unlikely that software and hardware problems will vanish completely—virus and spam show little sign of waning. Automobiles have been with us for more than 100 years but still break down, crash, and run out of gas. And children still emerge from school without basic skills of various kinds.

The only solution to these problems at the moment seems to be more student support—help lines, tutors, online support, and so on. But such support is expensive, and for students from educationally disadvantaged backgrounds, it will probably have to be proactive as they are less likely to seek support before they dropout. Proactive support will be more expensive than reactive support and—as suggested earlier—will be in danger of eliminating still further one of the most important reasons for promoting e-learning—its supposed lower costs.

Promoting E-Learning Retention

Are there then ways of overcoming retention problems in e-learning at reasonable costs? Tiffin and Rajasingham (2003) argue that the advance of the technology itself will develop in ways that will provide the answers. For example, they hypothesize the introduction of what they call JITAITS—"just in time artificial intelligence tutors"—which will pop up like Microsoft's animated paperclip when needed. Among other ideas they suggest is to promote student and tutor interaction students by using "avatars"—online simulacra of themselves to visit virtual classrooms for support.

It does seem likely that imaginative answers like these will be needed if e-learning is to have any success in fulfilling its potential for overcoming social exclusion. Or it may be that answers will lie in the creative use of other forms of technology. For example, there is also much interest in "m-learning" using mobile devices such as palmtop computers and WAP-enabled mobile phones that can access the Web. These may become important not least because the ownership of mobile phones in the United Kingdom and Europe generally is higher than the ownership of computers and the capital costs lower. But although there have been projects on m-learning, there is little evidence as yet as to how it might work effectively. Most m-learning relies on access to the Internet at some point, and perhaps it will find a role in promoting proactive contact with students to enhance retention.

CONCLUSION

So far there seems little evidence that e-learning will help solve the problems of social exclusion in either developed or developing countries. We will need, as

Robins and Webster (2002) note, "to be sceptical about the hype surrounding the idea of a virtual university." We will also need at the same time to be aware that, as one of the contributors to their book Martin Trow writes, "The future will see a combination of traditional and distance learning rather than a replacement of traditional forms. But the short history of the computer has provided us with many surprises, some of them even welcome."

REFERENCES

Bishop, A. (2002). Come into my parlour said the spider to the fly; critical reflections on Web-based education from a student's perspective. *Distance Education* 23(2), 231–236.

Clarke, A. (2002). *Online learning and social exclusion.* Leicester, England: National Institute for Adult Continuing Education.

Driver, A. (2001). *Studying T171 at a learning centre.* Unpublished manuscript.

Hulsmann, T. (2000). *The costs of open learning: A handbook.* Oldenburg, Germany: Carl von Ossietzky Universitat.

LearnDirect. www.learndirect.co.uk.

McGerty, L. (2003). *Online learning and social exclusion–an overview of the literature.* Retrieved November 1, 2004, from the Overcoming Social Exclusion through Online Learning Project Web site: http://www.niace.org.uk/online/index.asp

National Institute for Adult Continuing Education and U.K. Open University. (2003). Retrieved November 1, 2004, from the Overcoming Social Exclusion through Online Learning Project Web site: http://www.niace.org.uk/online/index.asp

Robins, K., & Webster, F. (2002). *The virtual university? Knowledge markets and management.* Oxford: Oxford University Press.

Simpson, O. (2002). *Supporting students in online open and distance learning.* London: RoutledgeFalmer.

Simpson, O. (2003). *Student retention in online, open and distance learning.* London: RoutledgeFalmer.

Tiffin, J., & Rajasingham, L. (2003). *The global virtual university.* New York: RoutledgeFalmer.

United Kingdom Government Department for Education and Skills. (2003). *Towards a unified e-learning strategy.* Consultation Document. Retrieved November 9, 2004, from http://www.dfes.gov.uk/elearningstrategy/strategy.stm

Woodley, A., & Simpson, C. (2001). Learning and earning: Measuring "rates of return" among mature graduates from part-time distance courses. *Higher Education Quarterly,* 55(1), 28–41.

⁂ SIX ⁂

INTERNATIONAL STUDY CIRCLES

Ben Salt

Online learning is constrained by (among other things) technology, language, education, and wealth, but need not be limited to particular populations or geographical boundaries. With neoliberal globalization increasingly eroding the ability of nations to respond to national needs, this chapter investigates an educational response that matches the global reach of the transnational corporations.

International study circles (ISCs) embody the spirit of progressive adult education. Combining the philosophy of the Grundtvig-inspired Scandinavian folk schools with 21st-century technology, ISCs fan the dwindling embers of popular, radical adult education and shed fresh light on the practicalities associated with empowering democracy internationally. Exploring the possibilities of this version of nonaccredited, voluntary adult education has lessons of interest to more than those engaged in workers' education. Questions to consider as you read this chapter include:

- What do international study circles reveal about the ability of e-learning to cross national boundaries?
- Do international study circles show the weakness or power of employees in relation to their employers?

- What are your suggestions to improve international study circles?
- What are the costs and benefits to adults who engage in this form of education?

BACKGROUND TO THE STUDY

The rapid growth of union Web sites (Lee, 1997) and the role that the Internet is playing in actual disputes are indications of the potential that new technology offers for international workers' education. The Association for Progressive Communications helps 50,000 nongovernmental organizations (NGOs) in 133 nations fight their causes electronically (Mathews, 1997). In Amsterdam the Transnationals Information Exchange (TIE), comprising some 40 research and activist labor groups, is attempting to similarly empower the victims of global capitalism (Brecher & Costello, 1994; Herod, 1997), as is the San Francisco-based International Forum on Globalization (Roberts, 1998).

The place of computers in international labor struggles is well established. Cross-border alliances of unionists have proven effective in resolving labor disputes involving Coca-Cola's Guatemalan operations (Frundt, 1987). Herod (1995) has written on the successful campaign fought by the United Steelworkers of America (USWA) and the International Trade Secretariat (ITS) of the International Federation of Chemical, Energy, Mine, and General Workers' Unions (ICEM).

The trigger for this dispute was the 1994 illegal firing of 2,300 workers at five Bridgestone/Firestone tire factories. To attempt to reinstate the workers, the USWA and ICEM utilized the Internet to orchestrate a campaign of negative publicity. Shareholders and Internet advertisers were informed of the illegal action of the company, and a boycott of their products was initiated. The company's own Web site was targeted for these actions, making the employers pay for this aspect of the campaign. The Internet also allowed the protesters to spread their campaign worldwide. The catchy phrase "to picket, just click it" was used to encourage supporters to send electronic letters of protest to the management and spread the action. The campaign was so effective that in September 1996 nearly all the workers were recalled.

The Bridgestone/Firestone campaign showed that computers can put the workers in the driving seat, forcing management to react. Herod (1998) expresses guarded optimism by writing:

> Nevertheless, the internet does offer possibilities for organizing globally which will become increasingly significant as the speed of planetary capitalism and the spatial reach of capital increase to even greater levels, and unions become increasingly concerned about global geo-economic strategy. It does enable those with access to the technology (which though still concentrated in the advanced industrial nations is slowly beginning to diffuse to other parts of the world) to develop contacts, share information, and harass employers in ways and at speeds not previously [thought] possible. (p. 187)

While transnational corporations (TNCs) and their political allies remain firmly in control, the response of workers' organizations to neoliberal globalization is a fertile area for both research and practice (Salt, Cervero, & Herod, 2000). This chapter focuses on the contribution that online learning can have to providing a democratic tool for workers in their continuing struggles.

International Study Circles in Theory

The ISC Web site (ISC, 2003a) and the Final Evaluation Report of the ISCs (ISC, 2003b) provide the basis for a discussion on the rhetoric and reality of the potential of the Internet for international workers' education. In addition to Web-based information, data for this research on ISCs come from interviews with leading figures in the International Federation of Workers' Education Associations (IFWEA) who both participated in the ISCs and were integrally involved in designing and managing the program.

This study concerns the ISCs that have run from March 1997 to February 2003, with in-depth analysis of the two pilot ISCs. These pilots involved 178 participants (100 men and 78 women) from IFWEA affiliates in the following 12 countries: Barbados, Belgium, Bulgaria, England, Estonia, France, Germany, Kenya, Peru, South Africa, Spain, and Sweden. The Final Evaluation Report succinctly states the goal of this program:

> ISCs are aimed at facilitating a global education programme on issues concerning globalisation. Experiences of globalisation world-wide have pointed to the need for organisations and communities to develop an understanding of local problems within the international context. This understanding can more effectively emerge if working people in different countries are able to share ideas and information, leading to common strategies and activities. (ISC, 2003a)

The rhetoric of shared experiences is plainly evident from the ISC Web site:

> The ISC methodology is geared towards making the international experiences of participants themselves an integral part of the course content. ISC courses have workers' lived experiences as an important component of the learning process with participants from different countries learning from each other rather than only relying on experts or secondary sources. (ISC, 2003a)

As a regional facilitator in an international study circle, Marlon Quesada from the Philippines was able to explain both why he feels it is a necessary response to globalization and its operation. In his case, participants from Taiwan, Korea, India, Pakistan, the Philippines, and Australia physically met to design a common curriculum, course and module outlines, common education materials, and guide questions and to agree on a common time frame to organize small study groups or study circle groups. These groups would use the course outlines and guide questions and education materials in their respective countries. Then, with the use of the Internet site maintained by the Finnish IFWEA affiliate, the Workers' Educational Association of Finland (TSL), these participants would transmit the results of their respective study groups in each country. TSL would make a summary and transmit back the reports from each country so that each country has the opportunity to review the results of the discussions in the other cooperating groups and use that as a reference in the succeeding study session.

The ISC that Quesada helped to coordinate ran six sessions on the concept of globalization and the participating countries' experience with globalization. For workers, globalization can mean the replacement of permanent, full-time jobs by fixed-term, temporary, or part-time work (casualization and contractualization). National governments can present themselves as having no other option than providing ever cheaper and more flexible labor to remain competitive in the globalizing economy. Quesada had clearly thought out the reasons for investing so much time in the ISC:

> Globalization, is basically, let us put it this way. Not all issues could be negotiated in the enterprise workplace level. Many of the issues normally arise from the national policies. That's the first phase. But many national policies in our countries, would depend on international developments. So, many national policies are being shaped because of the international changes and global changes. So, in other words, that is where international solidarity and connection would come into place. Because if you're not able to negotiate, for instance, for instance in the Philippines it's useless to negotiate to your employer the issue on casualization and contractualization, it's a national policy in the Philippines, but then, the Philippines, they're not really, easily change or, address the issue of casualization and contractualization on its

own because it was really introduced by the international global, capitalist community. In other words, if the struggle is global, there's an important need to put the connections, especially among workers and trade unions. So in this context the IFWEA tried to think of concrete measures as to how globalization will be understood in the context of the different experiences of various countries, and certainly how a dialogue could be undertaken, between and among different countries. (Personal communication with the author)

IFWEA's enthusiasm for new technology is revealed in the following passage from their Web site:

The potential to conduct global education has been strengthened enormously by new information and communication technologies. The ISC project explores how to make use of the technology in such a way that participants in different countries are able to engage in meaningful international discussion. We hope that the technology will facilitate a global education process whereby local experiences of the effects of globalisation can be communicated and discussed by participants in different countries. (ISC, 2003a)

International Study Circles in Practice

The two pilot projects fell short of the designers' expectations on several counts. The most glaring case of the failure of reality to match rhetoric concerns the scarcity of international links or actions. The one exception involved Volvo workers in Peru and Sweden whereby Swedish workers visited their Andean colleagues, with Peruvian unionists now involved with the International Metalworkers' Federation World Council for Volvo workers. If anything, this episode underlines the weaknesses of computer-assisted learning, as it was only after face-to-face meetings that substantive contacts were established. Although the ISCs were instrumental in establishing the initial ties, it is clear that human contact remains essential to the development of meaningful international workers' solidarity and that technology, bereft of human contact, has yet to establish itself as an adequate substitute for personal interaction. The Final Evaluation report (ISC, 2003a) spells out the goal of the ISCs being to "stimulate thinking and action on a global basis." The notes to the facilitators (ISC, 2003b) unequivocally state that, "Our main aim should be to build the confidence of workers to struggle and take action in the context of globalization." Looking at the rhetoric, it is clear that the action remains largely confined to paper.

Many of the facilitators mentioned that moderating the study circles was much more onerous than they initially envisaged. In addition to translating, sending and downloading reports, tracking down the often equally busy participants to attend demanded considerable time. With the study sessions coinciding with strikes and contract negotiations, all study groups suffered sporadic attendance. Several participants mentioned that their hectic schedules left them insufficient time to act on the ideas developed in the study sessions. The ISC (2003b) Web site reported that

> attendance of the Australian participants was "patchy," usually because of personal, family commitments. No single session produced a full complement of participants. Sadly, the last session had to be abandoned after the second attempt—3 of the participants were involved directly in industrial disputes, 2 more had prior personal commitments.

Another weakness of the ISCs relates to the members. The designers of the ISCs intended for the participants to be rank-and-file activists from both trade union and community organizations such as NGOs. In reality, all but 32 of the 178 participants in the pilots came from unions, with many of these organizers and officials rather than shop floor activists. IFWEA provides the following explanation for the failure of the reality to match their intentions:

> There were several reasons for the lack of participation from the community organisations. In some instances, facilitators did attempt to recruit participants from other organizations but were unsuccessful due to the internal organisational weaknesses of these organisations, and/or lack of interest in the topic. Several participants however did not target their recruitment drive beyond trade unions. (2003a)

During the two pilot projects, the role of computers evolved. Initially, the designers of the study circles envisaged that only the facilitators would manage the computer-based communications between the participant nations. The reasoning for this was that the project was intended to be focused on education about globalization, rather than technology, so that computers were simply a tool to allow this international education. However, participants expressed a desire for the Internet itself to be included in the curriculum, in order for participants to become better aware of the potential uses of computers for international workers' education and solidarity. Furthermore, feedback from the first pilot suggested that participants wanted to contribute to the writing of the reports themselves and also undertake online discussions on topics of specific interest. In the event, lack of familiarity with computers and the English language limited the online discussions.

The danger that computers create new elites is real. With the vast majority of the world's population unable to afford a computer and unfamiliar with the technology, the power of the technocrats is enormously enhanced. The facilitators' course evaluations reflected this concern:

> In the Australian group, we had two officials and two delegates who were experienced users of the internet. For the rest, the internet as a tool in the program seemed to be regarded as some other aspect which they could have nothing to do with. At times I was wondering whether we had two sub groups in the discussion: one group which would use the internet language and references in its observations and reflections, and another group who just politely shook their heads when they listened. (ISC, 2003b)

The study circles were held in the local languages, but the decision to use English as the language for international communication raised numerous difficulties. One of the first consequences of this was the withdrawal of the French and Belgium participants and their decision to establish a French-speaking ISC between themselves. Another result was the inevitable disempowerment of non-English-speaking members. The English-speaking facilitators had the demanding task of translating the reports into English. Especially in the first pilot project, participants expressed dissatisfaction with the somewhat bland and unimaginative summaries of the study circle discussions. Although well aware of the negative consequences of utilizing English, a satisfactory alternative has yet to be found.

The Final Evaluation reported that the participants were "extremely positive about the ISC focus on globalization," but involving affiliates from 12 countries resulted in many tensions. For many unionists, the traditional educational focus on health and safety, collective bargaining, and shop steward training is more immediately relevant than discussions on the global economy. Tying the international issues to local experiences was essential, but it proved problematic. Skilled facilitators are needed to establish these links and keep the ISCs relevant to all participants. In the course of discussing the global economy, the might of the TNCs also resulted in feelings of helplessness that led to calls for future ISCs to give greater prominence to case studies highlighting workers' victories. A further complication concerns the differing political orientations of the participating affiliates. The overtly socialist stance of South Africa's affiliate contrasted sharply with those, such as the Estonian participants, who were not as ready to take such a critical view of TNCs. By encouraging workers in different countries to exchange

Table 6.1 List of International Study Circles From Their Inception to February 2003

- Civil Society Regional Study Circle Project for Central, Eastern, and Southeast Europe, September 2002–February 2003
- Transformation, Economic Reconstruction, and Social Consequences: Regional Study Circle Project for Central, Eastern, and Southeast Europe, September 2001–February 2002
- Migrant Workers in the Global Economy Study Circle, December 2000–May 2001
- Women and the Global Food Industry Study Circle, November 1999–May 2000
- IMF Magna Internet Action Project, September 1999–September 2000
- Asia ISC Project, January 1999–May 1999
- Pilot Projects 1 and 2 Tackling Transnationals, March 1997–December 1998

experiences and opinions, the ISCs run the risk of heightening divisions, rather than nurturing greater unity.

IFWEA's Web site provides detailed insights into the ISCs that have taken place subsequent to the pilot studies that are the principle areas of investigation for this chapter.

As will be seen, many of the problems and issues encountered in the pilots continue, which have both direct and indirect impacts on the democratic potential of ISCs. The Migrant Workers in the Global Economy ISC originally included Angola, Cape Verde, Greece, Guinea-Bissau, Ireland, Mozambique, Pakistan, Portugal, São Tomé and Principe, Sweden, Trinidad and Tobago, and the United Kingdom. The following quote from the course facilitator for Trinidad and Tobago reveals the importance of more traditional tools for the effective use of online learning, and how planning for seemingly small details can fundamentally affect the learning outcomes:

> The financial assistance from IFWEA allowed us to purchase folders, pens, writing pads, maps and flip chart paper. We produced our own *ISC Migrant Workers* cover to paste on the folders to give a specific identity to the course material. It proved difficult to get the maps required and although we eventually bought a map of the world and one of the Caribbean region neither were quite what we really wanted. The world map, in particular, was more a geographical than a political map and so many continents did not give details of country names to any degree. This is an example of the limited resources that we sometimes have available. (ISC, 2003c)

The limits to the ability of the Internet to jump geographic boundaries were clearly demonstrated by the inability of any participants from Tobago to attend the Trinidad-based sessions. Evaluations reveal that attendance throughout the ISCs was reduced by the difficulty to reach the hosting building.

As occurred in the pilot ISCs, technical issues continue to weaken their potential. Only two of Trinidad's participants had access to e-mail, forcing the facilitator to rely on post, phone, and word of mouth. More dramatically, the union computer crashed halfway through the course.

This ISC also suffered from difficulties in completing the course work and the withdrawal of the Swedish and Greek groups. Trinidad's evaluation mentions their disappointment at the lack of reports from the African groups. The evident partial breakdown of this ISC is shown by only three of the original twelve groups completing evaluations. Interestingly, these are the three countries where English is most widespread, again underlining the sociolinguistic dimensions to the democratic potential of international online learning.

Despite all these problems, Trinidad's evaluation reported that

> when we were able to get reports they were read with great enthusiasm. The reports from the other countries often provided the highlight of any session and remained a talking point after sessions had finished. What also made the international links more personal were the photos that some groups, particularly Pakistan, provided. (ISC, 2003c)

Those who attempt to provide a voice to empower a bottom-up response to globalization run the risk of retaliatory measures from those setting the agenda. This was seen in the Women in the Global Food Industry ISC with Egypt's withdrawal due to government restrictions on NGO activities. With a further two countries withdrawing, this ISC also found that unforeseen events limited its potential.

In reality, ISCs have seen the facilitators wearing several hats: translator, interpreter, teacher, researcher, IT technician, and mediator. Although participants reported feeling empowered as a result of their new knowledge, the use of ICT can lead to "proxy democracy." This is due to the power engendered to the facilitators, who become a voice for the others on the Internet. Echoing sentiments of isolation found elsewhere in this book, participants called for greater opportunities for direct contact and using both tradition and new technology. Potential solutions to address this issue included the following:

- create an online "chat" mechanism for participants to make direct contact with each other;
- reports should be written less abstractly and give a voice to different people in the local group;
- photographs of the local groups should be put on the Web or exchanged between the groups;
- if possible technically, the use of video conferencing;
- an exchange of personal and organizational fax and e-mail addresses to encourage direct contact. (ISC, 2003d)

When analyzing ISCs for their democratic potential, the issue of who participates is central. Throughout the ISCs, a high proportion of those involved are union or NGO officials rather than the rank-and-file union members. The difficulties in including shop floor workers were experienced in the Women in the Global Food Industry ISC. Although not unique, the English group faced immense difficulties in sustaining the local group. The facilitator explains that much of this was because

> part-time shift workers are the "flexible" work force in England as elsewhere. In the food processing industry with 24 hour production schedules, part time workers can find their shifts being altered at the last minute, called in to cover for absent colleagues, and offered overtime on bonus rates when production gears up as at Christmas. However interested and committed women are in educational opportunities, they will not turn down the chance for extra wages when they have families to feed. (ISC, 2003d)

So although ISCs can attempt to stimulate reflection and action (praxis), the power of neoliberal globalization to dictate the working rhythms of employees to a large extent determines which voices are heard. As ISCs demonstrate, both the working patterns and reliance on an IT-trained facilitator place a barrier to direct worker representation, which runs the danger that workers' own voices are heard through a proxy.

Despite these constraints, evidence that study circles fill a needed gap in transformational popular education is seen by the projects that have developed from ISCs. The IFWEA Web site lists the following outcomes:

- As a result of their participation in the ISC, Peru's IFWEA affiliate, Programa Laboral de Desarrollo (PLADES), is initiating a regional Latin American ISC on the same topic.

- In the Philippines, ISC course participants have now become involved in a regional program on women workers initiated by the Education and Research Network (LEARN) and the International Union of Foodworkers (IUF).
- In the Philippines, participation in the ISC led to women workers attempting to set up women's forums in their unions.
- In Norway, a course on globalization has been developed for trade unionists as a direct result of the ISC. The local group will also continue to meet.
- Through the ISC, Nestlé workers in Bulgaria and South Africa exchanged collective agreements and established links.
- Through the ISC, Kraft workers in Bulgaria and Norway established links.
- National study circles on globalization will be developed in Zimbabwe, South Africa, and the Philippines.
- In Zimbabwe, the local group managed to win an agreement with two companies concerning women's rights in the workplace. (ISC, 2003d)

CONCLUSION

The Final Evaluation Report comes to the following conclusion regarding the potential of computers for international workers' education:

> It was felt that the technology does make a project of this nature possible. International education programs would otherwise consume vast amounts of resources. Within the existing limitations imposed by the technology, culture and other differences, it is possible to strengthen and improve the international communication so that it impacts meaningfully on the education process. (2003a)

Despite the varying technological capacities of the participating organizations and minor and major technical glitches, the basic infrastructure requirements for the ISCs show that information technology is already sufficiently developed for this type of international workers' education. With a desire for greater IT-facilitated international contact such as bilateral video linkups, ISCs are likely to continue to grow as technology becomes more widely available.

Given the enormous linguistic, political, and economic differences among the participating affiliates, the generally favorable reactions to the ISCs is reason to believe that technology can indeed provide a tremendous boost to international workers' education. Although these ISCs have emphasized that technology devoid of human contact can only result in the most superficial and short-termed connections, computers provide workers' organizations with the best chance yet of implementing an internationally coordinated, broad-based educational response to the might of the TNC-led global economy. As the participants reported, "We learned to appreciate how technology could be used for the benefit of the working class" (2003b).

Nevertheless, the disparate backgrounds of the participants resulted in few sustained international connections and actions. This was true for both the pilots and subsequent ISCs formed with workers in the same TNC or industry, or between more homogenous entities such as women or migrant workers. ISCs supply workers with the potential to become integrally connected to the international union movement. The cost-effective and efficient Internet has already proven itself an effective ally to labor in actual disputes. With increased resources and continued honest self-criticism, ISCs will nurture a more knowledgeable and internationally-orientated movement. Based on the cornerstone adult education concepts of experiences and praxis, ISCs offer solace to those who are concluding that the reality of technology rarely matches the rhetoric. The place of the English language for international workers' education remains a thorny, unresolved problem. English is currently the preserve of the elite but offers tremendous opportunities to the international social movements (Salt, 1998). In order for ISCs to reach their full potential, it is necessary that unions win the right for paid education leave. TNC executives utilize Web-based learning during regular working hours. It is unrealistic to expect the ISCs to be attractive to all but the most committed unionists unless workers have the opportunity to engage this technology in company-provided facilities while being paid. This sentiment was expressed in the ISC report:

> The participants felt that unless the workers had access to these tools nothing will work out. Some said that it's virtually impossible for a worker to have a computer and access to this information. Others thought that the computers at the workplace could be used for such activities but the management will never allow it. In this regard, some participants came up with the idea that there should be a workers' resource center established where a couple of computers should be available so that workers could come together and access all information. (ISC, 2003b)

The limited number of concrete actions resulting from the ISCs highlights the fundamental need for unions to attract more members. Time and again, the participants were forced to reflect on their current weakness in the face of the global economy and to recognize that this will continue unless unions become a more serious challenge to the national, international and supranational instruments of globalization (Salt, 2000). Computers can become an effective tool for re-energizing the union movement, but only if used as a complement to traditional person-to-person organizing, and not as a substitute. Waterman (1993) writes of networkers replacing labor agitators. Experienced unionists know that disputes are won or lost through solidarity on the picket line, not in virtual exchanges. Technology presents new challenges to the labor movement. Designed to serve the interests of government and business, it is wise to be suspicious of this new technology. Only the most rabid free marketers would argue that computers have positively impacted the lives of all workers. The Indian ISC facilitator is under no illusions about who is benefiting from the impact of technology:

> The TNCs have come with the New Technology as part of the globalization process, creating a bunch of new problems concerning employment, particularly in labor surplus countries like India, which makes a host of traditional skills redundant. Employers prefer to phase out workers with old skills and recruit new ones. The new jobs are likely to be managerial and supervisory positions. These can run an industry with very few unskilled, casual or contract workers. New Technology enables the management to have major control over the labor process. This erodes the power of the unions. (ISC, 2003b)

The implementers of the ISCs seem fully aware of the danger of encouraging a false consciousness of empowerment via computers. Their emphasis that the education should result in action is to be applauded. However, the virtual lack of this praxis raises concerns that technology may prove ineffectual as a solution to the very real hardships faced by millions of globally restrained workers. Despite these concerns, it is my firm conviction that the ISCs of IFWEA offer the best chance yet of utilizing the new emerging technology to dramatically improve the lives of the victims of globalization. There is plentiful evidence to conclude that ISCs are a genuine and successful initiative in democracy, empowerment, and praxis. Unions and other pro-labor institutions should do all they can to further the expansion of this exciting development in international workers' education.

REFERENCES

Brecher, J., & Costello, T. (1994). *Global village or global pillage: Economic reconstruction from the bottom up.* Boston: South End Press.

Frundt, H. J. (1987). *Refreshing pauses: Coca-Cola and human rights in Guatemala.* New York: Praeger.

Herod, A. (1995). The practice of international labor solidarity and the geography of the global economy. *Economic Geography, 77*(4), 341–363.

Herod, A. (1997). Labor as an agent of globalization and as a global agent. In K. Cox (Ed.), *Spaces of globalization: Reasserting the power of the local* (pp. 167–200). London: Guilford.

Herod, A. (1998). Of blocs, flows and networks: The end of the Cold War, cyberspace, and the geo-economics of organised labor at the . . . fin de millenaire. In A. Herod, G. O Tuathail, & S. M. Roberts (Eds.), An unruly world? Globalization, governance and geography (pp. 162–195). London: Routledge.

International Study Circle Programme. (n.d.). *Final evaluation report.* Retrieved August 16, 1999, from http://www.ifwea.org/isc/isc_final_evaluation_report.html

International Study Circle Programme. (2003a). *Final evaluation report: Responding to the global economy.* Retrieved August 12, 2003, from http://www/ifwea.org/isc/isc_final_evaluation_report.html

International Study Circle Programme. (2003b). *Asia ISC project: January 1999–May 1999.* Retrieved August 12, 2003, from http://ifwea.org/isc/pilot03/index.html

International Study Circle Programme. (2003c). *Migrant workers in the global economy: Trinidad and Tobago country report.* Retrieved October 1, 2003, from http://www.ifwea.org/isc/iw-isc/index.html

International Study Circle Programme. (2003d). *Women and the global food industry November evaluation.* Retrieved October 1, 2003, http://www.ifwea.org/isc/project4/index.html

Lee, E. (1997). *The labor movement and the Internet: The new internationalism.* London: Pluto.

Mathews, J. T. (1997). Power shift. *Foreign Affairs, 76*(1), 45–61.

Roberts, S. M. (1998). Geo-goverance in trade and finance and political geographies of dissent. In A. Herod, G. O Tuathail, & S. M. Roberts (Eds.), *An unruly world? Globalization, governance and geography* (pp. 116–131). London: Routledge.

Salt, B. (1998). English as a foreign language and its relation to international workers' education. *Adult Basic Education, 8*(1), 3–17.

Salt, B. (2000). Factors enabling and constraining worker education programs' responses to neo-liberal globalisation. *Studies in Continuing Education, 22*(1), 115–144.

Salt, B., Cervero, R. M., & Herod, A. (2000). Workers' education and neo-liberal globalization: An adequate response to the TNCs? *Adult Education Quarterly, 51*(1), 9–31.

Waterman, P. (1993). Internationalism is dead! Long live global solidarity? In J. Brecher, J. B. Childs, & J. Cutler (Eds.), *Global visions: Beyond the new world order* (pp. 257–262). Boston: South End Press.

※ SEVEN ※

A CRITICAL LOOK AT DISTANCE EDUCATION IN TURKEY

Husra Gursoy

Distance education is becoming increasingly popular throughout the world as economic forces continue to encourage the facilitation of new technologies. (Potashnik & Capper, 1998). Many countries are now integrating distance education programs into their existing programs using advanced technologies, promising equal opportunity to those who do not have access to or cannot afford a higher education. These countries perceive distance education as a way to liberate education from the restrictions of time and location. The governments, universities, and other organizations favor the distance education programs as an ultimate alternative to the conventional systems. Nonetheless, they ignore that distance education creates a system where standardization and efficiency are supported over diversity and individuality (Rose, 1997). They rarely discuss the inequalities perpetuated through the implementation of the distance education programs. As a result, students of distance education are disadvantaged in many ways compared to their counterparts in conventional universities.

Turkey, as well as other countries, took the initiative to create a distance education system with support of its government and the Turkish Council of Higher Education (TCHE). In recent years, large investments were established to bring advanced technologies into the existing distance education programs. Additionally, the universities are encouraged to open online courses with new policies established by TCHE. While the advanced technologies are welcomed in every way, the cultural, social, and economical realities of the country and their impact on distance education are rather neglected.

It is my intention here to present the gaps between the rhetoric and realities of distance education in Turkey. After I briefly introduce the distance education programs in Turkey, I will look at the potential barriers in accessing technology. Next, I will analyze distance education within the context of social problems, while examining the Turkish culture and underlying cultural differences that relate to globalization. Finally, I will suggest several strategies we can employ in overcoming inequalities in the Turkish distance education system. The following questions might also help to focus on more specific issues related to the Turkish distance education system.

- What are the challenges of educating large masses through distance education systems?
- In what ways do distance technologies, either old-fashioned or advanced, impact the educational opportunities in terms of time, location, and affordability?
- How do the cultural values and norms of the country impact the spread of distance education programs to other nations?

DISTANCE EDUCATION PROGRAMS IN TURKEY

The development of distance education in Turkey commenced in the early 1980s. At that time, Anadolu University (AU) was designated to provide distance education on a national scale. AU currently is the only institute conducting "distance higher education" in the country (Ozkul, 2001). Recently, several universities including Middle East Technical, Istanbul Bilgi, and Bilkent have initiated online certificate and degree programs. Similarly Sakarya, Karadeniz Teknik and Firat Universities are offering online courses (TCHE, 2003). The TCHE, a governmental agency, confirms that numerous other universities in the country have launched vocational oriented distance education programs using advanced telecommunication technologies:

To expand the higher education system, preliminary studies were started in 1996 for the design and construction of a nationwide distance education system based on advanced telecommunication and educational technologies. Now, some graduate programs in some universities are offered through the Internet after being approved by at the national committee and some undergraduate courses are also offered through Internet. Talks are being held with universities abroad to offer joint degrees through Internet. (TCHE, 2003)

It is clear from the report that the development of new distance education programs is encouraged with the regulations of communication-based distance higher education. The realization of the Internet as a potential way to deliver higher education emerges in the rhetoric, and it reflects the government's positive attitude toward globalization. At the same time, there is an open invitation to universities to consider the distance education options to a substantial extent. However, little discussion was initiated addressing pedagogical strategies emphasizing cultural differences and the technology access, while their absence might be an impediment to reaching intended practices. As a result, many problems are likely to surface in the implementation of distance education programs in Turkey. I will examine those problems in detail in the following subsections. Since AU continues to dominate as the major provider of distance education with more than 700,000 students and has had a huge impact on Turkey's higher education for the last 20 years, I will dedicate later sections specifically to AU to present examples of its implementation efforts and associated problems.

The Promise of Open Access in AU

Time and Location

AU serves as a dual-mode university with both conventional and distance educational systems. It has distance education programs in over 20 areas including business, health education, social sciences, and teacher training. In addition to nationwide distance education programs, AU offers bachelor's and 2-year associate's degree programs to Turkish citizens working in Western Europe as well as Turkish citizens residing in the Turkish Republic of Northern Cyprus.

The distance education system in AU mainly utilizes the old-fashioned technologies. The printed materials and TV broadcasts are major means to reach the large number of students. The Turkish Radio and Television (TRT) channel is currently in charge of broadcasting the distance education courses and can be viewed by all regions in Turkey. Even though the channel represents the Educational TV of AU, only half of the weekly broadcasting is related to the distance education programs. The remaining hours include musical and horse race programs. This, in itself, weakens the educational identity of the channel (Ulutak, 2002). In addition, lessons are broadcast during inconvenient times in the late morning or late evening. Students who have full-time jobs and other commitments cannot always equally benefit from educational broadcasting. Contrary to the premise of distance education, time becomes the major issue to be able to access the instruction. This situation further raises the question of whether educational opportunities are equally available within the student population of AU. It is clear that the existing resources are not adequate to serve students who have different priorities in their lives.

In order to compensate for the limitations of using one-way technologies, a number of local advising centers, and bureaus in different provinces were launched in recent years. The local advising centers complement the face-to-face aspect of the distance programs in more than 50 cities, while offering several courses in the area of business. However their variety and availability are limited to the number of AU's conventional locations. Similarly, the local bureaus are available in almost every city providing assistance in the areas of registration, maintaining academic and address records, transcripts, and distributing print materials. These bureaus function as an administrative-support unit of the AU. In Turkey's case, since other means of the registration and related services are not available, having access to the bureaus largely affects the access to the distance education programs. Those who live in villages and rural areas have to visit the bureaus regularly in order to maintain their records and academic progress. As a result, the conventional facilities make distance education favorable only to those who are free from the restrictions of location.

AU also attempts to increase the interactive learning opportunities by offering "live testing preparation broadcasting" on TRT, where students are able to reach their professors through new age videoconferencing. However, only limited numbers of students are able to ask questions in the short time intervals. The fact that these programs are broadcast just hours before the exams questions the credibility of instructional programs.

Affordability

With new developments in technology, the distance education programs in Turkey are starting to utilize more advanced communication technologies. This is predominantly because of the policies established by the TCHE. The council encourages the use of those new technologies as explained in the following quote:

> One of the aims of distance higher education based on communication and information technologies at the vocational, undergraduate, and graduate levels is to increase the effectiveness of education by making use of the interactive medium provided by information technologies, with multimedia features and the ability to access unlimited information. (TCHE, n.d.-b., para. 1)

The TCHE presumes that the effectiveness of distance higher education largely depends on the advancement of information technology and the integration of the multimedia features for information dispensation. Most favors the technology since it affords information dispensation more effectively than the various instructional methods employed in conventional classrooms. In a knowledge society, where both information dispensation and critical learning are valued, it is mainly the preference of the people to favor one of them over another. Nonetheless, access to information is possible when the access to technology is available, which returns me to my argument. Who will be able to afford the computer technologies and Internet?

The adoption of advanced technologies by large numbers of students is almost impossible in Turkey for several reasons. First, the access to the Internet is very costly and limited to those living in urban cities. The monthly charge for digital subscriber line (DSL) (256 kpbs) service, available only in metropolitan cities, is approximately $50 (Turk Telekom, 2004). Even though those expenses seem relatively similar to Americans, they are extremely high for an average Turkish citizen, whose salary is around $300 to $500 per month. The dial-up service is generally more expensive. For instance, a 10-hour dial-up connection costs approximately $10. Second, students' lack of computer knowledge and skills is the biggest obstacle in adopting computers in education in both rural and urban areas. As the knowledge of the educational technologies in elementary and high schools throughout the country becomes more sophisticated, problems relating to a lack of computer knowledge are expected to be solved rapidly in the near future. Finally, only a very small percentage of the population owns a computer in Turkey. Without carefully analyzing these problems and obtaining optimum solutions, it is simply not the best way to largely rely on those technologies in distance higher education, which will only intensify the educational inequalities between those living in urban and rural areas.

AU designed and developed Web-based courses parallel to the recent developments in advanced technologies, which integrate computer-based practice, TV programs, and print course materials. By making accessible the Web-based courses and other resources online, AU makes distance education an advantage for those who have Internet access and own a computer. It is apparent that students from low socioeconomic status cannot afford to access Web-based instruction. To address those problems, computer centers have been established in 15 city centers in past years. Since most of these centers are located in big cities, those who live in rural areas still cannot equally benefit from the proposed facilities. As a result, the solutions produced again only favor the students in urban cities and from prosperous families.

Social Obstacles

While the young populations and demand for higher education increase, the supply of institutions is very limited in Turkey. The Student Selection and Placement Center (SSPC) reports that in the 2002–2003 academic year, of 1,502,605 students who took the national exam, only 333,411 students were admitted to 2-year and 4-year degree programs. As a result, entrance to traditional programs becomes more challenging and competitive. With the capacity of accepting 200,000, distance education is considered as a means to meet the pressing demand for higher education (TCHE, n.d.-a). In a similar fashion, Ozkul (2001), dean of open education faculty at AU, points out that distance education in Turkey serves as an alternative to conventional education, since the universities have limited resources and cannot promise higher education to the millions of Turkish students:

> As a developing country with considerable economic and cultural potential, education is a vitally important issue for Turkey. Parallel to the population growth, the demand for all types of education is increasing whereas the resources, such as, schools and teachers are limited and not possible to reach adequate levels in short periods of time. Therefore, it seems quite difficult for

Turkey to achieve an overall educational level required by a modern society, using conventional educational approaches and techniques. (para. 2)

Ozkul continues:

> The educational needs of high school graduates, who, for *various reasons*, could not receive or continue their university education is the main target group for AU. In addition to awarding bachelor's and pre bachelor's (associate) degrees, AU has provided opportunities of improving academic or professional proficiency to people who are already engaged in professions. (para. 14)

Distance education in Turkey is available to everybody who receives the minimum score in university entrance exams. SSPC statistics show that in the 2002–2003 academic year, nearly half of the students registered to 4-year distance education degree programs were 20 years old and under, who, we can easily assume, were recent high school graduates. Since the competitive job market in Turkey pushes students to pursue at least a college degree, most of them consider distance education as only means to receive a college diploma. The "various reasons" stated by Ozkul then do not actually substantiate the argument of making education available to those who have family obligations, job commitments, or geographical obstacles. Rather, those reasons can be attributed to the void in the educational and social system, which presents distance education not as an alternative but as a "necessity." Consequently, the reasons most students pursue a distance education program at AU do not necessarily imply that those students in fact *want* to pursue a distance education. In Turkey's case, it is highly possible that most students who currently engage in distance education programs would prefer the conventional universities if they were more accessible nationwide and prefer the private universities if they were more affordable.

Job security seems to be another obstacle for distance education students. Even though graduates of these programs receive higher education diplomas equivalent to those earned by traditional universities, most of the business associations have not considered graduates as potential employees. Ozkul (2001) points out the social inequalities students confront after graduation:

> With regard to the social acceptance, when compared to the students of conventional universities, distance education students of AU are not accepted socially as formal students. This negative attitude is attributed to the relative

easiness of entrance to the open education. This attitude also brought the perception of the graduates of the system as inferior to their counterparts at the conventional schools. At present there is not a reliable assessment that measures the "quality" of the graduates of the distance education system. But when compared with the students of conventional universities the graduates of AU distance education system may stand a little below at the beginning because of their relatively low scores at the university entrance exams. But this is not a consequence of the distance education process. The distinction between the open education students and conventional school students appears as a result of the university entrance examinations. (para. 59)

Thus, Ozkul is asserting that low entrance requirements of distance education programs create a negative public attitude towards those programs. The public judges them not by the proven effectiveness of the programs but by their lower entrance requirements. They assume that the lower entrance requirements are generally associated with the less quality programs. However, distance education programs should not be part of this discussion since their entrance requirements are consciously set to the minimum to attract more students. Then, the quality of instructional approaches employed by the distance education programs becomes more and more important than the achievement scores of the students to minimize the inequalities, which actually contradicts Ozkul's argument. It seems that the lack of consideration to find appropriate instructional strategies to educate large masses is more likely to contribute to the social inequalities.

Social inequalities in distance education programs are further caused by the challenging university entrance examination. This challenge forces high school graduates to attend costly private courses and high schools in order to better prepare for the exam and enter the residential programs. While students from affluent families generally can afford those private lessons and schools, most others have to be satisfied with what the public high school offers them. Therefore, the exam process separates students not only on the basis of their achievement results but also on the basis of their socioeconomic status. It is possible to assume that the majority of the distance education students are likely to be from less affluent families who cannot afford to compete for traditional universities. As a result, many students, especially recent high school graduates, generally have minimum control of their education since their choices are limited to distance education programs in most cases.

Globalization and Cultural Sensitivity

The advancement of the new technologies combined with the increase in Internet use offers the possibility of sharing the educational resources with universities in other countries. In that regard, Turkey's efforts since 1986 primarily focus on supporting its own citizens living in Western countries and northern Cyprus. AU provides distance higher education to Turkish citizens living in various European countries who did not pursue a higher education after high school and who were unable to benefit from education offered in their new environment. This educational opportunity enables Turkish citizens to pursue education without having to quit their job. This, in turn, makes Turkish citizens in other countries productive individuals who will contribute to the values of the society they reside in (Cakir, 2002). Turkey also seizes this opportunity as a social investment to "re-acculture expatriate Turks to their language and culture" (McIsaac, M., Murphy, K. L., & Demiray, U., 1988). By educating younger generations, Turkey aims to protect the cultural values of the Turkish societies outside of their country while representing Turkey in a higher status abroad.

Turkey has collaborated with many other countries in the form of organizing symposiums to share its distance education experiences (Ozkul, 2001). However, the government managed to keep its own system and resources for only its citizens. Despite Turkey's past political efforts to provide education only to citizens, this view seems to have changed in recent years. Buyukersen (2002), Governance of Eskisehir and former president of AU, points out the importance of the globalization process in distance education:

> In different countries Mega universities providing distance education should get to know one another by producing close links and cooperate with one another in scientific and educational projects. If such a cooperational project takes place, then we will be able to make use of the information, communication resources, network systems, multimedia technologies and system practices all universities have. We can develop a new culture for students and teachers. We can develop and spread a multilingual educational system. By reducing the physical and geographical distance among people we can locate people closely.

Thus the rhetoric only reflects the optimistic view of globalization and does not emphasize the issues of homogeneity and cultural and contextual differences among the countries. Exemplifying Turkish cultural values and educational practices might help us to address those concerns. Murphy (1991) argues that Turkey's roots in an oral tradition, along with its emphasis on rote memorization and the sacredness of text, make learning independently with a textbook less suitable. Based on Islam's strong oral tradition, "It is the professor's responsibility to interpret text to students just as it is the students' responsibility to memorize the words of their professor" (Murphy, 1991, p. 43). Ongs, (1982) further points out that "those who live in cultures with strong oral roots are likely to express themselves in terms of practical situations rather than abstract terms" (cited in Murphy, 1991, p. 44).

These variations in Turkish culture are likely to affect the educational practices. In addition, the transition from teacher-centered education to individual-based learning, where students learn alone and support is minimal, creates many difficulties for Turkish distance education students. Therefore, the instructional methods, which will reflect the cultural values and educational practices of the country, might be quite different from strategies employed by other countries. In order to adopt the distance education courses from other countries, these courses should be examined in terms of the possible effects on Turkish cultural values and pedagogical approaches.

CONCLUSION

In conclusion, I have analyzed one of the major distance education programs in Turkey. I have further examined AU's distance education system in large scale by looking at the implementation effects of the programs in terms of social, cultural, and technological aspects. Despite the fact that the rhetoric focuses on positive features of the programs, various forms of inequality still exist in the implementation of distance education programs.

As shown in the AU example, both old-fashioned and advanced technologies have become the fundamental means of distance education programs. However, the technology favors those who have high socioeconomic status and those who live in urban cities, whereas it neglects those living in rural areas and those from low socioeconomic status. These inequalities will continue to exist until the universities and governments carry out large-scale projects distributing resources allocated for education equally. The new policies should concentrate on developing funding formulas that equalize technology spending throughout rich and poor districts.

The challenging university entrance exam, limited job opportunities, and negative public attitude towards the credibility of a distance education degree are the main problems causing social inequalities in the system. In order to minimize these problems, I strongly believe public awareness towards the distance education programs should be increased by involving the media and other communication channels. The private organizations should support the programs by allocating funds and providing equal job opportunities to the graduates.

Even though AU has managed to provide distance education programs to its own students without considering other opportunities in the international market, it is clear from the rhetoric that this political view might change in the future. Turkish cultural values, including respect and oral traditions, shape the educational practices in the country. Thus, the implementation of the courses developed in other countries might have negative effects on Turkish distance students, and therefore these courses should be carefully examined before they are employed as part of the distance education programs.

REFERENCES

Anadolu University Open Education Faculty. (n.d). Retrieved March 5, 2004, from http://www.aof.anadolu.edu.tr

Buyukersen, Y. (2002). *Yirminci yuzyildan yirmibirinci yuzyilin acik ogretimine* [From twentieth century's to twenty-first century's distance education]. Paper presented at Acik ve Uzaktan Egitim Sempozyumu, Eskisehir, Turkey. Retrieved March 1, 2004, from http://aof20.anadolu.edu.tr/program.htm

Cakir, M. (2002). *Anadolu Universitesi Bati Avrupa Acik Yuksekogretim Hizmetleri* [*Anadolu University Western Europe open higher education services*]. Paper presented at Acik ve Uzaktan Egitim Sempozyumu, Eskisehir, Turkey. Retrieved March 5, 2004, from http://aof20.anadolu.edu.tr/program.htm

McIsaac, M. (2002). *Global distance education: AU's rise to prominence.* Keynote Speech at the 20th Anniversary Celebration of Open Education, AU, Eskisehir, Turkey. Retrieved February 12, 2004, from http://aof20.anadolu.edu.tr/program.htm

McIsaac, M., Murphy, K. L., & Demiray, U. (1988). Examining distance education in Turkey. *Journal of Distance Education, 9*(1), 106–119. Retrieved February 10, 2004, from http://home.anadolu.edu.tr/~udemiray%20/&Exam.htm

Murphy, K. L. (1991). Patronage and oral tradition: Influences on attribution of distance learners in a traditional society (a qualitative study). *Distance Education, 12*(1), 27–53.

Murphy, K. L. (1996, November). *Enhancing interaction in Turkish distance education.* Paper presented at Turkey's First International Distance Education Symposium,

Ankara, Turkey. Retrieved February 17, 2004, from http://www.coe.tamu.edu/~kmurphy/writings/tdes97.html

Ozkul, A. E. (2001). AU distance education system: From emergence to 21st century. *TOJDE, 2*(1). Retrieved February 12, 2004, from http://tojde.anadolu.edu.tr/tojde3/2/ekremtxt.htm, paras. 2, 14, 59.

Potashnik, M., & Capper, J. (1998) Distance education: Growth and diversity. *Finance and Development, 35*(1). Retrieved February 1, 2004, from http://www.worldbank.org/fandd/english/0398/articles/0110398.htm

Rose, H. (1997). *Technology respecting culture: The impact of distance learning systems on diverse societies.* Retrieved March 15, 2004, from http://www.imprintit.com/TopicBody.html

Student Selection and Placement Center (Ogrenci Secme ve Yerlestirme Merkezi). (n.d). *2002–2003 academic year higher education statistics.* Retrieved February 11, 2004, from http://www.osym.gov.tr/BelgeGoster.aspx?DIL=1&BELGEBAGLANTIANAH=206

Turkish Council of Higher Education (TCHE). (2003). Uzaktan yuksekogretim ile Ilgili gelismeler ve calismalar [Studies and developments about distance higher education]. In *Turk yuksekogretiminin bugunku durumu* [Current situation of Turkish higher education] (pp. 97–103). Retrieved March 5, 2004, from http://www.yok.gov.tr/egitim/raporlar/mart2003/baslik.pdf

Turkish Council of Higher Education (TCHE). (n.d.-a). *The Turkish higher education system* (Part 3—Current status). Retrieved February 3, 2004, from http://www.yok.gov.tr/english/index_en.htm

Turkish Council of Higher Education (TCHE). (n.d.-b). *Regulations on interuniversity distance higher education based on communication and information technologies.* Retrieved March 5, 2004, from http://www.yok.gov.tr/english/distance.html

Turk Telekom. (n.d.-b). Retrieved February 17, 2004, from http://www.telekom.gov.tr

Ulutak, N. (2002). *Turkiye de ulusal egitim televizyonunun olusturulmasinin gerekceleri.* [The reasons to establish national television channel in Turkey]. Paper presented at Acik ve Uzaktan Egitim Sempozyumu, Eskisehir, Turkey. Retrieved March 1, 2004, from http://aof20.anadolu.edu.tr/program.htm

PART III

ONLINE EDUCATION IN NORTH AMERICA:

An Analysis of the U.S. and Canadian Contributions

Liberty without learning is always in peril;
Learning without liberty is always in vain.

John F. Kennedy

Naturally, North American online learning is strongly influenced by the United States. But here, we benefit from an understanding not only of the United States' issues but also those of Canada. Shade and Dechief's chapter, which highlights issues associated with online learning in Canadian public schools, focuses on K–12 delivery issues. Carr-Chellman's approach to understanding the boon and bust of online learning in the United States takes primarily a sociocultural perspective.

In the case of the United States, the primary concern for those who are left behind focuses on what has traditionally been the concept of the digital divide. Within the United States that has essentially centered on *class* as the issue of distinction both in access and retention. While some discussion ensues regarding the role of rural United States in the digital divide, the chief interest and the main funding has been focused on urban underclass. On the other hand, in

Canada, the First Peoples are the main population left behind and the issues are similar to other nations in terms of the primacy of "rural and remote."

Both of these chapters highlight the issues associated with confusions over public and private. In both cases, we see some blurring of what have traditionally been clear boundaries between the public and the private. SchoolNet shows that when public schools and private corporations mix, the powerful private interests are usually asserted. The U.S. higher education system clearly has some mixed-up funding occurring in terms of public higher education being funded with public dollars, offering "cash cow" online learning programs that are chiefly vocational in nature, saving corporate interests billions in training budgets. This mixing or blurring of public and private is a particular facet of the North American experience of online learning that expands far beyond what most countries would tolerate. As Shade and Dechief write, "These corporations have the financial means and technical expertise to assist in the SchoolNet mandate, but they are naturally concerned with self-promotion and profit—goals that are frequently in conflict with the aims of public education" (p. 135, this volume). This sort of general acceptance that corporations have no public mandate or moral obligation is not a universally accepted notion. In other nations— Sweden is one good example not represented in this text—corporations have certain obligations to the public good. Thus the notion that public and private interests are tending to be skewed toward private benefits seems to be a fairly unique aspect of the online learning experience in North America.

Technological determinism is a clear theme in this section of the text. It is perhaps most strongly noted here and in the section on Asia in this book. Shade and Dechief point to clear statements of public officials advocating that our children must have technology experiences in order to ensure that Canada "can become a competitive country where we can all enjoy a good standard of living" (p. 141, this volume). In North America, the idea that we simply have to prepare our children for a technological society is nearly an unquestioned premise. However, this theme needs to be carefully examined. As I've written elsewhere, "If we suggest that the information age economy demands a different kind of student, have we carefully considered the values that are inherent in that statement and who will likely be well-served or ill-served by a system that responds to socio-economic demands in such a functionalist manner?" (Carr, 1998, p. 8). And as Fuller (1998) even more clearly points out, there is a danger in this sort of technological determinism:

> The problem (with technological determinism) is, both the kinds of technology we develop and their effects are shaped by social systems that are by

their nature non-determinist. While technology may acquire a certain fixity in use, one cannot assume that it will necessarily be implemented in any one way across contexts. . . . Arguments about technology's effect on our future working lives that fail to consider how it is embedded in particular social relations must therefore be treated with caution. (p. 17)

Thus, while we might like to be able to make metanarrative statements regarding the potential impact of online learning or technology on the future of our children, it is really not as appropriate or possible as the rhetoric might suggest. It has almost become, in North America, an unquestioned assumption, and this is an excellent opportunity to question that mantra.

Another notable issue that seems to come up in both chapters for the North American online learning enterprise is the issue of exporting or distributing online learning internationally from Canada and the United States to other, mainly developing, countries. Perhaps it should not surprise us that two capitalist democracies would approach online learning as a potential market abroad. We might expect this approach more intensely from the United States than from Canada given the United States' slightly more capitalistic tendencies. It is interesting that some have suggested that online learning, or e-learning, is an "innovation thwarted" (Zemsky, 2003). Shade and DeChief indicate that SchoolNet's funding is likely to be cut. If the movement is dead, then what does it say about our societies that we are moving to export it to other developing countries?

Ultimately, this section on North American online learning clearly compares the political rhetoric around capitalism, access, and technological determinism to the reality of Canada's First People's and rural populations, the homeless and poor in the United States, and the exportation of online learning for profit to developing countries. There is clearly power in North America to help direct the future of this movement. Cogent analysis of benefits and needs can help bring into sharp relief the sociocultural nature of technology within the North American context. We expect this has been such a cogent analysis.

References

Carr, A. A. (1998). Educational change and technological determinism. *Review Journal of Philosophy & Social Science, 23*(1&2), 2–8.

Fuller, S. (1998). Economic restructuring and the future. *Review Journal of Philosophy & Social Science, 23*(1&2), 14–21.

Zemsky, R. (2003, January 17). *Thwarted innovation: What happened to e-learning and why.* Keynote address at the Research Institute for Higher Education, Hiroshima University.

EIGHT

CANADA'S SCHOOLNET:

Wiring Up Schools?

Leslie Regan Shade and Diane Yvonne Dechief

With the rapid rise in prominence of the Internet during the 1990s, most industrialized nations developed policies and programs promoting public access to the Internet in order to ameliorate the emerging "digital divide" that threatened to undermine social solidarity. In Canada, this was pursued most visibly through the federal "Connecting Canadians" agenda, led by Industry Canada. Its goal was to make Canada the most "connected nation on Earth," notably through its SchoolNet, Community Access (CAP), and LibraryNet programs.

SchoolNet, established in 1994 to increase "connectivity" to public schools across Canada, was one of the earliest federal government projects in support of access to what was then dubbed the "information highway." Its mandate—to work with public and private partners to extend Internet connectivity into K–12 classrooms—was also touted as an international model. But, despite millions of federal government dollars invested in SchoolNet over the

---

AUTHORS' NOTE: Thanks from the authors to the Social Sciences and Humanities Research Council of Canada through their INE Program and the Concordia University Faculty of Arts and Sciences for research and start-up support for this discussion.

last decade, little to no evaluation on the effectiveness of SchoolNet as a learning resource has ever been conducted. Indeed, the 2004 federal budget has downsized SchoolNet, notably discontinuing its Office of International Partnerships. An examination of SchoolNet raises many salient issues related to the efficacy and claims of "wiring up" K–12 classrooms, an increasing practice bolstered by policy and funding pushes, particularly across North America. As you read this chapter, concentrate on the following questions:

- What has been the rhetoric of government in promoting access to the Internet within the K–12 sector?
- What sorts of evaluative strategies should be initiated in order to assess Internet-based resources for K–12 education?
- How can one best measure effective of the Internet?
- What should be the role of the private sector in providing resources for public education?
- What role should the public have in determining Internet policy for education?
- What evidence is there for the claim that computers and classroom access to the Internet motivate students and provide beneficial pedagogical means?
- How can one best measure effective use of the Internet?

SCHOOLNET AND ITS STAKEHOLDERS

SchoolNet's origins were at Carleton University in Ottawa where in 1993, students, led by Karen Kostaszek, conceived of a network to increase awareness of science and technology educational materials. Initial support came from the federal government's Industry and Science Canada (later renamed Industry Canada), with a pilot program of 12 schools in the Ottawa-Carleton school district. Kostaszek's group epitomized the spirit of early Internet entrepreneurs, and their efforts were celebrated widely in the Canadian media, garnering Kostaszek several awards—the women's magazine *Chatelaine* named her a "Digital Women of the Year" in 1997, she won one of Caldwell Partner's 1995 "Top 40 Under 40" citations, and in 1996 the "Young Entrepreneur of the Year in Ontario" award.

These were heady days when the potential of the Internet seemed unbounded. The number of new high-tech firms in Ottawa exploded, venture capital and initial public offerings were munificent, and the Canadian government established the Information Highway Advisory Council (IHAC) to formulate their information infrastructure policy, focusing on job creation, Canadian sovereignty, and cultural identity, and ensuring universal access at reasonable cost. Deploying the Internet in learning institutions was widely promoted through SchoolNet and provincial government funding plans.

At one level, SchoolNet is part of the Canadian federal initiative "Connecting Canadians," a broad-based programming "strategy to keep Canada among the leaders in connecting its citizens to the Internet" (Welcome to SchoolNet, 2003). At another level, SchoolNet is a Web-based site linking educators to online pedagogical resources and education-focused news, as well as providing a vehicle for corporate sponsors to display their logos and links.

SchoolNet consists of several projects, including Computers for Schools, First Nations SchoolNet (FNSN), DirecPC™, Network to Savings, and SkillNet.ca, that are accessed through the SchoolNet Web site, which also hyperlinks to all of the public schools in Canada, other North American schools and resources, and international SchoolNet programs. Computers for Schools provides refurbished computers to classrooms and labs through industry and volunteer linkages. Network to Savings is a database on educational tools and "great deals on equipment, software and services" (Network to Savings, 2003). SkillNet is "a partnership of integrated recruitment services" advertised as a "one-stop shopping site for jobs and career-related information" (SchoolNet Home: Services, 2003) designed for secondary and postsecondary graduates. The 2004 budget axed two of the most successful SchoolNet programs: GrassRoots financially rewarded schools that created and shared Internet-focused lesson plans, while LibraryNet promoted Internet connectivity within libraries (IHAB, 2004).

FNSN was established to meet the distinct needs of Canadian First Nations schools, many of which are located in remote regions requiring satellite Internet connections. From 1993–1999, Industry Canada spent $7.3 million to pay for one computer in each of the 420 schools to be connected to the satellite technology DirectPC™. Partner Bell ExpressVu supplies Internet access and five regional help desks. Initially, feedback was positive: "Attendance rates of students . . . jumped from about 36% to 76% thanks to the use of computers" (Himmelsbach, 1999, p. 38). The principal of Koocheching First Nation School in northern Ontario said that SchoolNet "made everyone excited about education in general" (Ibid, C14). Unfortunately, barriers have increased, and at the time of a 2000 KPMG study, barely 60% of the schools were still connected to the Internet, with technical reasons commonly cited for the demise of connectivity.

These various projects link and serve the needs of geographically disparate students, librarians, teachers, administrators, the technical industry, and government at the provincial and federal levels. SchoolNet's objectives and achieved goals are described in quantifiable terms:

- On March 30, 1999, Canada became the first country in the world to connect its public schools, including First Nations schools, and public libraries to the Information Highway.
- As of May 2000, there were close to half a million connected computers in Canadian schools.
- To date, the SchoolNet Web site links to more than 5,000 teacher-approved learning resources, making it easier for Canadian teachers and students to access an immense source of online resources ("What is SchoolNet?", 2003).

SchoolNet's original mandate, enunciated in the federal government's Building a More Innovative Economy strategy of 1994, was to connect all 20,000 public schools and public libraries to the Internet by March 31, 1999 (Kainz, 1994). This goal was met just within its deadline, as each provincial or territorial minister of education signed a statement articulating that every public school within that minister's jurisdiction was connected to the Internet. In 1998, prior to the completion of SchoolNet's first goal, the mandate was expanded with the new "Connectedness Strategy," prompting the descriptors "SchoolNet 1" and "SchoolNet 2." SchoolNet 2's goals included increasing Internet access to classrooms, and by May 2000, SchoolNet estimated that nearly 500,000 connected computers were in Canadian classrooms across Canada. Current goals focus on First Nations SchoolNet and the development of e-learning content.

Stakeholders include Industry Canada, provincial and territorial education-focused government and teachers, First Nations school communities, the private sector, and the students. While considering the interests of these diverse stakeholders, it is useful to picture their interactions as an "ecology of games" (Dutton, 1999). SchoolNet's catalyzing stakeholder, contributing $82 million between the years 1995–2000, is the federal government (KPMG, 2000). The governance of SchoolNet that has taken place at this level as Industry Canada, along with the SchoolNet Advisory Board (SNAB)—composed of representatives from all of the following stakeholder groups—has leveraged relationships and partnerships with about 60 private corporations and various government sectors (KPMG, 2000, p. 42). While many of these relationships have been successful "several [of the] highly-visible partnerships are currently in danger of collapse due to a lack of sufficient program funding, and lack of co-ordination and vision" (KPMG, 2000, p. v). Highlighting visibility is key—tied to SchoolNet goals have been the federal government's desire to promote itself globally as an innovative and internationally competitive, knowledge-based economy. Specifically, through the Office of International Partnerships, the SchoolNet model was marketed internationally, with 22 countries using the model by 1999 (Brady, 1999, p. C14). Nationally, besides reminding Canadians of the effectiveness of the federal government, a key goal has been to reduce inequalities in Internet access. This has focused particularly on assisting rural and remote regions through its role as an "agent provocateur" and facilitator between other stakeholders, rather than taking on the full costs of connectivity. One initial method of catalyzing for connectivity has been to post educational materials and resources online in order to entice educators and librarians to make use of these materials (KPMG, 2000, p. 10–11).

The private sector's role in SchoolNet is the easiest to define; each corporation that contributes through donations of software and hardware and the provision of Internet access gains tax and "gift-in-kind" benefits, as well as opportunities to market to schools, and achieve brand loyalty from a guaranteed audience. When the Office of International Partnerships negotiated international agreements for use of the SchoolNet "brand," Canadian firms took part in the negotiations and benefited. Not all of SchoolNet's corporate partnerships are with Canadian firms; many are multinationals, including Microsoft, AOL, Cisco, Aliant, and Imperial Oil. These corporations have the financial means and technical expertise to assist in the SchoolNet mandate, but they are naturally concerned with self-promotion and profit—goals that are frequently in conflict with the aims of public education.

Canadian students and their parents, the last of the stakeholders identified here, are the people whose voices most need amplification in discussions of SchoolNet. The official rhetoric from Industry Canada is that kids love technology, but this notion is not above scrutiny and should not be taken as fact. Élise Boisjoly, former executive director of SchoolNet, asserts that students "are used to multimedia—[and] that's the way they want to learn now" (Himmelsbach, 1999, p. 38). A report from the annual conference of the Network of Innovative Schools, one of SchoolNet's projects, advocates, "Most young people are natural technology users, and the ones who aren't can quickly learn from their friends." One teacher at the conference argued, "The most important thing I do is get out of [the students'] way" (Keenan, 2000, p. 17). In the same spirit, the Connecting Canadians Web site boasts that "Canada is breeding new generations of IT workers by focusing on skills development in students from Kindergarten to Grade 12" (Licenik, 2000).

Rose (2003) argues that this rhetorical strategy of naturalizing children as innate computer users and Web surfers, propelled by both industry and government promotion, calls into question new narratives of childhood that need to be critically assessed:

> Would it be more accurate to view contemporary conceptions of computer-friendly youngsters as a throwback to the days when factory urchins were required to relinquish individuality and engage passively with technology, and to the days when harsh discipline was the primary means of achieving what inducing total absorption in the simulated, sensory-stimulated world of video games accomplishes today: the formation of "docile bodies"? (pp. 157–158)

Do computers and the Internet in the classroom motivate students and provide beneficial pedagogical means? Despite the political economic push and the heavy financial investment by governments and industry to wire up schools, educational researchers have continuously pointed out the lack of evidence linking technology to improved learning (Moll & Robertson, 2001, pp. 167–168). Cuban (2001), commenting on the U.S. imperative to computerize and wire up schools and through his assessment of early childhood, high school, and university classrooms in Silicon Valley writes:

> The billions of dollars already spent on wiring, hardware, and software have established the material conditions for frequent and imaginative uses of technology to occur. Many students and teachers have acquired skills and have engaged in serious use of these technologies. Nonetheless, overall, the quantities of money and time have yet to yield even modest returns or to approach what has been promised in academic achievement, creative classroom integration of technologies, and transformations in teaching and learning. (p. 189)

Absent from this technological imperative have been discussions and debates about the organizational culture of schools, the professionalization of teachers, and the public mandate of schools in a democratic society.

Measuring Connectivity

Although the federal government claims that SchoolNet has "helped improve social equity through provision of computers, Internet access, and technical advice to all Canadian communities, no matter how remote" (KMPG, 2000, p. 77), we need to ask whether these goals have really been met—or is it simply the case that computers have been put in place to help accomplish these goals? Questions about the effectiveness of connectivity remain even though rudimentary technical requirements are in place.

The digital divide is not simply a chasm that requires heroic efforts to bridge, but, as Warshauer (2002) writes, is "rather a gradation based on different degrees of access to information technology." He believes that "the digital divide framework" overemphasizes the importance of connectivity to the exclusion of other factors that allow people to use information and communication technologies (ICTs) for "meaningful ends" (pp. 4–5).

A criticism of the quantitative measurement of Canada's connectivity is that it promotes competitiveness but not a nuanced look at the social dimensions of access. If social connectedness is truly a goal of SchoolNet, this method of measuring connectivity is a losing prospect. The private sector stands to be the big winner as schools, provinces, and nations race to outfit themselves with the highest ratio of computers to students and the fastest Internet connections. Having a warehouse filled with high-end computers and broadband access waiting to be plugged in is of no benefit unless these tools can be used effectively. How then can effective use be measured?

Rather than looking solely at technical and quantitative measures, social and qualitative tools for measuring digital inequalities are required. Hargittai (2002) argues that "Merely offering people a network-connected machine will not ensure that they can use the medium to meet their needs because they may not be able to maximally take advantage of all that the Web has to offer" (p. 13). She delineates five dimensions of divides:

1. technical means (software, hardware, and connectivity quality);
2. autonomy of use (location of access . . .);
3. use patterns (types of uses of the Internet);
4. social supports networks (availability of others . . . for assistance, size of networks to encourage use); and
5. skill (one's ability to use the medium effectively).

With the exception of the GrassRoots program, SchoolNet has focused on Hargittai's first technical dimension, as its measures indicate how well this one dimension has been bridged; consider how the Industry Canada-sponsored KPMG report defines connectivity as "the process of getting schools and libraries hooked up to the Internet" (KPMG, 2000, p. 10).

The federal government has ignored the importance of training and support; provincial education ministries and teachers are forced to fill these gaps. The Canadian Teachers' Federation member survey on online learning indicated that teachers were very concerned about the impact of ICTs on their jobs—including workload issues; job security; impact on professional autonomy; collective bargaining; and training and content issues, including access to technical support; and ensuring quality in online programs, access to curriculum-based professional development and training, and increased commercialization and privatization of public education (Canadian Teachers' Federation, 2003, 42).

Another tool for evaluating connectivity is the Access Rainbow (Clement & Shade, 2000). Created as a sociotechnical architecture for analyzing access to network services, here it will be utilized to measure the effectiveness of SchoolNet's connectivity. The Access Rainbow consists of seven layers beginning with technical elements. Each of the seven layers is listed in Table 8.1, with essential aspects, SchoolNet elements, and policy questions used to describe each layer.

The particulars of the Carriage, Devices, and in part the Software Tools levels are determined by SchoolNet and the corporate partners. While corporate sponsorships may play a role in the types of activities at the Content/Services layer, this layer, along with the Service Providers and Literary/Social Facilitation layers, is the responsibility of school administrators and teachers. Looking at the layers sketched out in Table 8.1, it is easy to visualize the interplay of these elements and consider how critical it is that both social and technical components are intact and functioning in order to achieve the goal of connectivity. Without teachers to facilitate and plan lessons, connectivity could not be achieved; likewise, without Internet connections, workstations, and software, there is no possibility of accessing the Web.

The Governance level of the Access Rainbow poses a challenge to the SchoolNet model that requires further examination. The amount of public consultation process and research and impact assessment guiding decisions about SchoolNet's activities must be questioned. How much input were each of SchoolNet's stakeholders, especially teachers, parents, and students, invited to

Table 8.1 The Access Rainbow Applies to SchoolNet

Layer	Essential Aspects	SchoolNet Elements	Policy Questions
7. Governance: how decisions are made concerning the development and operation of the infrastructure.	Public consultation process, research and social impact assessment, conception of the electronic commons	SchoolNet Advisory Board (SNAB), Office of International Partnerships, the federal government	Who determines the composition of the SNAB? Are school boards and teachers consulted about the nature of SchoolNet? About Internet use in the classroom?
6. Literary/Social Facilitation: the skills people need to take full advantage of ICTs, together with the learning facilitation and resources to acquire these skills.	Computer literacy (keyboarding, Web navigation).	Teachers, librarians, technology specialists, Bell ExpressVu regional help desks (for First Nations SchoolNet)	Are teachers effectively trained on use of the Internet? Are they funded for training? Do teachers have an input into the development of curriculum-based material?
5. Service Providers: the organizations that provide network services and access to users.	Schools–classrooms, school libraries, computer labs, resource centers.	LibraryNet, AOL, Bell Canada, Aliant Group, Canarie, CA*net, Clearnet, Telus, SaskTel, Telesat	How can sustainable funding from service providers be provided to schools? What are the terms of the contracts?
4. Content/Services: the actual information and communication services people find useful.	E-mail, Web sites, online educational sites	GrassRoots Program, Digital Collections, SkillNet	Are teachers consulted about curriculum content? How much of the content is Canadian-based, in both English and French? Is the content updated? Is there commercial content?
3. Software Tools: the programs that operate the devices and make connections to services.	Web browser, educational software, Microsoft Office	Microsoft, Network to Savings	What is the role of corporate partners and branding in supplying software? Is the software interoperable? Are software upgrades provided?
2. Devices: the actual physical devices that people operate.	Classroom, computer lab, or library workstations.	Computers for School Program, Network to Savings	Are the devices interoperable? Easily expandable? What happens with obsolete devices? Who fixes/replaces broken devices?
1. Carriage: the facilities that store, serve, or carry information.	Local or satellite Internet connection.	Satellite through DirectPC™, Bell ExpressVu, Network to Savings, Cisco	What is the minimal essential bandwidth needed?

contribute as plans for their schools' increased connectivity were put into place? Given that Internet connectivity arrived in schools before teachers were consulted and trained about its pedagogical possibilities, SchoolNet initiatives, created in a top-down fashion, suggest that the federal government's intent to market the system internationally may have been a key motive for its creation. According to Lewis and Jenson (2001), "Education, long a 'goal in itself' [and] a 'public good' has become more purely a means to the end of a more efficient and competitive economy and workforce immutably situated within the notion of the 'knowledge economy'" (p. 28).

SCHOOLNET'S PUBLIC SCREEN

The federal government's initiative in selling the SchoolNet model internationally makes Canadian students the trial consumers and models of the social and educational effects of classroom connectivity; in industrial terms, our youth are the model "products" of this educational "process." By ensuring that the Internet is in classrooms in Canadian public schools, the federal government places great significance on this key symbol of the information economy. The seeming lack of concern with the way connectivity is being utilized echoes that the Internet's mere presence in the classroom is a goal met. This leads to the notion of the "public screen" (DeLuca & Peeples, 2002), a more empowering example of the convergence of business and education via technology:

> on today's public screen corporations and states stage spectacles (advertising and photo ops) certifying their status before the people/public and activists [and others can] participate through the performance of image events, employing the consequent publicity as a social medium for forming public opinion and holding corporations and states accountable. (p. 134)

Following DeLuca and Peeples's (2002) definition, consider how newspapers, television, films, museum exhibits, and the Internet, with their dense visual imagery, comprise the public screen. Sometimes the screen is used to advertise products, while at other times it promotes social norms. SchoolNet can be used to exemplify the public screen because it is both a product promoted by the federal government and it has the effect of increasing the presence of the Internet as a viewing medium. Industry Canada has made use of the public screen, as well as other less visual forms of media, to promote SchoolNet since its inception.

For the Canadian federal government, SchoolNet became their "poster child" for their ICT programs. Media coverage was extensive, with a special focus on political and celebrity branding: "Students show off Internet to Queen, Prince" (Bennett, 1998), one headline read, while other newspaper coverage highlighted staged events: students in Ottawa and inner-city Washington, D.C. demonstrating an interactive SchoolNet session with Prime Minister Chrétien's wife Aline and First Lady Hillary Clinton, and school children chatting with Bill Gates via satellite linkup about their experiences developing GrassRoots projects, an opportune time as well for Industry Canada to announce Microsoft's partnership with SchoolNet (Walker, 1998).

Internet use for K–12 education was exalted as an innovative pedagogical tool: "Students roam the world on Internet, through SchoolNet they can consult experts, share ideas" (Warwick, 1995), and as a requisite means for the future worker. Commenting on her department's $250,000 investment in the national Atlas on SchoolNet, then Natural Resources Minister Anne McLennan remarked, "These are new opportunities that all our children should have and we need it to ensure they have it so Canada can become a competitive country where we can all enjoy a good standard of living" (Moysa, 1995, p. B2). Digital Collections, a SchoolNet program where young students create theme-based online collections, was celebrated as a program to "turn young people into skilled techno-entrepreneurs while at the same time helping put Canada on the leading educational edge on the Internet's World Wide Web" (Shaw, 1998, p. C9).

But as Moll (2001) argues, providing Internet connectivity in schools did not grow out of educational needs, but rather "out of the perceived need to privatize and commercialize one of the last and largest unexploited markets in the world" (p. 113). Following the deregulation of the communications industry in North America and a heightened trade agenda, a vast marketplace—that of the K–12 sector—became ripe territory to infiltrate. An emphasis on computers and the Internet in schools fed into the school reform movement, which instituted standardized testing and "back to basics" curricula. Starting in the mid-1970s, North America, especially the United States, began to fear a loss of global economic competitiveness from Japan and Germany. Public schools came to be seen as a site for the production and training of a skilled workforce, particularly for the high-tech industry. Corporate and public officials thus promoted the use of ICTs in classrooms as a necessary component for the preparation of the future workforce in the knowledge-based economy. The computer, according to Cuban (2001), became a "high-status symbol of power and modernity" (p. 159). Given declining public school budgets, financing an ICT infrastructure became costly. Many schools resorted to cost-cutting measures; in Canada, this was seen, in many instances, in the closure of school libraries, the decline of the teacher-librarian, and parental fund-raising for computers. For the private sector, the public school market was lucrative—Industry Canada estimated it to be worth Can$41 billion in 2000, and business-education partnerships proliferated (Canadian Teachers' Federation, 2003, 31).

CONCLUSION

The notion of the public screen as a place for interaction provides a more positive perspective on the effects of SchoolNet than the focus of this chapter has maintained, even if it comes as a mode of triumphing in despair. What does remain, however, is the question of how SchoolNet can be considered a success without a nuanced examination of the social aspects of connectivity.

Given the lack of evidence that computers and the Internet contribute to learning effectiveness and the paucity of Canadian research to date on the particular linguistic, cultural, and geographical exigencies related to connectivity, there needs to be more accountability in the use of public monies spent on technology for public schools. A trip through several classrooms in Canada's public school system to examine how the Internet is being utilized (or not) is required. A focus on social barriers for SchoolNet's next phase would certainly be timely, although this is not likely, as the 2004 federal budget stripped away many of SchoolNet's initiatives—including the popular GrassRoots, Digital Collections, and LibraryNet programs. As noted previously, the Office of International Partnerships was also disbanded, and the main public screen of SchoolNet—its portal, will no longer be maintained, while portions of it will be hived off to other branch Web sites. While Industry Canada made ample use of this public screen to promote the idea that via SchoolNet equal access for all Canadian students is now in place, that accomplishment is not as simple as purchasing PCs and setting them up with Internet access. The complexities of access require that social as well as technical groundwork be laid in order for connectivity to be accomplished.

REFERENCES

Bennett, B. (1998, May 14). Students show off Internet to Queen, Prince. *The Evening Telegram* (St. John's, Newfoundland), p. 4.

Brady, M. (1999, April 26). Reading, writing and cyberspace. *Financial Post,* p. C14.

Canadian Teachers' Federation. (2003). *Virtual education, real educators.* Ottawa: CTF.

Clement, A., & Shade, L. R. (2000). The access rainbow: Conceptualizing universal access to the information/communication infrastructure. In M. Gurstein (Ed.), *Community informatics: enabling communities with information and communications technologies* (pp. 32–51). Hershey, PA: Idea Group Publishing.

Cuban, L. (2001). *Oversold and underused: Computers in the classroom.* Cambridge, MA: Harvard University Press.

DeLuca, K. M., & Peeples, J. (2002). From public sphere to public screen: Democracy, activism, and the "violence" of Seattle. *Critical Studies in Media Communication, 19,* 125–151.

Dutton, W. H. (1999). Regulating access: Broadening the policy debate. In W. H. Dutton, *Society on the line: Iinformation politics in the digital age* (pp. 285–308). Oxford: Oxford University Press.

Haney, C. (1999, April 23). Canada strives to be most connected nation. *Network World Canada, 9,* 8.

Hargittai, E. (2002). Second-level digital divide: Differences in people's online skills. *First Monday, 7.* Retrieved October 23, 2003, from http://firstmonday.org/issues/issue7_4/hargittai/index.html

Himmelsbach, V. (1999). Making the grade? *Technology in Government, 6,* 36–38.

Information Highway Applications Branch. (2004). *2004 budget update—Changes to the community access and schoolnet programs.* Retrieved June 30, 2004, from http://ihab-transition-dgaai.ic.gc.ca/pub/index.html?iin.lang=en

Kainz, A. (1994, December 6). Information highway gets a boost. *The Ottawa Citizen,* p. E1.

Keenan, T. (2000). Some schools really do get it. *ComputerWorld Canada, 16,* 17.

KPMG. (2000). *Evaluation of the SchoolNet1 initiative: Final report.* Retrieved November 10, 2003, from http://www.schoolnet.ca/home/e/documents/SN_evaluationE.pdf

Lewis, B., & Jenson, J. (2001). Beyond the workshop: Education policy in situated practice. *Education Canada, 41,* 28–31.

Licenik, Jitka. (2000, April). "Canada's SchoolNet: Making a difference." *Connecting Canadians.* Retrieved November 11, 2003, from http://www.connect.gc.ca/en/ar/1018-e.asp

Moll, M. (2001). Pianos vs. politics: Sustaining public education in the age of globalization. In M. Moll & L. R. Shade (Ed.), *E-Commerce vs. e-commons: Communications in the public interest* (pp. 109–127). Ottawa: Canadian Centre for Policy Alternatives.

Moll, M., & Robertson, H. (2001). A "high-wired" balancing act: Technological change and public education in Canada. *Canadian Journal of Educational Communication, 27*(3), 157–174.

Moysa, M. (1995, September 23). SchoolNet goes online. *Edmonton Journal,* p. B2.

Network to Savings. (2003, December 7). Industry Canada. Retrieved December 7, 2003, from http://www.connect.gc.ca/en/294-e.asp

Rose, E. (2003). *User error: Resisting computer culture.* Toronto: Between the Lines.

SchoolNet Home: Services. (2003, December 2). Industry Canada. Retrieved December 4, 2003, http://www.schoolnet.ca/accueil/e/services.asp

SchoolNet Home: What is SchoolNet? (2003, December 2). Industry Canada. Retrieved December 4, 2003, from http://www.schoolnet.ca/home/e/whatis.asp

Shaw, G. (1998, October 23). SchoolNet program turns out techno-entrepreneurs. *St. Catharine's Standard,* p. C9.

Walker, A. (1998, October 15). Students keen on satellite chat with Gates. *Edmonton Journal.*

Warschauer, M. (2002). Reconceptualizing the digital divide. *First Monday, 7.* Retrieved October 23, 2003, from http://firstmonday.org/issues/issue7_7/warschauer/index.html

Warwick, L. (1995, August 12). Students roam the world on the Internet. *The Montreal Gazette,* p. G2

Welcome to SchoolNet. (2003, December 2). *Industry Canada.* Retrieved December 4, 2003, from http://www.schoolnet.ca/

NINE

THE NEW FRONTIER:

Web-Based Education in U.S. Culture

Alison A. Carr-Chellman

E-learning has become one of the hottest new training modalities in the United States. More than one third of all 4-year colleges and universities offered some form of distance education in 1997 (National Center for Education Statistics, 1997), and the offerings are on the rise. By the year 2000, more than 56% of those same institutions were offering distance education programs (National Center for Education Statistics, 2003). In 2000, more than 3 million learners were logging in for distance education opportunities (National Center for Education Statistics, 2003). The growth in Web-based education is an explosion unparalleled elsewhere in the educational enterprise (Daniel, 1996; Jones, 1997), and it is mirrored in corporate training shifts to e-learning. Fueled by fear of open-market competition and recent advances in Web-based design tools, the economies of scale for distance education have become *very* attractive to a variety of organizations. Web-based learning offerings proliferate particularly in America because the enterprise appeals to some

AUTHOR'S NOTE: An earlier version of this chapter was published as Carr-Chellman, A. A. (2000), Web-based education in U.S. Culture. *Information, Communication, and Society Journal, 3* (3), 326–336.

of our most basic, stereotypically American values. This paper explores these cultural assumptions and then discusses the ways in which the rhetoric of democracy espoused by American politicians may not meet the realities of implementation in American e-learning programs today.

America has been perhaps the fastest growing of all international markets with regard to Web-based degree and certificate programs. There are many reasons why this is the case: an open, permeable higher education system; the efficiency value of Web-based degree programs; the independent nature of online learning; the history of vocations in higher education in America, and the myth of the meritocracy. As you read this chapter reflect on the following questions:

- How is the promise of open access being lived out in your experiences in distance learning or e-learning?
- What impact in terms of race, gender, class, and power dynamics results from these open access promises?
- In what ways does the rhetoric of democracy match or mismatch the realities of e-learning in America today?
- What are the possible predictable failures of our current efforts to democratize higher education in the United States through e-learning?
- What sorts of systemic impacts and unintended consequences may result from current implementation for online learning in the United States?
- What ideas do you have for solving some of these problems?

OPEN HIGHER EDUCATION SYSTEM

Although Web advocates would certainly take issue with me on this (see Olsen, 1999a), the relatively open and permeable boundaries of the higher education system in America have led to a rapid proliferation of Web programs of varying quality. Many involved in the movement feel that the requirements of governmental and university accreditation bodies are slowing down the potential of Web-based learning. However, because much of the training in online learning is vocational in nature, the need for a name brand university degree may be decreasing in certain areas. It is my view that, increasingly, the need for university certification is less a requirement and more a note of status. Jones University is the first all online university to gain regional accreditation (Olsen, 1999a), which they proclaim prominently on their Web site and in their advertising. Jones University is a large online university offering a wide variety of primarily master's and bachelor's degrees in business, education, and communications. Their accreditation has caused quite a stir among traditional academics. The American Association of University Professors (AAUP) objected strenuously to this accreditation, pointing out that Jones International does not have many of the specific requirements that the accreditation has been enforcing for traditional universities, such as adequate facilities, sufficient numbers of full-time faculty, and established curricula. While the debate may go on, the accreditation has not been revoked, and in fact, it is this openness that encourages many new and entrepreneurial businesses in America to flourish . . . a perceived cause of our excellent economy.

As Web degrees grow, the possibilities for gaining knowledge necessary for vocations will also become less and less dependent on the university for certification. As with any economy where the quality control mechanisms are relatively loose, some unscrupulous entrepreneurs will take advantage of the public. In the case of online learning, this phenomenon easily leads to the problems of diploma mills such as Monticello University, which the *Chronicle of Higher Education* (Olsen, 1999b) reported was sued by the state of Kansas for selling doctorates and law degrees online for as much as $8,000. State officials claim that Monticello, headed by a former insurance agent, was in violation of the Consumer Protection Act. However, Monticello countered that the Consumer Protection Act does not apply to businesses engaged in "the dissemination of information," and therefore they had not committed any crime. Whenever there is a lack of consumer protection, there is also the potential for rapid growth and entrepreneurialism in an economic sector (in this case education); however, there is also a corresponding opportunity for unethical and clearly undemocratic capitalist advantage.

Efficiency Value

For many in America, a Web-based education system promises to be more efficient than the traditional system (Daniel, 1996; Jones, 1997). With online learning, there is no more need for travel, there are potentials for streamlining a huge bureaucracy full of administrators and expensive faculty, time is saved, money is saved, and, presumably, the educational goals are met. For a Fordist culture still under the influence of industrial work models and efficiency studies, the idea that this time-consuming endeavor could be less expensive and more efficient is not merely attractive, it is seductive. When the Louisiana legislators learned about Web-based education, they fell into a fiscal love affair with online learning in the hopes that many professors could be eliminated and the system could be totally automatized. Their hopes had backing. In May 1998 Coopers and Lybrand (accounting firm) released a white paper saying, "Instructional software could easily substitute for campus-based instruction, or at least be a substantial part of the delivery system" (Woody, 1998, 1).

Computers are not neutral tools, they express certain values at the expense of others, and one of their primary values is efficiency. In many other cultures, the value of efficiency may be more elusive, or there may be a more balanced recognition that efficiency at the expense of quality of life or effectiveness is not a good bargain. But in America, we almost always seek the most efficient, cost-effective solution. We put family farmers out of business with this value, and we may do the same to our current system of higher education. Perhaps only the educational equivalent of agribusinesses will survive this latest assault of efficiency values. As Berry (1996) writes of the plight of family farmers,

> The governmental and educational institutions, from which rural people should by right have received help, have not helped. . . . They have eagerly served the superstition that all technological innovation is good. They have said repeatedly that the failure of farm families, rural businesses, and rural communities is merely the result of progress, and such efficiency is good for everybody. (p. 410)

It is not important to us that the overall impact of this choice may be to homogenize our dietary or educational products, or that we may eliminate a way of life for a treasured segment of our society. Where distance education is concerned, we don't even seem terribly concerned that there may indeed be differences between face-to-face modes and distance education. We have tried very hard to convince ourselves that, in fact, it is the same experience—even though fundamentally everyone does understand that it is different. The debate as to whether it is better or worse could go on for decades, and probably will, but the idea that it is no different seems wholly disingenuous. A recent Sloan Consortium (proponents of online learning) press release touts, "Online learning is as good as being there" (Sloan Consortium, 2003a). The complete report (Sloan Consortium, 2003b) surveys academic leaders and administrators and indicates that "a majority of academic leaders (57 percent) already believe that the learning outcomes for online education are equal to or superior to those of face-to-face instruction" (p. 3). Meanwhile, faculty everywhere toiling away with heavier workloads because of online learning programs question whether or not the experience is really the same or really superior. The tools have indeed improved dramatically over the past decade, but the experience of being in a face-to-face experience cannot so easily be dismissed. As Sclove (1995) points out,

> Even nascent or hypothetical new electronic media that convey a dimensionally richer sensory display are not a substitute for face-to-face interaction, because electronic media implicitly choose how to decompose holistic experience into analytically distinct sensory dimensions and then transmit the latter. At the receiving end, people can resynthesize the resulting parts into a coherent experience, but the new whole is invariable different, and in some fundamental way less than the original. (p. 108)

Why would we accept an educational system that is in some fundamental way "less than the original"? It is likely that we are able to overcome our concerns about the quality issues because it is seen as a highly efficient system that allows each of us to pursue our own goals individually. It is interesting that so many academic leaders and administrators have such faith; in my experience, it is not so wholeheartedly mirrored among their faculty counterparts.

Independent Nature of Online Learning

We, in America, love our independence. There is almost nothing that is more precious to us than the ability to determine our own individual destinies and to pursue them with all vigor, potentially alone. The recent rise in libertarianism may be a hallmark of the sort of culture that fosters a reticence toward increased governmental or communal action to the benefit of many (sometimes at the expense of a few). Libertarians eschew all sorts of governmental intervention and control over our everyday lives. It is not my aim to credit or discredit libertarianism, but the nature of such a movement, and its growing popularity along with the growth in mainline politics of a "smaller government/less intrusion" attitude in America, is on the rise. We *like* our independence. We want to be able to carry guns even if that causes lethal errors. We want to allow bizarre performance art to exist (as long as tax dollars do not pay for it) as a statement that anyone in America can do as they please. Online learning is directly in line with this stereotypical

American value. In Web-based education, you can select from among many consumer-oriented choices and pursue your dreams. You can work all by yourself, and you can attain your success completely independently. It is not important that the American Psychological Association recently reported that all this independence usually also leads to isolation—even from your own family—or that recent reports suggest that the Internet can even be addictive.

However, this independent learner that we are quite interested in encouraging may experience negative feelings of disconnectedness. This has led to a good deal of scholarship raising questions about the building of community within online learning spaces (e.g., Lock, 2003; Lindner & Murphy, 2001; McCarty, 1999). In addition, we are looking for all sorts of different *tools;* technological tools, naturally, to create community where there really isn't a natural tendency toward community. We look to Web logs, discussion boards, bulletin boards, text messaging, chat rooms—anything that we think might reconnect us without actually bringing us into direct contact. Nevertheless, the lack of community has caused increased feelings of isolation and eventual withdrawal from online learning programs (Rovai, 2002; LaRose & Whitten, 2000; Wegerif, 1998).

Here again, the immutable nature of technology manifests itself. It is not a neutral tool that can create anything. I am reminded of a recent Star Trek episode in which the beings of a certain planet capture a sick creature and keep it alive just enough to take advantage of its ability to form itself into any shape or thing that is desired by those around it. In the end, there is terrible pain for the creature that has a specific nature and is trying to please those around it by becoming a neutral tool for them. In the long run, is incapable of this because it has an underlying nature which is muted when it is manipulated in this way. It reminded me of online learning. We start with a tool that is all about efficiency and information dispensation; that is what it is good at—computation, dispensation, and so on. We discover certain efficiencies and decide it may be a useful tool for learning, even though there is nothing about its nature that causes us to believe this. After exploring this possibility, we find that the tool is useful for information dispensation, but not so useful for other forms of learning, and that, in fact, it tends to disconnect people rather than connect them. So we try to retrofit the basic nature of the thing so that it *can* connect people. The basic nature of the tool, however, the existential nature of the experience of online learning is isolating. It is more isolating than if you were to go to a classroom and attend face-to-face learning experiences.

VOCATIONAL HIGHER EDUCATION

The history of American higher education has been a tale of evolution away from liberal education and toward increasingly vocational goals. Abraham Flexner (1930), in his strident and remarkable review of universities in England, America, and Germany points out the vocational nature of American higher education with great disdain:

> Is it strange that the general American public is utterly at sea as to what education is, as to what purpose the college serves, as to where the line should be drawn between mere tricks, vocational training, practical experience, and intellectual development . . . (pp. 66–67)

> Some of the reasons for the low quality of college education I have already given, but there is one more, reflective of the tone and spirit of American life that is especially important. The American wants to get ahead . . . It is no exaggeration to say that most college students look upon college as a means of getting ahead in life, for them the college is largely a social and athletic affair. Intellectual concentration would take too much time; it would restrict the student's social contacts. . . . There is another strange feature that keeps our colleges down to a low intellectual level. As a nation we believe in initiative, as all pioneers must. . . . Almost no one at the top has been deliberately trained for his post; anybody may, if really able, become anything—banker, executive, general, diplomat, scientist, editor—what not. (pp. 72–73)

This rather scathing critique of the system of higher education as it existed in America in 1930 has certainly only increased over time. The extent to which our football coaches are paid more than our university presidents speaks rather directly to the athletic angle that Flexner takes, but the increase among vocational degree programs, and the consequent decline among undergraduates majoring in philosophy, comparative literature, and sociology speak clearly to the importance of getting ahead in America. College students in the United States are wooed by the promise of human capital. Not surprisingly, online education offerings are almost exclusively vocational. One of the hottest topics and fastest growing online degree program areas today is within the field of information technologies. Everything from management information systems to Web mastery to network administration is being offered online in increasing numbers.

Robert Reich recently suggested on National Public Radio that many large corporations are asking for more and more foreign nationals to fill positions in the high tech industry claiming that they cannot find qualified workers in the United States. Dr. Reich explained that while we have many programs in these areas available at universities, there is little interest among undergraduates to pursue such degrees not because starting salaries are too low, but because there is no real way to get ahead within that industry—at least not to the satisfaction of traditional undergraduate students. He suggested that if corporations would offer a sincere attempt at increasing wages over time and developing career paths that make work increasingly satisfying, there would be far more interest among our own undergraduates and less of a need for foreign nationals to labor in these areas. I would add to this argument the position that expecting relatively poorer students (who cannot afford to quit their jobs and who, therefore, enroll in online courses) to take positions in such an industry creates a classist or two-tiered system. In this case, those with degrees from face-to-face or traditional institutions will have more opportunities to advance and to have enjoyable work lives, while those with degrees from online institutions will suffer with vocational skills that do not serve to advance them to the highest salaries and leadership positions.

MYTH OF THE MERITOCRACY

In general, Americans believe in the myth of the meritocracy—it is perhaps one of our most powerful shared beliefs. This myth essentially states that, as Flexner suggested earlier, anyone can become anything in America. Nothing is really needed except dedication. One need not be born into money, or endowed with innate intelligence or talent. Anyone can become anything in America . . . it is one of our most treasured beliefs and the reason why so many immigrants hope to come to America. A recent report from ABC News' *20/20* exposed some of the fallacies of this argument in an extensive examination of nepotism. The reporters kept lamenting that what is fundamentally American is that anyone can get ahead, and that those with privileged backgrounds do not enjoy any more breaks than those with poor backgrounds—not so in nepotism they remind us. Certainly, the idea of a meritocracy is close to some people's fundamental understandings of what a democracy is. If we threaten the foundation of this myth, for many in America, we essentially threaten democracy. Programs that seek to create more level playing fields, such as Head Start, are sometimes supported but are often seen as an attempt to bring those with advantage down to a level even with those who have not applied due diligence in trying to move out of disadvantage.

We have, as a society, been frustrated over the years by the apparent failure of the meritocratic system. IQ and SAT scores, college admissions, and subsequent income levels are too strongly linked to family wealth and parental education levels. This stymies our belief in the myth of the meritocracy but we hope that technology will offer us a new way out of this conundrum. For example, former U.S. Secretary of Education Richard Riley stated in an address to the National Conference on Educational Technology,

> Most of you are pioneers in this area. You've seen first hand how teaching and learning that uses technology effectively really can make a difference in the lives of students. You know how it can open doors that would otherwise be closed for many—the economically disadvantaged, the disabled, and those who live in rural areas far away from large libraries, museums, or universities.

We see that technology may be a way to *really* allow anyone to become anything. Online learning programs generally speak to this underlying belief. However, the menu of online learning programs does not include all the degrees necessary to "get ahead" in America. For instance, U.S. Supreme Court Justice Ruth Ginsburg raised great suspicion with regard to the pursuit of online law degrees. Objecting to an all-online law degree granted currently by Concord University, a subsidiary of Kappan Testing Service, Justice Ginsburg said,

> I am uneasy about classes in which students learn entirely from home, in front of a computer screen, with no face-to-face interaction with other students and instructors. So much of legal education and legal practice is a shared enterprise, a genuine interactive endeavor. The process inevitably loses something vital when students learn in isolation, even if they can engage in virtual interaction with their peers and teachers. (Mangan, 1999)

Thus, you can become anything you like, except possibly an attorney, a CEO, a medical doctor, or other highly paid professional. Most fields would feel as Justice Ginsburg does, that something may be or is lost in the process of putting their field online. Those with power will fight this movement to maintain high standards for their discipline.

However, the politicians see technology as the way to appease many factions in America who are unhappy with the current system of education. Corporations gain because many "lifelong learners" are learning vocationally oriented skills during their off hours, sometimes funded by their employers, but more often funded by themselves or the federal government. Perhaps the most corporate friendly aspect of current U.S. online learning policy is the apparent shift in the financial burden for training corporate needs from private to public dollars. The nature of federal funding as contributing to a shift from private training dollars to public monies is perhaps most clearly exemplified in the move by the U.S. federal government to include online learning programs at the same level of assistance as traditional programs. Thus, someone who is enrolled in an online learning program can apply for the same grant and loan programs available to any other student in the United States.

Corporations may be happy about this shift, but the politicians are also finding ways to make the general American public happy about it. American politicians are only too quick to extol the virtues of technology and the promise of democracy as delivered through this "open access" medium. In a 1998 speech to the 15th International ITU (International Technology University) Conference, Al Gore said,

> We have a chance to extend knowledge and prosperity to our most isolated inner cities, to the barrios, the favelas, the colonias and our most remote rural villages; to bring 21st Century learning and communication to places that don't even have phone service today; . . . to strengthen democracy and freedom by putting it on-line, where it is so much harder for it to be suppressed or denied.

It may be true that there isn't the same level of direct control on the Internet that mass media enjoys; however, there is really no evidence that the Internet will democratize our political discourse—or even facilitate it (Winner, 1998). It is only through careful and conscious design that we might be able to create democratic uses of technology, (Sclove, 1995) and thus far, the online learning system in America has been anything but consciously designed to advance democracy.

Perhaps we should be glad that online learning is not really a part of Bush's policy agenda. His official technology agenda (White House, 2004) focuses on promoting innovation and competitiveness through a number of corporation-friendly policies, including a moratorium on Internet taxes and speedier depreciation schedules for technology investors. These policies are consistent with the trickle-down philosophy of the administration in that there is no direct assistance or aid for impoverished American populations in this policy. The expectation, rather, is that breaks for corporations will encourage private investment in technology infrastructure, which will eventually increase access for all. However, because corporations are driven by profits, they will search for ways to gain the economic advantages offered by Bush's policies while maximizing their own income, thus catering to those who can pay for the services rather than catering to the homeless, for example, who are powerless to contribute to the corporate bottom line.

THE REALITY OF OPEN ACCESS IN AMERICA

Recent figures from the Congressional Budget Office show that the poorest 20% of U.S. households will average $8,800 in after-tax income this year, down from $10,000 in 1977, while at the same time the average income of the richest 1% has more than doubled to $515, 600 after taxes. The nation has lost 1 million manufacturing jobs in the past decade. Average pay for top executives has quadrupled since 1990, but roughly 45 million Americans—including many in low-paid service jobs—lack health insurance (Crary, 1999, p. 3A).

Most public initiatives in America serve certain populations more than others. For example, the Rails to Trails Program—a noble initiative to transform old railway paths into bike trails—really only serves those with bikes and the necessary leisure time to utilize them. On the face of it, there is nothing wrong with this, unless our public officials insist that any given public initiative is aimed at helping the entire public. In the case of online learning and the public expenditures necessary to build the infrastructure and support students in their pursuit of higher education, not all the public will be served. What is most inconsistent about the rhetoric and the reality, however, is that the politicians and advocates of online learning are insisting that this system will help the "least of our brethren." Always pointing to the poor and underprivileged, politicians insist that open access to educational opportunities is delivered through Web-based education. However, this system cannot truly serve our most needy. I have never been in a homeless shelter or soup kitchen that had Internet hookups available to the patrons. In fact, the concept is ludicrous. What shelters and welfare workers need is not online education opportunities for the homeless. Solving the poverty problem in America may be too much to ask of Web-based education admittedly, so let's look at who is actually served.

Recent reports indicate what many of us suspect: More wealthy people than poor people have access to the Internet, particularly if you qualify that as in-home access, which is critical to the "anywhere-anytime" learning advertised in most Web-based education marketing. As of 2001, more Americans were online than were not; that is, more than half the U.S. population (54%) was using the Internet. However, in April of 1999, the College Board released a report indicating that the government should endeavor to close the gap between haves and have-nots as they proceed with online learning. In their report, they indicate that it is impossible to know who can benefit from online learning because currently no tracking of enrollees or their characteristics is maintained. The report indicates that while online learning shatters barriers of time and space, it erects new barriers that are primarily financial. It states:

> Students who come from low-income and minority backgrounds are less likely to have been exposed to computers and computer networks at home and school. Not all students have equal access to computers and the Internet. In fact, there is evidence that students with the greatest need get the least access. (College Board, 1999)

This is continuing to be the case with most recent reports in 2001 indicating that 85% of households with incomes over $75,000 have Internet access, while only 14% of households with incomes between $5,000 and $9,999 have access. What is also interesting about these statistics is that there are very little other differences in terms of other demographics such as rural or urban—the primary determinant of access in the U.S. today is income levels. We also know that issues of gender and age enter into access and comfort levels with online learning which must be addressed. Issues surrounding cultural impediments within America to accessing online learning have not yet even begun to be addressed, but they are certainly an issue. In the end, a publicly funded "open access" system is serving relatively more white young working male adults with some financial advantage and relatively fewer minority, female, homeless, or poverty-stricken members of our society.

CONCLUSION

Corporations need to fill their high-tech jobs. And they would prefer to fill them with lower paid employees if they can find them. Those who are pursuing online degrees are often working in jobs that are less attractive than those sought by new college grads from traditional programs. They may be more willing to accept a lower paying service sector job that will serve current corporate needs. Now this is not to suggest that no one who gets an online degree will ever make it to the highest ranks. Our wealthiest American is a Harvard dropout after all, but public policy is not made on individual anecdotes; it is made based on the vast majority of the populace and their experiences and expectancies. In many cases, these policies are friendly to capitalist ventures and corporate needs; in some cases this may be good, but in others, it may serve to control rather than liberate. As Dorothy Nelkin (1997) suggests,

> Advocates of electronic democracy fail to see the difference between the inundation of information and reflective political exchange. And computer advocates fail to see the broader issues of manipulation and loss of political accountability as problems; to them, the technology appears to enhance individual choice. (p. 25)

Certainly I would wager that Al Gore believes technology will indeed enhance individual choice—and it *may*. The issue is that we have to carefully design it to do that; otherwise, it will serve the purposes of the most powerful factions in American society. The innate nature of technology will serve our American instincts for efficiency, individualism, and vocation rather than liberation, democracy, diversity and community. A careful study of unregulated markets and deregulation in America may serve to help us predict failures and design online learning technologies that *truly* advance democracy.

This has been only a brief review of some of the recent rhetoric and realities of online education in America as seen through the traditional, stereotypically American beliefs that have contributed to the rapid proliferation of online learning programs. As one of the most powerful forces for corporate colonialization (McDonalds and Wal-Mart infiltrating all corners of the earth), I cannot imagine the cultural impact of aggressive American online learning programs on a global economy. Should the movement create an open market in which American universities can compete, they will—and they will probably—do very well. American higher education has brand name appeal and an excellent reputation, ripe to be sold on the Internet wires. And we should expect predatory marketing techniques, digital diploma mills, shoddy products for cheap, better products for high expense, and all the other ills and benefits of any American success story. However, with that expanding system of online education goes a whole set of cultural beliefs (some of which we have reviewed here) that may be passed on to online learners worldwide: There's no better method to expand the American Way and the American market.

REFERENCES

Berry, W. (1996). Conserving communities. In J. Mander & E. Goldsmith (Eds.), *The case against the global economy: And for a turn toward the local* (pp. 407–417). San Francisco: Sierra Club.

Carr-Chellman, A. A. (2000). Web-based education in U.S. culture. *Information, Communication, and Society Journal, 3*(3), 326–336.

College Board. (1999). *Virtual universities and educational opportunities: Issues of equity and access for the next generation.* Retrieved January 10, 2000 from http://www.collegeboard.org

Crary, D. (1999, October 3). Low-paid workers grope for share of prosperity. *Centre Daily Times*, p. 3A.

Daniel, J. S. (1996). *Mega-universities and knowledge media: Technology strategies for higher education.* London: Kogan Page.

Flexner, A. (1930). *Universities: American, English, German.* New York: Oxford University Press.

Gore, A. (1998). Remarks from Vice President Al Gore to the 15th International ITU Conference, October 12, 1998. Retrieved December 12, 1999, from http://www.itu.int/newsroom/press/PP98/Documents/Statement_Gore.html

Jones, G. R. (1997). *Cyberschools.* Englewood, CO: Jones Digital Century, Inc.

LaRose, R., & Whitten, P. (2000). Re-thinking instructional immediacy for Web courses: A social cognitive exploration. *Communication Education, 49,* 320–338.

Lindner, J. R. & Murphy, T. H. (2001). Student perceptions of WebCT in a Web-supported instructional environment: Distance education technologies for the classroom. *Journal of Applied Communications, 85*(4), 36–47.

Lock, J. V. (2003). Laying the groundwork for the development of learning communities within online courses. *Quarterly Review of Distance Education, 3*(4), 395–408.

Mangan, K. S. (1999, September 13). Justice Ginsburg raises questions about Internet only law school. *The Chronicle of Higher Education*, pp. A14–A15.

McCarty, J. E. (1999). Cyberjunctions: Building learning communities in cyberspace. *Journal of Experiential Education, 22*(2), 74–79.

National Center for Education Statistics. (2003). *Distance education at degree-granting post secondary institutions.* Retrieved January 10, 2004 from http://nces.ed.gov/pubsearch/pubsinfo.asp?pubid=2003017

National Center for Education Statistics. (1997, October). *Report, distance education in higher education institutions.* Retrieved May 1998 from http://nces.ed.gov

Nelkin, D. (1997). Information technologies could threaten privacy, freedom, and democracy. In M. D. Ermann, M. B. Williams, & M. S. Shauf (Eds.), *Computers, ethics, and society* (pp. 20–32). New York: Oxford Press.

Olsen, F. (1999a, August 6). "Virtual" institutions challenge accreditors to devise new ways of measuring quality. *Chronicle of Higher Education*, pp. A29–A30.

Olsen, F. (1999b, September 3). Kansas sues on-line university that allegedly sold degrees. *The Chronicle of Higher Education*, p. A57.

Riley, R. W. (1999, July 12). Speech to the National Conference on Education Technology, Washington, DC. Retrieved January 2, 2000, from http://www.ed.gov/Speeches/07-1999/990712.html

Rovai, A. (2002, April). Building sense of community at a distance. *International Review of Research in Open and Distance Learning,* 3(1). Retrieved August 6, 2003, from http://www.irrodl.org/content/v3.1/rovai.html

Sclove, R. (1995). *Democracy and technology.* New York: Guilford Press.

Sloan Consortium. (2003a). Press release. Retrieved February 1, 2004, from http://www.sloan-c.org/resources/survey.asp

Sloan Consortium. (2003b). Sizing the opportunity: The quality and extent of online education in the United States, 2002 and 2003. Retrieved February 1, 2004, from http://www.sloan-c.org/resources/survey.asp

Wegerif, R. (1998). The social dimension of asynchronous learning networks. *Journal of Asynchronous Learning Networks,* 2(1). Retrieved November 24, 2003, from http://www.aln.org/publications/jaln/v2n1/v2n1_wegerif.asp

White House. (2004). Retrieved January 10, 2004, from http://www.whitehouse.gov/infocus/technology/tech2.html

Winner, L. (1998, June 2). Tech knowledge review. *NETFUTURE: Technology and human responsibility,* 72, 4–10.

Woody, T. (1998, June 12). Academics rebel against an online future. *The Industry Standard.* Retrieved June 8, 1999, from http://www.suite101.com/discussion.cfm/higher_education/6062#message_1

PART IV

ONLINE EDUCATION DOWN UNDER

An Analysis of Aotearoa/ New Zealand and Australia

"Don't worry about the world coming to an end today. It's already tomorrow in Australia."

—Charles Schultz

Australia is a land of wit and fervor. New Zealand is a place of great pride and independence, innovation, and egalitarianism. In many ways, Australia and New Zealand are perhaps the cultures most similar to America. These countries value independence and individualism. Perhaps because of a similar history as British colonies finding independence relatively recently (as history goes), the connection with the United States is fairly strong. However, the culture is markedly different. Perhaps partially because of Captain Cook's history there, a great navigator and explorer, or perhaps because of the separation and thus independence from their past that the early inhabitants felt, this culture is exquisitely adventurous.

Interestingly, the New Zealand case points to expansion from a few primary providers to several tertiary providers. Is this possibly the future for other cultures that have traditionally had only a few or even only one distance education provider? When online learning comes into being, perhaps because it commands greater respect or because it is seen as a potential for profit, more players want to get into the game. Anderson makes some excellent points regarding the explosion of online learning in New Zealand. Latchem also recognizes the potential pitfalls of splitting things up between public and private providers, noting that the public universities are scrambling onto the online bandwagon and private providers are trying to cream off the more lucrative courses and fee-paying students.

Both authors in this section do a good job of problematizing the subject matter, pointing out the "real" issues associated with access such as who can afford the access, and who is able to take advantage of the technologies, "at our fingertips" (Anderson p. 174, this volume). Anderson supports the idea that Latchem posits: that the issues associated with internationalizing distance education, "requires far more than a fostering of technology. It calls for organizational envisioning, strategic thinking, course design, teaching and learner support systems and strategic alliances that are sensitive to cultural diversity" (Latchem, p. 195, this volume). This is absolutely the case throughout all the international contexts in this book, and I suspect the main offender in terms of attempting to its impose values and practices on other societies is likely to be the United States, where people tend to bullishly refuse to recognize that their culture is not the world's culture. While multicultural societies from Australia to the United States may pay lip service to the need to be culturally sensitive, it is going to be increasingly important that we recognize intra- as well as intercultural compassion and understanding as we move e-learning into global contexts.

Latchem perhaps poses one of the clearest questions in the entire text: "Who will write these rules and to whom will the providers of international distance education be accountable?" (p. 185, this volume). This is a particularly striking question when combined with the critical issue of who is gaining and who is losing in this game.

※ TEN ※

NEW ZEALAND:

Is Online Education a Highway to the Future?

Bill Anderson

New Zealanders are often told that as citizens in a small nation they can expect to be buffeted by powerful global forces. In the area of online education, there are certainly such forces. For example, globalization, technology development, and the commodification of education continue to impact the way online education develops. The powerful internal dynamics of a country run alongside these global forces in shaping the development and practices of an education system. This chapter specifically focuses on some of those internal issues in relation to online education in New Zealand.

A combination of factors molds and raises issues about adoption of online education within New Zealand. I note two here to illustrate the specific nature of New Zealand's situation. First, distance education is an integral part of the New Zealand education system. At a tertiary level, almost one quarter of all students study at a distance (Ministry of Education, 2004), while in the compulsory sector, 98% of all high schools have students who are involved in some form of distance education (Education Review Office, 2003). The promise of openness provided by online education is thus not new or surprising, but its reality is a long way from its promise. Second, a treaty between Māori and the Crown (Government)—the major funder of education in New Zealand—creates specific obligations in relation to education for Māori. Māori are the indigenous people of Aotearoa/New Zealand and currently make up around 15% of the total population. (New Zealand has the Māori name Aotearoa, meaning land of the long white cloud.) This chapter suggests it is unlikely that online education currently helps meet the Crown's obligation.

New Zealand has a small but comparatively open education system. As a nation, we pride ourselves on the quality of that system and the high levels of participation in education at all levels. The growth in online education, in both compulsory and tertiary sectors, raises some particular questions for urgent consideration that are considered in this chapter. At a more general level though, as a reader of this volume, you might consider the questions below as you read through the sections that follow:

- How does a country's educational history impact on the uptake of online education?
- In what ways, if any, can a technology such as online education drive an education system to greater democratic involvement?
- To what extent does the cost of information and communication technologies used in online learning limit their value to indigenous cultures?

THE CONTEXT OF EDUCATION IN AOTEAROA/NEW ZEALAND

Three elements are shaping the form of education as Aotearoa/New Zealand moves into the 21st century: the changes in governance and management set in train in the final decade of the 20th century, the perceived need for educational institutions to engage with new information and communication technologies in their teaching and administration functions, and the commitment to act in accordance with the principles of the Treaty of Waitangi. These factors are operating within an education environment with an ongoing commitment to the notion of equality, conceived of in terms of first, access; then opportunity; and more recently outcomes. The remainder of this section briefly elaborates on this context.

A strong nationally expressed egalitarian ethic led to the 1877 Education Act that provided for free, secular, compulsory education for children up to the age of 14 throughout New Zealand. Simon (2000) points to a major reason for this act being the concern to bring about equal access to schooling for all children. In 1939, the notion of egalitarianism was still strong, but the then-Minister of Education Peter Fraser turned attention to the idea of equality of opportunity and a liberal-progressive approach to education. This approach continued for several decades with particular support, despite some concerns, from the Currie Report of 1962. Another turning point came through the late 1980s and early 1990s.

The Picot Report of 1988 initiated a series of changes that dramatically altered the education system. There was a transformation that saw schools, polytechnics, and universities facing changes in funding mechanisms and management structures and engaging more actively than ever before in competition for students. Institutions became self-managing; they faced fewer of the traditional constraints that had bound them, and, of particular interest to this chapter, the monopoly over distance education provision held by preferred traditional providers was broken. For schools in particular, emphasis moved from equality of opportunity to equality of outcomes (Ministry of Education, 1990).

This change in the education system was accompanied by two other important factors that, together, have changed the context and the manner in which education is offered in New Zealand. One factor was the growing acknowledgment that rapid strides were being made in the development of telecommunications technology.

In attempting to continue to drive forward economic growth within Aotearoa/New Zealand the Government has looked to develop a local version of the global "knowledge society." In Aotearoa/New Zealand this means broadly that the government is seeking to develop and apply new information technologies in computing, communications, and biotechnology to areas where the country has existing competitive advantage. A central aspect of the move to develop this new economy is involvement in education and development of the nation's intellectual capital. As might be anticipated in line with the thrust toward a knowledge economy, the education sector is expected to engage closely with new computer-based information and communications technologies. Documents published by the Ministry of Education (2002a, 2002b) such as *Digital Horizons: Learning Through ICT*, related to school information and communications technologies (ICT) use, and *Highways and Pathways*, concerning online education in the tertiary sector, reflect this expectation.

The third factor is the development of awareness of and subsequent action related to the implications of the Treaty of Waitangi and the need for equitable provision of education within Aotearoa/New Zealand for all citizens. The Treaty of Waitangi is a distinctly national document, described in 1990 by Sir Robin Cooke, then president of the Court of Appeal, as "simply the most important document in New Zealand history." Although the Treaty is not legally enforceable, it imposes considerable moral obligation on the Crown. This obligation is grounded in the principles of the Treaty, of which there are three: the principle of partnership; the principle of active protection, whereby the Crown is required to take positive steps to ensure that Māori interests are protected; and the principle of redress.

The Treaty of Waitangi, through its second principle, places an obligation on the Crown in relation to the provision of education within Aotearoa/New Zealand. To some extent, this has been visible throughout the last two decades in the establishment and growth of Kura Kaupapa, Whare Kura, and Whare Wānanga. These face-to-face institutions, at the primary, secondary and tertiary level of education respectively, operate with particular emphasis on the application of knowledge concerning ahuatanga Māori (Māori tradition) and tikanga Māori (Māori custom). But as we shall see, there are serious issues in the field of online education and provision for Māori.

EDUCATION AT A DISTANCE IN NEW ZEALAND: TO, AND THROUGH, THE 1990s

Distance education in Aotearoa/New Zealand has always been seen as one of the means through which equality of access and opportunity can be attained. There has never been a sense in which a distance education has been considered inferior. At least in part, this is due to the length of time that distance education has been offered as part of the public education system.

The heavily centralized nature of the Aotearoa/New Zealand education system through most of the 20th century saw the development of singular distance education institutions. The Correspondence School (Te Kura a Tuhi) was established in 1922 to serve as the sole provider of distance education to schoolchildren throughout the country. At a tertiary level, two institutions were involved in the distance delivery of courses as publicly funded distance education providers. The Open Polytechnic of New Zealand was founded in 1946 to retrain returning World War II servicemen and servicewomen. In 1963 it changed focus, offering training nationwide in trades subjects. Just one year later, Massey University was chosen as the university to develop and offer extramural (distance) courses to students throughout the country.

As the 1990s progressed, tertiary institutions began to take advantage of the developments that had occurred in the information and communication technologies (ICT) area to make their courses available more widely. These moves were underpinned by the (then) recent changes to the education system. A number of institutions began to provide distance education opportunities for tertiary students through developments in the online education area. In contrast, the compulsory sector did not move markedly toward distance delivery of courses for the following reasons: First, it comprised a large number of comparatively small self-managing schools that did not have the resources of the large tertiary institutions; second, those schools had a focus on providing face-to-face education for students in their immediate area; and finally, the Correspondence School was still providing an effective national distance education service. Developments in the compulsory sector in the area of online education took longer to occur and arose from an evolution in the role of ICT in classrooms. Developments at tertiary and compulsory levels are discussed further in the next section.

THE ROLE OF GOVERNMENT AND RECENT INITIATIVES IN ONLINE EDUCATION

The move to online education, rapidly in the tertiary sector and more slowly elsewhere, heralded a shift in the traditional conception of distance education. From a comparatively centralized system with three major providers and an emphasis on print material, sprang a collection of providers emphasizing the currency of their online course material and their ability to create "communities of learners." Opportunities for the education "enterprise" abounded, at least in the tertiary sector. The tertiary-sector developments occurred largely without direct Government intervention, although some decisions (such as the decision to fund distance education students at the same rate as on-campus students) had considerable indirect effect. Through the 1990s, however, Government interest in the ICT and education area was focused on the compulsory education sector. The approach of Government at all levels though has been to increase infrastructural capability and provide strategic direction.

Compulsory Education Heads Online

The Sallis Report of 1990 (Consultative Committee on Information Technology in the School Curriculum, 1990) was the first indication that ICT use in schools had achieved some prominence as an educational issue. However, the years following the Sallis Report were comparatively bereft of central direction until the late 1990s. In 1997, the Minister for Information Technology's Advisory Group (ITAG) published *ImpacT 2001: Learning With IT. The Issues* (ITAG, 1997). This report made reference to the "knowledge society" and the economic importance of information technologies being taught in schools was highlighted. That same year the Education Review Office (1997) released its own report, *The Use of Information Technology in Schools*. This report was highly critical of the lack of planning for ICT use at both a school and national level.

Two national strategy documents have attempted to rectify the planning vacuum. In 1998 the Ministry of Education published its first national strategy for ICT use in schools. That document was the Ministry's first real attempt to provide a sense of order and cohesion to the scattered initiatives and projects being undertaken throughout the education system. In 2002 a new strategy document, *Digital Horizons*, was published (Ministry of Education, 2002a). Linking this document with the education past was the foreword provided by the Minister of Education. Drawing on former Director General of Education Clarence Beeby's innovative spirit and his advocacy of the right of all New Zealand children to access good-quality education, the foreword suggests that digital technology is a key tool for education. The developments in and use of ICT in schools are seen as a natural extension of Beeby's philosophy and approach to education. The egalitarian principle that drove the New Zealand education system through the 20th century resurfaced as a rationale for the extensive adoption of ICT.

This new strategy document places considerable emphasis on learning through ICT, which it explains by saying that it involves "using ICT to support new ways of teaching and learning" (Ministry of Education, 2002a, p. 8). Online education features prominently in this strategy, with specific mention being made of virtual classrooms being linked by video, audio, or online conferencing; online discourse and collaboration using email, chat, discussion groups, and Web pages; and online resources giving general information, courses, learning objects, and Web links (Ministry of Education, 2002, p. 10).

Digital Horizons has been subject to considerable criticism. Brown (2003) points to the hidden curriculum that will teach students to be "high-tech consumers and low-tech post-industrial data-entry workers in the global economy of the future" (p. 34). He suggests there are strong but unquestioned assumptions underpinning the social, economic, and pedagogical rationales for ICT use expressed in the document—assumptions related to the value of globalization, the economic imperative for ICT uptake, and the nature of deskilling of teaching.

Implementation of projects related to *Digital Horizons* continues. Apart from strategic leadership, the Government indicates it is committed to funding professional development for teachers and "developing digital resources and a national infrastructure to maximize the benefits of ICT in education" (Ministry of Education, 2002a, p. 6). Some prominent initiatives concerning this latter promise are noted below.

Te Kete Ipurangi

TKI is a Web site (www.tki.org.nz) funded by the Ministry of Education. Originally conceived as a portal site for teachers, it has also become a point of access to official Ministry of Education information and resources, and a storehouse for education-related content. In addition to the content, both pointed to and on-site, TKI developers have created spaces for discussion in an attempt to establish various interactive communities, whose members might share information and provide feedback about TKI.

Project PROBE

PROBE is a project intended to roll out high-speed Internet access to all schools and provincial communities by the end of 2004. The emphasis on education is for the reason that

> there is huge opportunity for schools to use the Internet and related technologies to support learning and ensure that New Zealand children are able to succeed in our emerging Knowledge Society.
>
> High-speed bandwidth will give additional access, particularly for remote and rural schools, and *kura* (Māori language medium schools), to
>
> - existing digital resources;
> - use of ICT for administrative efficiency and teaching effectiveness;

- online communication and professional development for teachers;
- the expansion of e-learning; and
- wider curriculum choice and teacher expertise, including through two-way video-conferencing (Ministry of Education, 2002c, p. 2).

KAWM and Other Networks

Kaupapa Ara Whakawhiti Mātauranga (KAWM) is an example of the projects that have the potential to follow on from PROBE. KAWM is a project involving a number of Māori language medium schools with the goal of raising the achievement of Māori learners. The three areas where KAWM contributes to this goal are

- strengthening current curriculum delivery;
- broadening curriculum options (particularly at the senior secondary level) by linking classrooms by videoconferencing;
- facilitating professional development and governance and management initiatives.

The KAWM model of linking schools was derived at least in part from earlier school network examples that used audiographics. In turn, KAWM has been the catalyst for additional networks of mainly secondary schools. These networks, usually linking between 4 and 10 schools, have developed on a regional basis throughout the country. They typically work to attain goals similar to those of KAWM but without the specific Māori emphasis.

Leadspace

Leadspace is an online project that includes a network for principals of schools. The Leadspace Web site is designed to bring together information for principals and to provide a forum for discussion of general educational and educational leadership issues.

Tertiary Online Initiatives

Two initiatives serve as landmarks for governmental involvement in online education at a tertiary level, and both are comparatively recent. In contrast with the compulsory sector's relative reluctance to move online, tertiary sector institutions, without any form of government strategic direction, moved with some haste to take advantage of the possibilities—predominantly increased enrollment and thus increased revenue—they saw in online education. Institutions have used a wide range of learning management systems, and there has been considerable duplication of courses in a small student population. In response, we see initiatives that demonstrate the governmental reaction to this situation. These initiatives are the report of the E-learning Advisory Group *Highways and Pathways* (Ministry of Education, 2002b), the Tertiary Education Commission's e-Learning Collaborative Development, and Innovation and Development Funds (eCDF and IDF). E-learning can be considered almost synonymous with online education.

Highways and Pathways

The *Highways and Pathways* report was the result of deliberations by a government appointed E-learning Advisory Group. That group was tasked with advising the Ministry of Education on ways to achieve a strategic direction for e-learning in the tertiary-education sector. Eight recommendations came from the group. In particular these focused on the importance of collaboration between Government, tertiary education providers, and other stakeholders; Māori participation in e-learning; quality assurance; and closer links between compulsory and tertiary sectors.

eCDF and IDF

The e-Learning Collaborative Development and the Innovation and Development Funds arose from recommendations of the *Highways and Pathways* report. These funds provided Government funding for a range of projects that were seen to either demonstrate a collaborative approach to e-learning or to increase the e-learning capability of institutions in Aotearoa/ New Zealand. Funding was on a competitive basis. Examples of the projects that were successful demonstrate the emphasis placed on the recommendations of *Highways and Pathways*. Those projects include the following:

- A project to develop a Centre for Māori Innovation and Development
- The National Secondary Tertiary Curriculum Alignment Project to align secondary school and polytechnic curriculum at a local level

- Te Ako Hikohika Wānanga to increase the ability of Māori communities to research what e-learning works best for them (undertaken by the three Wānanga)
- The Quality Standards, Framework and Guidelines Project to develop guidelines and standards to ensure the quality of e-learning in a New Zealand context (six tertiary institutions collaborating)

The initiatives mentioned here, in compulsory and tertiary sectors, are all relatively recent, having occurred since 1999. The move to online education seen so clearly in these initiatives springs from the overall vision of Aotearoa/New Zealand as a knowledge society, and from the role that online education is believed to play in the development of such a society. The move has been speedy, even hasty, and questions about the impact of online education in the national context remain. The following section reviews some of those questions and points to areas of concern as well as aspects of value.

Holes in the Highway? Moving Ahead With Online Education

Education in Aotearoa/New Zealand has concerned itself with the democratic ideal of egalitarianism. Egalitarianism has been variously expressed as equality of opportunity, equality of access, and equality of outcomes. At the conclusion of her discussion of education policy change, Simon (2000) suggests, "Both the policies and practices within schools have continued in varying degrees to reproduce social inequalities" (p. 63). Simon was writing of education before the online era.

There is no doubt that Aotearoa/New Zealand is committed to an educational path that involves extensive use of online education. The question to ask is whether online education will exacerbate or reduce social inequalities. Will the policy and strategic directions currently set help to democratize and provide greater opportunity for all New Zealanders, or are they likely to provide scattered opportunity and access, acting to marginalize sectors of the population?

Access

In the compulsory sector, where Internet access at schools is the issue, it is possible to be reasonably positive. The initiatives associated with the ICT strategy development have enlarged the capacity of schools to engage in aspects of an online education. A recent survey of schools (BRC Marketing and Social Research, 2003) shows that 100% of primary and 96% of secondary schools have Internet access. However Internet usage is biased markedly toward teacher use, not student use. For example, just over half of all primary schools reported 25% or more of their students use the Web at least once in a typical school week, in contrast with 72% of such schools reporting use by 25% or more of staff. In addition, it would appear that much of the Internet access is simply for accessing resources (lesson plans, etc.) for later use in face-to-face lessons. This finding from a Government-commissioned evaluation of one of the ICT initiatives (Ham & Wenmouth, 2002) suggests that online education in the compulsory sector is not yet well advanced.

Access to online education within the tertiary sector brings different issues. At a tertiary level, the development of online education is underpinned by the notion of access for all—an "anytime-anywhere" education. To what extent is it "anywhere," and for whom?

Who Can (Afford to) Access the Internet?

Figures about access to the infrastructure and equipment needed for the general population to take advantage of online education are quite stark in broad terms. The 2001 New Zealand Census of Population and Dwellings provides information about Internet access—the "sine qua non" of online education (Department of Statistics, 2002).

Thirty-seven percent of New Zealand households have access to the Internet. As might be expected, this access is not equally distributed across income groups, ranging from over 70% in households with an income over NZ$100,000 to just over the 10% mark in households with income in the NZ$5,000 to NZ$15,000 range. Only one in four Māori live in households with access to the Internet.

Household Internet access in Aotearoa/New Zealand is currently dominated by the dial-up modem—broadband access is not widespread. Thus it is useful to note that 96% of all households have access to a telephone, with the rate falling to just below 90% for households in the $5,000 to $15,000 income range. In addition, one in nine people of Māori ethnicity live in households that do not have telephone, fax, or Internet access.

Broadband access for Internet access purposes is limited in New Zealand but is being pursued. Project PROBE is consistently cited as bringing the

Internet to the provinces as in the following from the Associate Minister for Information Technology:

> The New Zealand Government has taken a number of initiatives to deepen and broaden the reach of broadband throughout our country, especially in our more remote and rural areas. We intend that all schools and their surrounding communities will be able to access broadband by the end of 2004. (Cunliffe, 2003)

The disjunction between Internet access and telephone access leads to an obvious but important conclusion. Internet access is largely determined by income, where lack of access arises from the inability to meet the economic demands of computer purchase and ongoing payments to an Internet service provider for dial-up access. The value of Project PROBE to households is even more limited because of the even higher costs that need to be met for a broadband service.

Beyond the Wires

The issue of providing physical infrastructure and the economic difficulties of accessing that infrastructure to obtain Internet access comprise only part of the picture. Although it is an essential element, I want to put aside the question of the economics of online access at the moment—the point is clear and has been made. Providing an infrastructure is akin to what Perkins (1985) calls a first-order fingertip effect that he describes by saying "technology has a venerable history of putting things at our fingertips to be seized and used widely for their designed objectives as well as for other purposes" (p. 11). The question that Perkins goes on to ask is, "Does the opportunity that is placed at our finger tips get taken?" This second-order question recognizes that the provision of opportunity does not ensure the uptake of whatever it is that is on offer.

Difficulties of access faced by some groups in Aotearoa/New Zealand are well recognized. Crump and McIlroy (2003) quote a recent Government strategy paper in saying:

> In New Zealand the government has identified those more likely than others to be left behind in the information revolution. These groups include Maori and Pacific peoples, those on low incomes, sole parents, older people, people with no or low qualifications or poor literacy, the unemployed, people with disabilities and people living in rural areas that lack a sound

telecommunications structure. (Connecting Communities: A Strategy for Government Support of Community Access to Information and Communications Technology, 2002)

As Crump and McIlroy show, access is not the issue, however.

The Crump and McIlroy (2003) study concerned use of a community computing facility in a lower socioeconomic area in Wellington, the capital city of Aotearoa/New Zealand, and served people identified in the Government's community access strategy as less likely to have Internet access. The facility was situated in a city council high-rise apartment block and offered free access to the Internet. Investigations into usage revealed that after six months the majority of residents in the apartment block still did not use the ICT facilities. A survey of nonusers within the apartment block was undertaken to obtain information about computer access and usage, tenants' knowledge of and interest in the facility, factors that would encourage ICT usage, and reasons for tenants not using the facility.

Analysis of the survey results led Crump and MCIlroy to conclude, "The digital divide will not be addressed in environments like the Newtown Park Flats through universal physical access to computer technology." They added,

> With approximately 70 percent of the apartment population on state benefits the struggle to meet basic needs is greater than for those people in work. Interest in accessing computing, even when situated in a convenient social space, and offered at no charge, is unlikely to be seen as a priority for daily living. (Crump & McIlroy, 2003)

The first-order issues of economics and physical access are, for some, irrelevant to the question of actual use, and second-order questions of motivation, need, and contribution to one's daily world do not necessarily meet positive responses.

Depending as it does on resolutions to first- and second-order questions, online education does not and cannot currently represent a breakthrough in the provision of access to education in New Zealand. It certainly does provide an additional means of access for a segment of the population, but that segment of the population—middle and higher socioeconomic groups—is already privileged in terms of education access. Those who are less privileged will not find advantage here. While not denying the potential that online education has, and the opportunity it provides, literally at the fingertips, the issues facing online education are those that have faced all forms of education—power, privilege and interest. Online education will become an additional site of argument rather than being the holy grail of democratic education access.

Online Education for Māori

In the case of Aotearoa/New Zealand, two questions arise in relation to the use of online education by Māori. The first of these relates to the obligations of the Government under the Treaty of Waitangi. Māori are over represented in that segment of the population without Internet access, as the previous section shows. Thus Māori ability to access education from "anywhere" is severely limited. As Irwin (1999) points out though, "transforming Māori education is not an intellectual challenge. It is a political challenge" (p. 68). The antecedent of an effective online education for Māori is political action. Online education does not precede or bring democracy; its effective and universal delivery is conditional on democracy and the political action that occurs within a democracy.

The second question relates to the arguments that Bowers (1998) makes concerning the cultural biases inherent in the computer technology used as the basis for online learning and discussed in the introduction to this book. Within Aotearoa/New Zealand, Māori educational institutions have been willing to turn to online education in both synchronous and asynchronous forms to complement other means of education.

Māori education is customarily undertaken in face-to-face (kanohi-a-kanohi) situations, recognizing the need for an intimate connection between teacher and learner. Given this, synchronous forms of online education have the potential to be more successful. Indeed, the KAWM videoconferencing network showed that although there may be some loss of immediacy, the sense of oneness between teacher and students was still present. It has been welcomed as a valuable innovation by the schools involved and not seen to detract markedly from the richness of a teaching context not mediated by technology.

The Wānanga have developed asynchronous systems of online education, reflecting the path followed by other university and polytechnic providers. Te Whare Wananga o Awanuiarangi, one of the three Māori tertiary-education providers, delivers a number of its programs of study online using material delivered by Web and CD-ROM. It has developed student support systems to allow for the potential isolation of students and makes face-to-face blocks of time a compulsory element of courses. In many respects, these measures are the response of an institution to traditional distance education issues. We need to recognize that they are more than that. The Wänanga are tasked by legislation to provide teaching that is based on the application of knowledge regarding *ahuatanga Mäori* (Mäori tradition) according to *tikanga Mäori* (Mäori custom). Their acceptance of online education suggests that although Bowers's (1998) claims about bias have intellectual force, the practice of education, by a people, for a people, finds ways to meet and possibly counter those biases.

CONCLUSION

Since its genesis in the 18th century, the system of education in Aotearoa/New Zealand has been premised on a principle of egalitarianism—the promise of equality of access, of opportunity, of outcomes. Online education, brought to the fore in the drive to re-create Aotearoa/New Zealand as a knowledge society is seen to be a way to meet these promises. However, as has been argued in this chapter, online education falls short for many. We must recognize online education for what it is. It is surely another form of education that allows access to education for some. But it does not deliver universally even when universal free access is possible. Those who are traditionally disadvantaged in our system of education face the same disadvantage when confronted with the online world. Online education does not bring democracy; it requires it.

REFERENCES

Bowers, C. A. (1998, *Spring*). The paradox of technology: What's gained and lost? *Thought and Action,* 49–57.

BRC Marketing and Social Research. (2003). ICT in schools 2003 report. *The Learning Centre Trust of New Zealand.* Retrieved January 22, 2004, from http://www.learningcentretrust.org.nz/pdfs/final_report_2003.pdf

Brown, M. (2003). Beyond the digital horizon: The untold story. *Computers in New Zealand Schools, 15*(1), 34–40.

Consultative Committee on Information Technology in the School Curriculum. (1990). *Report of the consultative committee on information technology in the school curriculum.* Wellington: Author.

Crump, B., & McIlroy, A. (2003). The digital divide: Why the "don't–want–tos" won't compute: Lessons from a New Zealand ICT Project. *First Monday, 8(12).* Retrieved December 6, 2003, from http://firstmonday.org/issues/issue8_12/crump/index.html

Cunliffe, D. (2003). *Statement on behalf of New Zealand at The World Summit on the Information Society.* Geneva, Switzerland.

Department of Statistics. (2002). *2001 Census. Snapshot 2. Who has access to the Internet?* Retrieved January 25, 2004, from http://www.stats.govt.nz

Education Review Office. (1997). *The use of information technology in schools.* Wellington, New Zealand: Author.

Education Review Office. (2003). *The Correspondence School. Overview report.* Wellington, New Zealand: Author.

Ham, V., & Wenmouth, D. (2002). *Educators' use of the online learning centre (Te Kete Ipurangi) 1999–2001.* Christchurch: Christchurch College of Education.

Information Technology Advisory Group. (1997). *ImpacT 2001: Learning with IT. The issues.* Wellington: Ministry for Information Technology's Advisory Group.

Irwin, K. (1999). Maori Education Policy 1989–1998. *New Zealand Journal of Educational Studies, 34*(1), 66–76.

Ministry of Education. (1990). *The Charter Framework.* Wellington: Author.

Ministry of Education. (2002a). *Digital horizons: Learning Through ICT.* Wellington: Learning Media.

Ministry of Education. (2002b). *Highways and pathways.* Wellington: Learning Media.

Ministry of Education. (2002c). Project PROBE Update 1. *Ministry of Education.* Retrieved December 14, 2003, from http://www.ecommerce.govt.nz/broadband/probenewsletter1.pdf

Ministry of Education. (2004). *Students at tertiary education providers.* Retrieved April 3, 2004, from http://www.minedu.govt.nz/index.cfm?layout=document&documentid=7548&indexid=7552&indexparentid=6142

Perkins, D. N. (1985). The fingertip effect: How information-processing technology shapes thinking. *Educational Researcher, 14*(6), 11–17.

Simon, J. (2000). Education policy change: Historical perspectives. In J. Marshall, E. Coxon, K. Jenkins & A. Jones (Eds.), *Politics, policy, pedagogy: Education in Aotearoa/New Zealand.* Palmerston North: Dunmore Press.

Te Puni Kokiri (2001). He Tirohanga o Kawakite Tiriti o Waitangi: A guide to the principles of the treaty of Waitangi as expressed by the Courts and the Waitangi Tribunal. Wellington, New Zealand: Te Puni Kokiri.

ELEVEN

TOWARDS BORDERLESS VIRTUAL LEARNING IN HIGHER EDUCATION

Colin Latchem

By definition, distance education is borderless, and as Blight, Davis, and Olsen (1999) show, enrollments in distance education programs have progressed from local to national to regional to international. Such a transition means that distance education can be a means of forging international networks and partnerships, internationalizing the curriculum, promoting virtual staff and student mobility, and generally encouraging higher education to become more international in its outlook.

As you read this chapter, reflect upon the following questions:

- To what extent are globalization, satellite communications, and the Internet shrinking our world and bringing every nation to a fuller realization of where it stands in relation to others in terms of human capacity, understanding the world and the knowledge-based economy?
- How can higher education mobilize the educational, technological, human, and financial resources to provide distance education that helps developed and developing countries achieve their full potential?
- How can distance education provide greater, faster, cheaper, better and more equitable educational delivery in all parts of the globe?

- In what ways are international distance education programs helped or hindered by being for-profit and user pays?
- What lessons can be learned from the successes and failures of international distance education and consortia?

INTERNATIONALIZING THE CURRICULUM

The British Columbia Task Force on Internationalization (1993) argues that universities need to prepare their students for living and working in a diverse but increasingly interdependent world. The Australian National Board of Employment, Education, and Training (NBEET) (1992) suggests that Australian graduates should be capable of contributing to intellectual, cultural, economic, and social development at the international level and operating anywhere in the world at a level of professionalism commensurate with best international practice. In his comparative study of Australian, Canadian, European, and U.S. educational systems, de Wit (1995) sees the need for a curriculum infused with international, intercultural, and international development studies; cross-border teaching and staff/student exchange; and international collaboration in credit transfer and credentialing. All of these are achievable through distance or virtual learning.

The Commonwealth Secretariat (1985) suggests that international distance education involves a continuum of activities, ranging from "low risk-modest benefit" (sharing information and experience; collaborating in staff development; exchanging students; and acquiring or sharing distance education materials) to "high risk-major benefit" (collaboratively adapting and developing courses; establishing credit transfer arrangements; and creating common open learning systems). The remainder of this chapter examines how these approaches are being applied around the world and their ramifications.

INTERNATIONALIZING DISTANCE EDUCATION

With the exponential growth of the Web, learners are no longer limited to local resources or lockstep, one-size-fits-all courses of study. They can select, contextualize, and apply their learning according to their needs and seek out, analyze, verify, and utilize knowledge and experience from anywhere in the world. Being essentially dialogic, the Internet also provides learners with opportunities to learn with and from teachers and students in other countries and cultures.

An increasing number of institutions are taking advantage of the opportunities offered by international distance learning, some to gain strategic advantage, some to generate extra income, and some (less commonly) to help the disadvantaged in the poorer nations.

MIT's 2001 announcement of its intention to post 2,000 OpenCourseWare programs on the Web (http://ocw.mit.edu) is a particularly dramatic expression of institutional commitment to making courses freely available (Kumar, 2003). It is yet to be shown whether this will inspire other universities to collaborate in creating a worldwide web of knowledge to benefit humankind. Cross-border access to digitized collections of learning objects is also being pursued in the U.S. MERLOT project (Hanley, 2003) and the European ARIADNE (www.ariadne-eu.org/en/about/general/benefitsd/index.html) and CANDLE projects (Wetterling and Collis, 2003).

Case Study 1—The University of Melbourne Institute of Land and Food Resources Global Seminar

The University of Melbourne's Institute of Land and Food Resources has been involved in an award-winning international distance education program, the Global Seminar (www.unimelb.edu.au/HB/2000). Compressed video, Web conferencing, and e-mail have been used to involve Australian, American, Dutch, Swedish, Honduran, Costa Rican, and Indian students in virtual seminars, tutorials, and collaborative examination of such topics as population demographics, food security, environmental sustainability, ecotourism, waste management, biodiversity, biotechnology, forest fire ecology, and irrigated and dryland agriculture. The program has helped students appreciate that perspectives and roles in seeking solutions to global problems are influenced by sociocultural, political, technical, environmental and ethical/philosophical considerations at the local level.

Summaries of group positions on the various issues are posted on the listserv, and the students undertake project work based on the seminar series and present their findings at their respective institutions and on the Global Seminar Web page.

Case Study 2—Curtin University of Technology Business School, Western Australia

In an initiative believed to be unique in Australia, Curtin University of Technology in Perth, Western Australia, has used videoconferencing for its third-year commerce students and business students in Singapore Polytechnic to practice international business negotiation.

Curtin's school of management and marketing students were split into two teams—one representing a brewery company and the other a food company—and instructed to negotiate a hypothetical joint venture in frozen and canned foods in the Peoples' Republic of China with their Singaporean counterparts. Before the videoconferenced negotiations began, the students researched the Singaporean and Chinese cultures, the relevant industries, joint venturing, government assistance, restrictions and legal requirements; exchanged emails with the Singapore Polytechnic students; and received briefings from local companies on the finer points of penetrating the Chinese market. The intensive, real-time face-to-face meetings then took place over a period of eight weeks by means of integrated services digital network (ISDN) videoconferencing.

The exchanges brought into focus everything the students had learned during their three years of study. They also revealed differences in Australian, Singaporean, and Chinese values and practices and gave both sets of students valuable lessons in cross-cultural communication, exercising patience, gaining understanding, and building trust—all of which are essential in conducting business in Asian contexts.

However, as Perraton (1997) observes, the rhetoric may emphasize the value of international cooperation and exchange, but the reality is an agenda primarily driven by the financial ambitions of the providers. Farrell (1999) observes that public universities are scrambling onto the online bandwagon and private providers are trying to cream off the more lucrative courses and fee-paying students, while Duke (2002) concludes that the overriding concern is not with curriculum and content but with commercialization and commodification.

Cain and Hewitt (2004) suggest that selling online education to the world represents a regrettable transition of the university from public institution to corporation and ask whether this is a case of money for learning or money before learning. These are regrettable developments, given the need for greater equality of educational opportunity across the globe.

Case Study 3—The University of Southern Queensland, Australia

Like all other Australian universities, the University of Southern Queensland (USQ) (www.usq.edu.au) has a rapidly growing international program. Originally serving students in regional and rural Australia, USQ now also provides undergraduate and postgraduate programs for 6,400 international students from over 100 countries. It offers a choice of three modes of study: on-campus, external (pursuing the same academic programs in their home countries), or a combination of these plus USQOnline (studying through the Internet).

The strategic importance of internationalization to USQ is shown by the fact that its Global Learning Services Division is headed up by a deputy vice-chancellor (vice-president). The international distance education students are helped with enrollments, contact with staff, and linking with other students through USQNet, a worldwide network of USQOnline liaison officers, local support offices and online support services.

USQ's online global learning has been recognized as state-of-the-art in international delivery, content, and form by the Australian Government's Evaluation and Investigations Program. USQ has also been recognized as an international leader in e-learning by the Australian University Quality Agency, has received an International Council for Distance Education Prize for Institutional Excellence, and has been the joint winner of the Australian University of the Year Award for its work as an e-university. It is also the world's first distance learning institution to have been granted an ISO 9001 Quality System Certificate of Registration.

Case Study 4—United Kingdom Open University

The UK Open University (UKOU) (www.open.ac.uk) laid the foundations for open learning across the world by widening opportunities for those without the necessary entry qualifications and by providing distance education through public funding rather than private enterprise. Today, it has a total enrolment of about 230,000 students, more than 130,000 of whom are online, and it serves 30,000 students a year outside the United Kingdom, mainly in Western Europe.

Most of the UKOU's overseas students study at a distance in English, take the university's examinations, and are awarded its own degrees. Franchise arrangements and accreditation agreements with institutions in the UK and overseas help to further the UKOU's reach and influence. Overseas partners can enter into course licensing agreements with the UKOU through the university's international division, OU Worldwide Ltd. (OUW), and use the OU's courses and materials for their own award programs. OUW also enables overseas students to enroll in UKOU courses and receive UKOU materials and tutorial support online as well as from local partner institutions. UKOU Validation Services (OUVS) allows those partner institutions that are unable to award degrees to reach accreditation. OUW also sells stand-alone learning resources—there are currently over 2,500 on offer—through a network of distributors in more than 30 non-European countries.

UKOU distance learning courses are considered among the world's best and regularly receive national and international awards. The university ranks among the top U.K. universities for teaching quality.

Over the past 7 years, the university has invested £30 million in online learning. An increasing number of its programs are Web-enhanced (where e-learning is an option), Web-focused (with a required element of online learner support), and Web-intensive (in which the course is wholly online).

FREE TRADE IN EDUCATION

Globalization transforms every activity and every resource into a commodity, including education, and free trade in educational services is being heavily promoted, particularly by the United States (Duke, 2002). In 2003, countries were invited to notify the World Trade Organization (WTO) of those service sectors, including education, that they wished to see included in the General Agreement on Trade in Services (GATS). However, as Hawkridge (2003) observes, whether or not GATS affects trade in educational services is not an issue because the globalization of education is proceeding apace.

The global drive to deregulate education raises important questions about quality. The World Bank (2002) asks how national authorities can exercise quality control over overseas educational providers operating within their own borders and how rulings by the WTO and decisions under GATS will affect national governments in exercising such control. Farrell (2001) observes that many countries are already discovering that the policies and regulations they have developed to limit the activities of overseas providers, control recognition of learners' credentials, restrict the use of the term "university," and safeguard copyright, intellectual property and quality assurance arrangements no longer apply in the new globalized environment. Who will write these rules and to whom will the providers of international distance education be accountable?

INTERNATIONAL DEVELOPMENT PROGRAMS

International agencies such as the World Bank, UNESCO, UNDP and the Commonwealth of Learning (COL) are helping in the development of institutional and technological capacity, fostering alliances, and providing models of exemplary practice to support distance education in developing countries. National aid agencies such as the Japanese International Cooperation Agency (JICA), the Canadian International Development Research Center (IDRC), USAID, the U.K. Department for International Development, AusAID and the New Zealand Agency for International Development are also helping to enhance knowledge and practice in distance education and establish telecenters and other systems providing e-learning, e-commerce and e-governance in Latin America, the Caribbean, Africa, and Asia (Latchem & Walker, 2001). Global distance education development is also being supported by professional associations such as the International Council for Distance Education (ICDE) and the Asian Association of Open Universities (AAOU).

Case Study 5—JICA and the University of the South Pacific

The University of the South Pacific (USP) is the premier higher education provider in the Pacific region. The university is multiethnic and regionally governed by 12 member countries—Cook Islands, Fiji, Kiribati, Marshall Islands, Nauru, Niue, Solomon Islands, Tokelau Islands, Tonga, Tuvalu, Vanuatu, and Western Samoa. It is also the major provider of distance learning for the region's students who live across four time zones in islands and atolls spanning 33 million square kilometers, and comprising at least 60 cultures and 265 language groups.

In 1999, the Japan International Cooperation Agency (JICA), Australian AusAID, and New Zealand Overseas Development Agency (NZODA) collaborated in enabling USP to establish its own satellite-based USPNet that is now used extensively for audioconferencing, videoconferencing and Internet and Web access for distance education and intercampus teaching and learning.

JICA's ICT Capacity Building at USProject, which is scheduled to run from 2002 to 2005, aims to enhance USP's capacity in ICT, strengthen ICT usage throughout the region, and provide more students with access to improved educational programs and services. There are three components to this program. The computing science course component trains the ICT specialists needed for the other two components of the program through a mix of face-to-face and online learning. The distance learning component provides USP staff with on-the-job training and e-learning from Japan and helps them develop model online programs, enhance USPNet, and develop a multimedia knowledge management system. The ICT research and training component is concerned with helping South Pacific communities to embrace these new technologies and methodologies and apply them to e-learning, e-health, e-government, and e-commerce.

Recognizing that reduced trade barriers and increased economic activity require increased educational integration, particularly between the "old Europe" and the newer eastern European members, the European Union (EU) is promoting cross-border distance education and virtual mobility. Such initiatives are also being supported by the European Association of Distance Teaching Universities (EADTU), European Distance Education Network (EDEN), EuroPACE 2000 consortium, and other organizations.

Case Study 6—AED LearnLink Community Learning Centers

The Washington-based Academy for Educational Development LearnLink project team has collaborated with local organizations in Ghana and Paraguay to establish community learning centers (CLCs). These centers, described in Latchem and Walker (2001), are designed to provide disadvantaged rural and urban communities with access to ICT, education, support for local enterprise, and government and other information services. The project has had to cope with poor infrastructure, poverty, a lack of education in the targeted communities, and a complete lack of familiarity with information and communications technology.

Locally appointed LearnLink advisors work with various government, nongovernment, and community organizations to ensure that the centers and their services are relevant to community needs, train the CLC staff, develop business plans and affordable fee-for-service systems, and promote and seek community and private-sector involvement.

The voluntary or salaried CLC staff are drawn from the local communities and trained to manage the centers; provide the technical services; create environments conducive to learning; help the communities use the technology, resources, and services; and monitor the use and impact of the centers.

Case Study 7—The Virtual Colombo Plan and African Virtual University

The World Bank and Australian Federal Government's Virtual Colombo Plan (www.ausaid.gov.au) is designed to combat global poverty through a distance education initiative designed to improve education and information access in developing countries.

The World Bank has initially earmarked approximately Aus$1.3 million over five years for this global information and knowledge sharing network. The Australian Government has pledged Aus$200 million to the project. Australia has internationally recognized strengths in distance education, and this project provides a platform for the country's educational providers, researchers, and technology companies to share their knowledge and skills with partners in developing countries and co-develop online degree courses and materials.

The first stage of the Virtual Colombo Plan program will involve teacher education, education system policy development, and development of the distance learning infrastructure. The second stage will provide training for development of country policy-makers. The third stage will provide training and support for staff and students in higher education. The activities also include expanding the World Bank Global Development Learning Network in Asia and the Pacific, providing ICT-based training through 200 virtual scholarships, and using Australian university courses and materials to improve the capacity of the African Virtual University (AVU) (www.au.org).

The AVU was originally conceived as an international ICT-based portal allowing engineering, science, computing, and business students in universities in sub-Saharan Africa to access lectures by overseas professors and an online international library and database. It currently serves students and researchers at 31 partner institutions in 17 countries. Australia's Curtin University of Technology in Perth, RMIT University in Melbourne, and other institutions are now collaborating with African partners in providing online programs.

PLANNING FOR SUSTAINABILITY

There is no guarantee that international distance education will prove profitable or sustainable for every institution or course. Some ventures have failed, some have yet to show a profit, some have relatively small enrollments, and some have yet to reveal how well or badly they are actually doing.

Long-term sustainability in international distance education depends upon sound business planning and achieving the right balance among the three critical issues of access, cost, and quality. This is not easy. Increasing enrollments may require higher student-teacher ratios, heavier teaching loads, and/or reduced contact times—all of which can affect the quality. Constraining costs may adversely affect quality. And assuring quality may require considerable investment in instructional design, technology, and student-teacher interaction.

The jury is still out on the cost benefit of distance and online learning. Mayadas (2001) suggests that online learning can be less expensive than on-campus education, but only by 20% or less. Contrary to what some politicians and institutional managers may believe, Bates (2000) claims that introducing technology is more likely to increase costs, at least in the short term. And Karelis (1999) argues that technology-mediated instruction is more expensive unless enrollments are large and lower-paid teaching assistants are employed—both of which run counter to the aim of providing learners with distance education programs of the same quality as their on-campus equivalents. Moreover, any full cost assessment of international distance education must take into account the token payment or unpaid extramural work by staff and the direct and indirect costs incurred by students. Ignoring or underestimating any of these may result in failure.

CULTURE AND PEDAGOGY

Hanna (2000) suggests that differences in culture and teaching methods may prove to be the greatest barrier in international distance education. Faculty members may argue that their courses have an international focus and include overseas examples, but closer examination may reveal content and methods that are essentially Eurocentric. Course writers and tutors involved in international distance education need to be sensitive to cultural and educational differences, cultural assumptions embedded in their programs, and the imposition of cultural values and practices on those of different persuasions.

Critics of globalized distance education argue that it is incompatible with the concept of cultural diversity. All cultures have their own values, norms, perceptions of reality, and points of intransigence, and all educational systems are founded upon these standards and beliefs about the origins, ownership, and transfer of knowledge. Goldsmith (1993) warns that there is no surer way of destroying a culture than through its education system and that countries with a legacy of colonialism, racism, or fear of hegemony will reject anything they see as paternalistic or culturally imperialistic.

Mason (2003) has found both benefits and difficulties in involving students from different cultures in online learning environments. The benefits are found in the richness of multiple perspectives. The difficulties arise in supporting cross-cultural interaction and preventing certain students from dominating the proceedings—problems that arise particularly when English is the students' second language and/or their schooling has imbued them with a less critical, more deferential, teacher-dependent approach to learning.

Mintzberg (2003) argues that globalization should not blind us to the need to help individuals and groups build on their own cultural traditions and unique strengths. Spronk (1998) recommends that global distance educators should develop the ability to look at the world through two pairs of eyes—their own and another culture's. Matthewson and Thaman (1998) suggest that cross-cultural understanding comes through developing the navigational skills to work through cultural contexts, examine cultural assumptions, and determine appropriate courses of action. Ghanaian writer Afele (2003) argues that all nations, rich and poor, can gain greatly from incorporating the knowledge of other countries and cultures into their thinking and actions and suggests that international learning networks should be conceived as horizontal (localized), vertical (globalized), and bottom-up as well as hub-periphery.

TECHNOLOGY

The challenge in using technology in international distance education is not simply to provide teaching that is as good as in the traditional classroom but to use the instructional tools and methods in ways that achieve *better* or *different* learning outcomes. There is also the digital divide to take into account. Technology that is available, accessible, and affordable in the developed world may not be so in the poorer nations. Even having a private place for study is a privilege not shared by all distance education students in all countries.

COLLABORATION AND CONSORTIA

International distance education consortia are being established on a university-university or university-corporate basis. Such strategic alliances allow institutions to position themselves globally, take advantage of opportunities too great to tackle on their own, spread risk, capitalize on each others' brand names, share new ideas and practices, and avoid regulatory constraints on overseas providers. They also enable international curricula to be developed, students to gain internationally portable credentials, and borderless professional networks to be created.

In the case of public-private partnerships, the universities provide the intellectual capital, courses, teaching expertise, accreditation, and international linkages, while the corporates, who may be publishers, broadcasters, carriers, software producers, and so on, provide the delivery, marketing, and funding. In many countries, it is virtually impossible for private providers to be recognized as award granting institutions. For example, Japan is deeply suspicious of external providers, China limits direct investment by foreign providers, and in many countries, there is a government monopoly of local institutions (Larsen, Martin, & Morris, 2002). By partnering with universities, the corporates can circumvent these hurdles.

Case Study 8—Global University Alliance

The Global University Alliance (GUA) (www.gua.com) is an international company owned by six New Zealand, Australian, United Kingdom, and U.S. universities and the Hong Kong-based systems integrator, NextEd Limited. GUA is not currently an accrediting body. Its courses are available online globally, accredited by institutions in the major English-speaking higher education jurisdictions, and recognized towards degrees from these institutions. Each GUA member and approved university provider has policies and procedures in place to assure quality in system and program design and delivery, student support, communications, and assessment.

GUA markets itself on its capacity to provide students with readily accessible and quality learning experiences through a global ne work of academic expertise, campus resources, interactive technologies, and Education Centers. The Education Centers (currently only operational in Korea and Singapore) provide GUA's points of presence, computer labs, access to the online programs, and meeting rooms for local study groups. They also have student advisors to assist in selecting study pathways, applying for study, and providing academic support.

GUA's technical platform for the teaching and learning environment is developed and maintained by NextEd Limited, which operates on both a fee-for-service basis and as a risk-sharing partner in the enterprise.

Case Study 9—Universitas21 Global

Led by the University of Melbourne in Australia, Universitas21 is a consortium of Australian, New Zealand, United States, Canadian, United Kingdom, Swedish, German, Chinese, and Singaporean universities.

Originally conceived to achieve staff and student exchanges, U21 evolved into Universitas21 Global, a consortium and joint venture with Thomson Learning aimed at entering the e-learning market on a world scale and headquartered in Singapore. In 2003, Global launched its first online course, an MBA. It also plans to offer a Master of Information Systems.

Global sees itself as uniquely positioned to capitalize on its members' international credibility, brand names, and experience in using ICT for teaching and learning. It plans to operate mainly in the Asia–Pacific region and offer courses costing about one third of their on-campus equivalents with fees tailored to the purchasing power of the students' home currencies. Thus for example, it is envisaged that for a U.S. student, the MBA will cost US$19,500; for an Australian student, US$12,500; and for an Indian student, US$9,000.

The original plans were for the respective universities to collaborate in developing and delivering the programs. However,

> Thomson will now be responsible for the course design, development, test assessment, student database management, and translation, and Global will contribute the brand-name, marketing power, quality assurance and multijurisdictional certification.
>
> Fourteen investing universities own 50% of this venture with member equity shares ranging from 2% to 16% and the University of Melbourne providing the largest investment—US$5 million. Thomson owns the other 50%. Despite early optimism about leveraging the reputations, resources, and experience of the partner universities to achieve maximum-shareholder value, the project has been slow to develop, the benefits are as yet difficult to quantify, there has been no income because of delays in creating courses, and there are no projections of income stream over the next few years (Cain & Hewitt, 2004).

Such consortia and alliances may not be that easy or quick to achieve. Duke (2002) observes that while some consortia such as Global University Alliance and UNext Inc. have been able to move fairly briskly into online operation, the fast-track ambitions of others, for example, Universitas21 Global, have been repeatedly frustrated by unsure partnerships. This experience confirms the Commonwealth Secretariat (1985) observations noted at the start of this chapter that the highest risks in internationalizing distance education arise in collaboratively developing courses and programs, establishing credit transfer arrangements, and creating common open learning systems.

Moran and Mugridge (1993) identify three prerequisites for successful collaborative distance education: an ability to accommodate different institutional cultures, practices, and assumptions about curriculum and pedagogy; shared values, personal trust, and institutional champions; and perceptions of mutual benefit. It is shown that for consortia to succeed, there must be agreement on how they are to be led, managed, and marketed; the roles and status of the various members; how their crests and logos are to be used; how the programs and services are to be provided and the degrees awarded; how much start-up funding is required and who is to provide this; and how the profits and other benefits are to be shared.

TOWARDS BORDERLESS VIRTUAL LEARNING: CONCLUSIONS

Reporting on a worldwide survey of virtual learning for the Commonwealth of Learning, Farrell (1999) concluded that there was more rhetoric than reality in what was actually occurring. But in a follow-up study (2001), he finds that the reality is beginning to match the hyperbole and that the majority of universities now recognize that distance education can add value to their operations and are mainstreaming it into their planning and operations. In their global survey of borderless education for the Australian Federal Government, Cunningham et al. (2001) confirm that technology, economics, and global competition are propelling universities into collaborating in delivering programs across international boundaries. However, Farrell (2001) notes that there is still very little international *virtual learning,* in the sense that all of the administration, course delivery, tuition, and learning support are online. He also observes that the programs are predominantly text-based and that there will probably be no increased use of multimedia until broadband and wireless technology become more widely available and affordable.

Distance education represents a major revolution. It provides great opportunities for those institutions that can comprehend the nature and extent of this revolution and see beyond the mere digital transmission of content and a market-driven philosophy to the fuller possibilities of global e-learning. Farrell (2001) observes that the Web is both a means and a metaphor for education across political and socio-economic borders. Afele (2003) reminds us that globalization and global equity are built on the premise of peace and that many of the visions and tensions within and between the world's communities are attributable to the imagined or real gain of financial or other assets at the expense of others. Hence the need for distance education and partnerships to share knowledge and prosperity around the globe.

Various predictions are made for how this might be achieved. Bates (2001) envisages that many universities will internationalize their programs and foresees an increasing number of for-profit universities and university-university and university-industry consortia also operating globally. Dhanarajan (1998) predicts the emergence of a number of pan-global open learning systems, some funded from the public purse and others formed by entrepreneurial agencies. It therefore seems likely that some international distance education programs will be driven by commercial imperatives and user-pays, while others will be open source and free. However achieved, there must be provision for the countless millions currently denied access to the technologies and educational opportunities we take for granted in the developed world, and the focus should be on cooperation, not competition or market dominance.

The world must become more inclusive. New networks and alliances are needed and curricula and pedagogy need to be widened and enriched by capitalizing on the wealth of cultural, ethic, social, and linguistic diversity in the teachers and learners. Those in the wealthy nations need to learn from, as well as help, those in the developing nations. In providing such learning, it is important to ensure that the necessary learner advisory, support, and mentoring services are provided locally and/or virtually, that account is taken of the learners' varying capacities to use and pay for the technology, and that careful heed is given to business planning and quality assurance.

Globalizing distance education can have important consequences, both bad and good. Opening up educational opportunity and widening the choices of study can be positive for progress. Limiting distance education to market-based methods will fail to address the development needs of many communities. The vision must be to develop global citizens without the diminution of indigenous culture. Such a vision demands leadership, organizational envisioning and strategic thinking, course design and delivery that educates, empowers, and respects cultural diversity, and the pursuit of excellence.

REFERENCES

Afele, J. S. C. (2003). *Digital bridges: Developing countries in the knowledge economy.* Hershey, PA: Idea Group Publishing.

Bates, A. W. (2000). *Managing technological change: Strategies for college and university leaders.* San Francisco: Jossey-Bass.

Bates, A. W. (2001). The continuing evolution of ICT capacity: The implications for education. In G. Farrell (Ed.), *The changing faces of virtual education.* Vancouver, BC: The Commonwealth of Learning. Retrieved November 8, 2004, from http://www.col.org/virtuald/index.htm

Blight, D., Davis, D., & Olsen, A. (1999). The internationalization of higher education. In K. Harry (Ed.), *Higher education through open and distance learning* (pp. 15–31). New York: Routledge Falmer.

Cain, J., & Hewitt, J. (2004). *Off course: From public place to marketplace at Melbourne University.* Melbourne: Scribe Publications.

Commonwealth Secretariat. (1985). *Summary report on Commonwealth cooperation in open learning.* London: Author.

Cunningham, S., Ryan, Y., Stedman, L., Tapsall, S., Bagdon, K., Flew, T., & Coaldrake, P. (2000). *The business of borderless education* (Evaluations and Investigations Program, Higher Education Division, Department of Employment, Education, Training and Youth Affairs) Canberra, ACT: Australia Government Publishing Service.

de Wit, H. (Ed.). (1995). *Strategies for internationalisation of higher education: A comparative study of Australia, Canada, Europe and the United States of America.* Amsterdam: European Association of International Education (EAIE).

Dhanarajan, G. (1998, April 20–22). International and inter-institutional collaboration in distance education. In J. M. Barker (Ed.), *Learning together–collaborating in open learning, Proceedings of the International Conference hosted by the John Curtin International Institute* (pp. 1–10). Perth, Australia: Curtin University of Technology.

Duke, C. (2002, Summer). Cyberbole, commerce and internationalisation: Desperate hope and desperate fear. *Journal of Studies in International Education: Special Issue: Models of Change: ICT and the Internationalisation of Higher Education, 6*(2), 93–114.

Farrell, G. (Ed.). (1999). *The development of virtual education: A global perspective.* Vancouver, BC: The Commonwealth of Learning. Retrieved November 8, 2004, from http://www.col.org/virtualed/index.htm

Farrell, G. (Ed.). (2001). *The changing faces of virtual education.* Vancouver, BC: The Commonwealth of Learning. Retrieved November 8, 2004, from http://www.col.org/virtualed/index2.htm

Fullan, M. G. (1993). *Change forces: Probing the depth of educational reform.* London: Falmer.

Goldsmith, E. (1993). *The way: An ecological world view.* Boston, MA: Shambala

Hanley, G. L. (2003). *Enabling educational institutions' success in distance learning: MERLOT's facilitation strategy.* Paper presented at the Networks Without Borders: Towards Cross-cultural Learning Communities International Symposium 2003, National Institute of Multimedia Education, Japan.

Hanna, D. E. & Associates. (2000). *Higher education in an era of digital competition: Choices and challenges,* Madison, WI: Attwood.

Hawkridge, D. (2003). *Models for open and distance learning 2: Globalisation, education and distance education,* Cambridge, UK: International Research Foundation for Open Learning & Vancouver, BC: The Commonwealth of Learning. Retrieved November 8, 2004, from http://www.col.orig/info/2003_MODL_Globalisation.pdf

Karelis, C. (1999, February). Educational technology and cost control: Four models. *Syllabus Magazine,* 20–28.

Kumar, M. S. V. (2003). *Opening up educational possibilities through content, pedagogy and technology.* Paper presented at the Networks Without Borders: Towards Cross-cultural Learning Communities International Symposium 2003, National Institute of Multimedia Education, Japan.

Larsen, K., Martin, J. P., & Morris, R. (2002). *Trade in educational services: Trends and emerging issues* (Working Paper). Paris: OECD.

Latchem, C., & Walker, D. (Eds.). (2001). *Telecentres: Case studies and key issues, Perspectives on distance education series*. Vancouver, BC: The Commonwealth of Learning. Retrieved November 1, 2004, from http://www.col.org/Telecentres

Mason, R. D. (2003). *Online learning communities for global course*. Paper presented at the Networks Without Borders: Towards Cross-Cultural Learning Communities International Symposium 2003, National Institute of Multimedia Education, Japan.

Matthewson, C. & Thaman, K. H. (1998) Designing the Rebbelib: Staff development in a Pacific multicultural environment, in C. Latchem & F. Lockwood (Eds.) *Staff Development in Open and Flexible Learning*, pp. 115-126, London & New York: Routledge Falmer.

Mayadas, F. (2001). Is anyone making money on distance education? *Chronicle of Higher Education*. Retrieved November 8, 2004, from http://chronicle.com/colloquylive/2001/02/distance

Mintzberg, H. (2003, October). *Africa lacks enterprises, not enterprise*. Copyright Project Syndicate. Retrieved November 8, 2004, from http://www.project-syndicate.org/ commentaries/commentary_text

Moran, L., & Mugridge, I. (1993). Trends in inter-institutional collaboration, in L. Moran & I. Mugridge (Eds.), *Collaboration in distance education*. London: Routledge Falmer.

National Board of Employment, Education and Training (NBEET). (1992). *Achieving quality: Report of Higher Education Council*. Canberra: Australian Government Printing Service.

Perraton, H. (1997). *The virtual wandering scholar: Policy issues for international higher education* (Keynote paper, annual HERDSA Conference, Adelaide).

Spronk, B. (1998). Seeing the world through two pairs of eyes: Staff development issues in distance/open learning programs for First Nations peoples in Canada, in C. Latchem & F. Lockwood (Eds.), *Staff development in open and flexible learning* (pp. 127–136). London: Routledge Falmer.

Wetterling, J., & Collis, B. (2003). Sharing and reuse of learning resources across a transnational network. In A. Littlejohn (Ed.), *Reusing online resources: A sustainable approach to e-learning*. London: Kogan Page.

World Bank. (2002). *Constructing knowledge societies: New challenges for tertiary education*. Washington, DC: Author.

PART V

ONLINE EDUCATION IN AFRICA:

An Analysis of Namibia and Sub-Saharan Africa

Ivory
The damnation of the African elephant—
To provide exotic cultures
With piano keys and billiard balls.

—Timothy Wangusa

Africa, the dark continent, a sense of danger, a clear sense of native, indigenous culture, a culture of development. This section of the book deals with only two of many African communities—Namibia and Sub-Saharan Africa. To the Western mind, Africa has been a place of plunder throughout history. Will e-learning turn African minds into ivory?

One of the interesting words that comes up consistently in both chapters is *development*. Shalyefu and Nakakuwa point to Kofi Annan's comments to the United Nations as evidence that information technologies (ITs) are thought of as having particularly strong impact on developing nations. Developing nations have particular needs for learning. Certainly, the need for a growing and increasingly skilled workforce is a thread that runs throughout this book, but it seems to be more of a theme in developing and non-western cultures. In the case of

Sub-Saharan Africa, this need translates into the massification of higher education. This is a level of development that is in fairly stark contrast to western cultures where universities see e-learning as a potential cash cow, but not as a way to grow the university itself. While e-learning has had the unanticipated outgrowth of establishing a number of e-learning friendly administrators within the ranks of western higher education, growing the e-university has not really taken hold in North America or Europe. In some ways, North America is searching for a way to reach a global audience with an already "fat" higher education system. Africa, on the other hand, is searching for ways to make more universities faster than ever before in the history of higher education.

Another word that comes up in these two cases is risk. What is the danger, what is the risk associated with implementation of ICTs in Namibia? Naturally, there is the risk that the culture of indigenous peoples will be eroded. What is the possible exchange? What will Namibia, or any developing nation, have to give up in order to afford e-learning and the massive infrastructure that accompanies the technology? As Mackintosh points out, in nations with significant political instability, there is the danger that regulations may not be tight enough to prevent large expenditures for infrastructure from being siphoned into other initiatives or far more nefarious applications. But perhaps the most obvious and real danger is the risk of widening the gap between the haves and the have nots. There are many ways this might happen, ranging from expensive infrastructures that serve industrial or corporate needs using public monies, to catering to those learners who can pay.

Naturally democracy comes up throughout this book. And it usually is about access. The rhetoric associated with access and democratization of learning through Internet wires may seem particularly questionable in a developing continent such as Africa. At what cost are we building the infrastructure? As Mackintosh points out,

> [Sub-Saharan Africa's] mission to expand tertiary education provision will need to find solutions that will take education to the remote rural regions despite the hopelessly inadequate ICT infrastructure and find innovative ways to roll out quality distance education provision covering the full curriculum, notwithstanding desperately insufficient funds to finance potential solutions. (p. 235, this volume)

So it may be *possible* to create the infrastructure, but will that manage to reach the poorest of the poor in Africa where people are daily starving to death? As many reformers have said, people cannot eat democracy.

In the case of Africa, democracy is not just about access. Democracy is about freedom of expression, peace, and equality far more than equity. The concept of democracy is significantly different in its treatment here than it is in Asia, where democracy in e-learning is almost purely about open access. There is a clear understanding that we cannot import the kind of solutions that are necessary to solve the problems of Africa and other developing nations from industrialized countries. As Mackintosh points out, the West has never faced the sorts of issues that Africa faces in the implementation of e-learning, and we have to understand that the indigenous need for peace and overcoming apartheid is unique to this context. They are the foundations of new democracy in Africa. Georges Nzongola-Ntalaja (2002) points to democracy in Africa as going beyond free elections. He asserts it as a moral imperative:

> For democracy is meaningless without economic and social rights. It means nothing to people who cannot eat properly, have a roof over their heads, find a steady job, send their children to school, and have access to a minimum of decent health care. A more solid foundation for democracy lies in the enjoyment by all long-term residents of a national territory of political, economic, social and cultural rights, including the rights to citizenship itself and a separate cultural identity within that citizenship; property ownership (land, housing); basic human needs in nutrition, shelter, healthcare and *education*; and the freedom to choose and replace their own rulers. Democracy, in other words, is a continuous social process of expanding fundamental human rights. [emphasis mine]

Rather than leading the ICT revolution, Africa hopes to be able to benefit from ICTs in their own countries as part of their development and connection with global economies. Despite Mackintosh's exploration of leading from behind, there is no indication in these cases that Africa hopes to export e-learning to other global neighbors. There is also no indication that Africa anticipates leading other nations in the use of ICTs. Rather, the hope is that Namibia, for example, can utilize ICTs in a country where radio is the most widely accepted technology, to leapfrog and put technologies to use for building up human resources to assist with national development. Mackintosh also recognizes the hope that in Africa, "new technologies provide a vehicle to 'leapfrog' legacy communication infrastructure" (p. 236, this volume).

Namibia understands that ICTs and e-learning must be culturally sensitive and adapted to fit with indigenous values. Perhaps they understand this better than other cultures, since, as Western cultures, we have tended to export e-learning as one-size fits all, and "culturally generic." It is a more humble, yet very African hope. As Shalyefu and Nakakuwa suggest, "When parents are poor, the first thing they think of is how to bring bread to the table, and education will be amongst the last things they could think of." It is too much to think that a culture that so deeply understands this level of poverty and hunger would imagine itself a leader in ICTs or e-learning. We need to understand African implementation and rhetoric within the framework of developing nations. Nevertheless, this disparity runs the risk (danger?) of creating a two-tiered system globally wherein Namibia and other developing nations import their hardware, pay others for expertise and content, and import, with great expense, the infrastructure necessary to deliver e-learning to its people. By the time the national debt of any African nation is finished with paying for these costs, the haves and have-nots may simply translate to global proportions putting developing nations even more in the hole. While we cannot expect Africa to lead, it is perhaps patronizing to expect less. As Mackintosh and Nzongola-Ntalaja and many others point out, it is our moral obligation to do it right this time. Our charge is to implement e-learning in a developing nation such as Africa with culturally sensitive curricula and an infrastructure that reaches the poor rural populations. And perhaps it is most possible to do this properly in this context where there is need—deep, developing, hopeful need. Yet at the moment, Wanqusa might suggest, in the words of our opening poem, that ivory from Africa—the minds of the African people—is used to make piano keys and billiard balls for wealthy nations.

This very issue, who wins and who loses is central to the entire book, and understanding this will probably take different forms of measurement so that we can more deeply understand what "accountable" means in online learning. This is why the text closes with a chapter from Drs. Zemsky and Massy who assert that e-learning is in fact a thwarted innovation. They do an excellent job of explaining why this is the case and then discuss the possibilities of new measurement techniques, which may help us to have a deeper understanding of online learning. In this case, the Weatherstation project which was utilized in the United States is proposed as a possible application for international contexts so that we can have a clear understanding of what is going on throughout the world in online learning.

This chapter was chosen to close the book because it has the most positive potential for international contexts. While many of our authors are hopeful, most of us are asking critical questions, which is, of course, the purpose of this book. However, I felt it was a good opportunity to think deeply about what a possible positive step might be toward caring for the "least of our brethren" through online learning. It is possible that this is too ambitious a demand of Zemsky and Massy, but it is a positive step without devolving into grand narrative.

References

Nzongola-Ntalaja, G. (2002). Democracy assessment and indicators: Introductory remarks at the international IDEA Democracy Assessment Seminar. Oslo, Norway, October 21-22,2002. Downloaded February 1, 2004, from http://216.239.41.104/search?q=cache:heAEC-dfX_MJ:www.undp.org/oslocentre/docsoslo/publications/Democracy%2520assessment%2520and%2520indicators.doc+people+cannot+eat+democracy&hl=en&ie=UTF-8.

⁂ TWELVE ⁂

DEVELOPMENT AND DEMOCRACY IN NAMIBIA:

The Contribution of Information and Communication Technologies (ICTs)

R. Kavena Shalyefu
and Hilda Nakakuwa

Namibia became a nation independent from South Africa only in 1990. It still depends on imports from South Africa, and the legacy of apartheid continues to trouble the country. The prolonged ruling of Namibia by colonial South Africa made it little known outside of Africa. In general, it can be said that the knowledge of South Africa throughout the world has overshadowed that of Namibia. Its current population is 1.8 million, and the cities and towns are sparsely populated. This makes it hard to establish a high-tech corridor. Though Namibia might not be typically associated with information and communication technology (ICT) advances, the country is said to have one of the most modern, progressive, and democratic constitutions in the world. Most, if not all, governments programs can be obtained at the government Web sites. Anybody who has access to the Internet can access information on all government operations through relevant ministries and departments' Web sites. If a person has a concern or contribution to make with regard to government operations, one can do so via e-mail to the relevant ministry, department, or person in such an institution. This access has broken barriers of distance, time, and class.

It is our belief that if Namibia does not respond to new global realities that include embracing promptly ICTs' knowledge, skills and information, there will be a widening gap between it and the rest of the world. Nevertheless, consideration of Namibia as one of the technological innovators in Africa offers some very important insights about the ways the realities align to development and democracy.

This chapter explores the benefits associated with improving the quality of life for all Namibian citizens through the use of ICTs. These inputs are drawn from various resources: studies, policy documents, observations, and the authors' experiences.

The chapter consists of five sections: Section 1 will briefly examine the historical development of ICT infrastructure, Section 2 will examine the benefits of ICTs to development, Section 3 will focus on the role of ICTs in education, Section 4 will discuss the role of ICTs in democracy, and the last section will discuss access to ICTs in Namibia. As you read this chapter, reflect on the following questions:

- Critically reflect on the risks of using ICTs in the developing countries.
- What are the other contributory factors that would promote democratic participation through ICTs?
- What are appropriate measures to minimize the risks of social, political, economic, and cultural exclusion that could be associated with these revolutionary technologies?
- How does ICT lack of access to ICTs relate to power and control, gender, equality, equity, and empowerment in your own context?
- Are the benefits of the diffusion and application of these technologies outweighing the risks for developing countries and Namibia in particular?
- What should be done to improve access to ICTs?

ICT INFRASTRUCTURE

The inequalities of the past were not only discrimination by race, religion, and gender, but also by allocation of resources. The immediate challenge that faced Namibian government after independence was therefore to transform a society divided into "ethnic administrations" and distorted by colonialism and apartheid into a modern, harmonious, and functioning democracy.

Many populous areas of the country were economically underdeveloped and lacked infrastructure. Addressing poverty, sociopolitical advancement, and sustainable development also means promoting access and services to the areas in need.

Since independence, the Namibian government has partnered with foreign agencies to provide funding to develop ICTs in the rural side. The ICT sector has developed rapidly into construction and provision of the needed infrastructure, mostly in the telecommunication service. This includes a wide range of fixed and mobile telephone services. Telecom Namibia is currently the sole supplier of fixed telephone lines in Namibia, and a fiber-optic backbone is installed countrywide. The growth in main lines is particularly striking. Even in rural areas 20 kilometers off the main road, some rural households are connected. One will find telephone booths at least as frequently as every 10 kilometers along roadways, while in the countryside they are found less frequently, only about every 20 kilometers. Extending a telecommunication network requires not only equipment but also investment in skills.

Namibia opted for the Global System for Mobile Communication (GSM) as the standard of the cellular network. Since 1995, when mobile phones were introduced in Namibia, only one company, the Mobile Telecommunication Corporation (MTC), has been issued with a mobile license so far. The wireless service is spreading at a higher rate. Access to mobile phone services, mostly in the northern regions of the country has grown significantly. The users of the wireless phones are people of all ages including some middle-aged working persons, but the majority are young people (even the jobless) between 16 and 40 years of age. These mobile phones are used, among other things, for general communication, business purposes, e-mail, storage of information, daily planning, and so forth.

In 1995, the Internet service was first introduced in Windhoek, the capital, and today, this service is throughout the country, however, with limitations on rural communities. The Internet has become a vital tool if not a basic need for those who have access to it. It provides access to information, to the world, and to the global exchange of knowledge.

Basic ICT infrastructure such as computers, solar energy, Internet services, and telephones are provided to Namibian schools through projects like SchoolNet, iNET, and LearnLink. These projects are funded by international donor agencies like the United States Agency for International Development (USAID). Through these projects, tools and skills are provided to develop computer-assisted training, educational management systems, basic dial-up or wireless connections, and so forth. In addition, unemployed youth are trained in software or computer literacy and the hardware and operating systems to enhance the teams of technicians installing networks in schools is provided. These projects thus provide technology skills training to teachers, students, and the communities.

Although ICTs might cost money, research shows that its application is cost-effective. The findings of a study done by a working group on informatics attest to it in concluding that "although the cost of using ICTs is high, the cost of not doing so is likely to be higher" (Oxford University Press, 1998, p. 1).

ICTS AND DEVELOPMENT

The barrage of information that is largely associated with ICTs constructs a world of glamour, excitement, knowledge, and fulfillment in attempt to appropriate and transform our thoughts and desires, our buying habits, political preferences, and more general ways of life (Gergen, 1999).

ICTs are believed to shrink borders and create many opportunities, such as having access to e-learning, e-medicine, e-agriculture, and e-commerce and ensuring that communities have access to expert opinions at the press of a button (MIB 2003: Information and Communication Policy for the Republic of Namibia).

The free flow of information provided by ICTs has the capacity to empower and motivate people to meaningfully participate in the democratic process to determine their own destinies (The Second National Development Plan (NDP2, 2001/2002–2005/2006). This can support and contribute to effective democratic decision-making and governing, international cooperation, trade and commerce, socioeconomic development, and lifelong learning.

The contribution of ICTs to development is also highlighted by Kofi Annan's remarks to the First Meeting of the United Nations Working Group on Informatics in 1997, when he stated that "communications and information technology have enormous potential, especially for developing countries and in furthering sustainable development" (Mansell & Wehn, 1998, p. 6). ICTs' role in development has become dramatically intensified, although the sources of development and the developers remain candidates for critical inquiry (Gergen, 1999).

According to the UNESCO Medium Term Strategy for 2002–2007 document, ICTs contribute to the "eradication of poverty, especially extreme poverty" (UNESCO, Medium Term Strategy for 2002–2007, p. 207). These contributions determine patterns of learning, cultural expression, and social participation and provide opportunities for development that are more effective to poverty reduction and preservation of peace. This UNESCO Medium Term Strategy for 2002–2007 document further states that ICTs open up new horizons for building inclusive knowledge societies through education, the exchange and sharing of knowledge, and the promotion of creativity and intercultural dialogue. In addition, the document argues that ICTs also bring about new challenges for freedom of expression, which is an essential condition for sustainable development, democracy, and peace. Contrary to these assertions in the UNESCO document are the realities that ICTs can also discourage critical thinking, and promote lack of creativity as people tend to use technology to do all things for them like planning, budgeting, calculating, and so forth. Some people are becoming too lazy to think as all they need can just happen at the press of a button.

ICTs have brought opportunities for working at home. Home-working improves productivity and brings a more flexible attitude to the working environment. This further reduces unnecessary travels and brings advantages to those balancing their professional life, child care requirements, and household chores. Home-working also brings a lot of management issues related to work standards, consistency, confidentiality, performance evaluation, and monitoring.

ICTs make life easier through e-banking. E-transactions have become a daily activity in Namibia through the automatic teller machines (ATMs) that are everywhere in all towns and accessible 24 hours a day, 7 days a week. Also, Internet banking with Namibia from anywhere is a commendable achievement. Unfortunately, e-banking has also made it possible for thieves to encroach into other people's bank accounts.

There are claims and counterclaims about benefits and risks of ICTs. Some authorities say that ICTs bring widespread social and economic benefits, while others say they make "no difference to the people," or worse, ICTs are "even having harmful effects" (Mansell & Wehn, 1998, p. 1).

To provide security, protection, monitoring, and legal liabilities against the harmful effects, the Southern African Development Community (SADC)

Protocol on Transport, Communication and Meteorology established fundamental principles as the framework for policy making for ICTs. Those principles will help build the general knowledge base in a way that maximizes the benefits of ICTs. This framework for action will help to develop strategies that provide leadership in contributing to efficient and transparent use of ICT for both public and private sectors in Namibia. This fundamental principle framework is further supported by a study done by the Working Group on Informatics. The study recommended policy-oriented perspectives on ICTs on promotion of access and construction of ICT infrastructures; capability building and skills training for ICT production, use, and services; and a strategy framework that will help the development of policies and regulation to ensure innovative knowledge societies that support the development goals.

ICTs stimulate people's thinking, help create values and ultimately create a sense of identity that has a possibility of shifting to the "global identity." The dream of Namibia to rebuff the shadow of South Africa, to be known, to be visible, to be documented for all to see, is possible with the presence of ICTs through the Internet, the World Wide Web, television, radio, magazines, and so on.

ICTS AND EDUCATION

The government of Namibia, in partnership with international donor agencies, has expanded ICT services to schools and educational institutions with an objective of strengthening and exploiting ICT benefits.

Many remote, rural schools have unqualified or underqualified teachers. Namibia has a limited number of institutions of higher learning, and many teachers do not have the opportunity to obtain higher qualifications.

Through the old education system, it was less possible for the people—mostly those in rural areas, the poor, and the marginalized—to further their education or upgrade their skills. However, those in the working class—for example, teachers, nurses, and public administrators—opt for distance learning. Most of the communication and interaction with the institutions at which they register use ICTs such as audio cassettes, videos, CD-ROMs, e-mail, and Web-based resources for learner support services and learning materials.

ICTs have become part of teaching and learning in Namibia at all levels, from basic to higher education as well as lifelong learning. Professionals and working adult learners are now utilizing ICTs to either obtain additional qualifications or just to broaden their horizons in terms of information, knowledge, or skill. ICTs are thus providing greater opportunities and flexibilities for professional development.

Teachers upgrade their qualifications via distance education through South African institutions that offer a wide range of courses. Some of these South African institutions, such as Technikon South Africa (TSA), Rands Afrikaans University (RAU), and the University of South Africa (UNISA), have branches and centers in Namibia, where examinations are taken.

Some educational supporting services are offered through the national radio service. These services benefit the individual teachers or learners, the community, and the government and are economical. Where radio waves are not picked up, programs are recorded on cassette and delivered to the areas as needed.

Very little has been done in the area of broadcasting, by either TV or radio, to provide distance education particularly geared to skills or qualifications attainment, although much has been provided in the way of general information or education on basic social issues, HIV/AIDS, and other compelling current events.

In trying to reach out to the remote areas, the government, through the Ministry of Information and Broadcasting and the Directorate of the Audiovisual and Communications Commission, started a project called "Audiovisual Education Network Consolidation." The aim of the project is to collect and provide information and education to and from those remote rural communities and the other marginalized populations that the National Broadcasting Corporation (NBC) cannot reach. This project acquired video cameras and vans with build-in broadcasting facilities. Information on government programs and policies is disseminated to the targeted communities and community concerns are also recorded and presented to relevant authorities for consideration. The equipment is also used in national campaigns by line ministries and nongovernmental organizations (NGOs). The project is to serve as a link between government and the people. In 2003, through this project, the government provided all 13 regions with audiovisual equipment able to record and duplicate audiovisual materials. The equipment is to be used by all government institutions and NGOs dealing with developmental issues.

To add to these services, Web-based learning resources and interactive learning environments are offered by institutions of further education to make it possible for learners to exchange ideas and access information to improve learning and reasoning. Interacting with other people through the Internet prepares people to learn from various cultures and languages. Through the Web, both teachers and learners access different views of the same subject matter. ICT and the Internet can be used in distance education to create repositories of study materials that can be transmitted via TV and radio broadcasting or e-mail. Study materials can also be reproduced on CD-ROMs and videos at low cost. Support, resources, and opportunities for professional development are provided by the Namibian Educational Developmental and Support Network Web site at www.edsnet.na.

The University of Namibia does provide some of its courses through videoconferencing, but only to students at the northern campus in Oshakati. Most distance education students registered with Namibian institutions of higher learning communicate with their tutors via e-mail, mostly for receiving and submitting assignments and projects.

ICTs have made enormous contributions to the improvement of education and to the enhancement of learning. Applications of ICTs will thus create potential benefits and help in alleviation of human resource constraints in the education system.

ICTS AND DEMOCRACY

In order to empower people to participate in decision making in their country, they need to be informed and acquire the necessary knowledge and skills. To help them identify their needs and have the desire to satisfy those needs, there must be a strategy to motivate them. Meaning "access to ICTs is necessary albeit not a sufficient condition for participatory democracy" (MIB, 2001, p. 3). ICTs open new horizons for building inclusive knowledge societies if awareness of the benefits has been created and people have been motivated to acquire knowledge and skills in the use or production of ICTs through education, the exchange and sharing of knowledge, the promotion of creativity and inter-cultural dialogue. For example, prepared, knowledgeable, and highly-skilled people can consciously exercise their rights to make decisions on using ICTs in managing and preserving their environment thereby benefiting their entire nation.

In order to empower the citizens of Namibia, the Parliament built a Web site, www.parliament.gov.na, nicknamed "Parliament Online," as a constitutional obligation to solicit and incorporate public views on legislation. With assistance from the National Democratic Institute for International Affairs (NDI), this initiative aimed at fulfilling the constitutional mandate and taking

Parliament to the people through the Internet. Parliament Online provides direct access to the National Assembly and the National Council, the Constitution of the Republic of Namibia, the Parliament calendar listing schedules and events, legislative proceedings, draft legislation, acts and policy documents, summaries of bills, minutes, public discussion forums, online public opinion polls, reports, and other documents. The system also provides contact information for all members of Parliament, including their regions, party affiliation, biographies, and individual legislative profiles. The system allows the public to engage with their elected representatives through online discussions and submissions.

At the launch of this particular Web site on May 31, 2001, Kandi Nehova, chairperson of the National Council, concluded his remarks with an important caution that "parliamentarians should never take it for granted that all their decisions would enjoy the support and acceptance of the people if the people are not consulted and given the opportunities to participate in the legislative process" (www.parliament.gov.na). With that caution in mind, the government of the Republic of Namibia has created an enabling environment for the public to have direct access to express their views and provide input on legislative matters.

Considering that the Internet may be only accessible to the elite and the haves, the government initiated "phone-ins" to include the very remote, the poor, and the marginalized. Namibia Broadcasting Corporation television and radio, the public broadcasting system, has initiated programs such as the "Open Line," a radio program where anybody can phone in and talk about anything, from politics to fashion. This program can be very educational and informative as well as, sometimes, a nuisance—but that is part of democracy, too. There was another radio program, the "Prime Minister's Questions Time," that is now off the air. Another public program is the television show "Talk of the Nation" that airs every Monday. People feel a sense of empowerment when they hear their own voices over the radio and when they get feedback on issues or concerns raised. The radio phone-in program empowers the presenter to follow up issues with relevant institutions or authorities, and as a result, concerns are addressed properly.

Another initiative in the attempt to get the government closer to the people is the Parliament's "Constituency Outreach." This is a mobile training unit, a bus nicknamed "Democracy on Wheels," loaded with a server, generator, projection equipment, and ten computers. The training unit staff goes around in constituencies to give civic education and train councilors, the civil society regional and constituency representatives, and school staff and learners to access the Parliament Web site.

This opportunity is mostly utilized by the male population. Those who are not utilizing this opportunity need empowerment education.

ACCESS AND ICTS

Some parts of Namibia that are remote and sparsely populated do not have the basic infrastructure for the ICT revolution, such as computers, electricity, telephone lines, and Internet services. Although the telephone lines are growing fast as mentioned previously, there are those who have access to ICTs and those who do not. Lack of access is caused by unequal distribution of wealth, age, and the political legacy of the colonial era.

The majority of Namibians still live below the poverty line, and inequality prevails and will continue for some time in the future. The fact that Namibia is sparsely populated and that communication corporations focus on building infrastructure or offering services in heavily populated areas results in limited access to ICTs for some areas.

The lack of resources that affect access also include money for purchasing radios, TV sets, and computers, the Internet service, and proficient educators for teaching technology skills. Without income, even poor people in populated areas with solid infrastructures are left out. Usually, poverty militates against education and development. When parents are poor, the first thing they think of is how to bring bread to the table; education will be among the last things they could think of. Uneducated people are the poorest, and people normally do not crave for what they have not eaten before. A parent would not bother if his child does not have that kind of food. In short, when parents are poor, education for their children, whether formal, distance, online, or otherwise, follows after many other considerations. First, they must be completely free. To overcome this challenge, there is a need for "good social policies" and multisectoral efforts for long-term benefits.

Not having access makes it hard to communicate, network, pursue education, acquire skills to become employable, apply for a job, work or study at a distance, call for police or medical assistance, or participate in a political process (Hammond, 1997).

The majority of Namibians have access to radio, and they use it for communication and sending messages. However, in the 13 regions of Namibia, there are remote areas where no radio or TV signals are picked up, and communities in those areas are really excluded. Interestingly, 80% of the Namibian population, both urban and rural, listens to the national radio service. Radios are popular because they are affordable and can make information reach everywhere. The other reason for radio popularity is that one can carry the radio to the field, the office, the classroom, or community hall or under the tree. One can conveniently receive or provide informal education through radio almost anywhere at an affordable price. There is so much one can do through radio in Namibia to contribute to the achievement of national development goals, ranging from personal to community development.

Lack of access does not refer only to infrastructures, but also to lack of the skills and knowledge of the value of information. Some people who live close to ICT infrastructure have problems because they do not know the value of information or how to use and apply it. These people in technologically developed areas need thus to be trained how to critically consume and evaluate the information and knowledge available.

Many senior professionals in the Government and private sector are reported to need training in the use and value of ICTs. Since recruitment and human resource development is a managerial responsibility, lack of knowledge about ICTs can lead to lack of commitment and accountability or lack of awareness of the importance of the contribution of ICTs to achieving development goals. "Currently ICT technical staff in the Government is the lowest paid, compared with industry and other professions in Government (MIB, 2001, p. 62). This phenomenon of personnel having no skills in utilizing ICTs and lacking knowledge of the potential benefits of ICTs can significantly contribute to managers' decisions not to even bother putting recruitment or training of ICT staff among the priority areas or activities considering the ever lack of enough financial resources in Government.

The above situation is of concern to the government; in almost every speech, the president of the country expresses his wish for Namibia to advance in science and technology, and he encourages research and human resource development in that regard. The same can also be said of the hopes and aspirations of the legislature in increasing peoples' participation through the use of ICTs.

The report of the Namibian 2001 Population and Housing Census of 346,455 households out of a population of 1,773,235 indicates that the majority of the population has access to basic ICT infrastructure such as telephone, computer, newspaper, and radio by household, as shown in Table 12.1.

Table 12.1 Namibia: Totals of Households by Access to Selected Facilities

Type of facility	Households	Population
TV	126,424	612,913
Radio	276,134	1,450,386
Newspaper daily	62,447	292,247
Newspaper occasionally	157,696	770,686
Telephone	133,722	629,345
Computer	29,091	119,420

Source: Republic of Namibia 2001 Population and Housing Census, p. lxi.

Table 12.2 Namibia: Urban Households by Selected Facilities

Type of facility	Households	Population
TV	90,867	407,501
Radio	115,729	499,525
Newspaper daily	47,271	199,155
Newspaper occasionally	101,420	432,149
Telephone	87,026	373,834
Computer	24,917	98,988

Source: Republic of Namibia 2001 Population and Housing Census, p. lxi.

Tables 12.2 and 12.33 show the households with basic ICT infrastructure broken into urban and rural areas.

In addition to the lack of ICT infrastructure, technology skills, and awareness of the value of information and how to apply it is the lack of equipment maintenance. This not only hampers full utilization of ICTs but also makes it difficult to keep equipment that is acquired. Some institutions are still lagging behind in addressing the ICTs skills and capabilities to contribute to national development.

The factor of lack of maintenance skills has been supported by the findings of the e-Government Baseline Survey on capacity and utilization of ICTs within the Ministry of Regional, Local Government and Housing Sub-National Structures. The survey reported limited capacity to support the existing ICTs (1,341 computers). The report provided the statistics in Table 12.4 as evidence for its argument.

The other exclusion factor is that ICT training is usually found in private institutions that are very expensive. Ordinary people cannot afford the training. The only public institution offering affordable ICT courses is the Namibia

Table 12.3 Namibia: Urban Households by Selected Facilities

Type of facility	Households	Population
TV	35 557	205 412
Radio	160 405	950 861
Newspaper daily	15 176	93 092
Newspaper occasionally	56 276	338 537
Telephone	46 696	255 511
Computer	4 174	20 432

Source of Tables 1-3: Republic of Namibia 2001 Population and Housing Census, p. 1xi

Table 12.4 Computers and Information Technology (IT) Technical Staff in Local Governments

Institution	No. of Computers	No. of IT Technical Staff
13 Regional Councils	116	None
17 Municipalities	1052	38 (36 in Windhoek)
13 Town Councils	143	1
14 Villages Councils	27	None
4 Settlement Areas	3	None

Source: Foster. S.S Mijiga, 2003, p. 25

College of Open Learning (NAMCOL), a parastatal institution that offers alternative education services to those who seek to obtain their high school qualifications. Another concern related to ICT courses offered is a general concentration on computer literacy only. There is no training in fundamentals of hardware, diagnostics, hardware refurbishing, server configuration, local area network (LAN) construction, wiring and basics of networking. This type of training could contribute to the alleviation of the high unemployment rates of Namibia and also promote sustainable development.

People can also be excluded from ICTs benefits because information, knowledge, and learning content are not contextualized. Contextualizing can be done, without forgetting to take globalization into consideration. While contextualization is an important aspect, this should not overshadow Namibia as part and parcel of the global knowledge and information society.

The globalization of ICTs' contents can put cultural resources of the indigenous people at risk with the emergence of the new knowledge that transform into new cultures. There is therefore a need to put in place programs and policies that will contribute to the presentation of resources and indigenous content through ICTs. In addition, there is a need to encourage and promote the creation and dissemination of local content reflecting the local cultures, morals, and values.

The disparity between those who have access to technology and those who do not has been highlighted in the Namibian 2001 Population and Housing Census. There are higher percentage rates of male representation for almost all advanced areas. These areas include literacy attainments, tertiary education, technical training, and employment. This situation needs thorough examination and perhaps action. Lack of access to ICTs and the associated skills promotes inequality and lack of equity as well as lack of inclusiveness. This supports the idea that the poor and women are excluded from the benefits of ICTs.

Perhaps it is not only that Namibia has women that face serious challenges that are sociopolitical, economical, and cultural. Though Namibia has quite a number of women who have broken into the decision-making circles, traditionally only available to males, still control and power to decide includes where, how and when ICTs are used and tends to be limited to males. Also when it comes to the use of ICTs, old perceptions and common stereotypes of women being "scared of technology or mechanical matter" still prevails. Only a few women are brave enough to explore other uses of ICTs apart from such purposes as using computers for wordprocessing and e-mails. Experience from elsewhere has supported that inequalities in both access to ICTs and the distribution of relevant competencies risks the opportunity of widening the gap between the haves and have-nots.

In addition to the earlier mentioned central government mobile ICT initiatives that try to reach even the very remote, the Department of Adult Education in the Ministry of Basic Education, Sport and Culture has also established community learning and development centers in the regions and each center is provided at least with a computer. These are the only centers where even the poorest can have access to the computer. However, the question still remains: If there are only one or two computers at the center, how many people will be able to access them? Another concern is that these are like pilot centers, with the majority of people in the regions still out of reach. The elite and the urban people will continue to benefit for quite some time. To reach and include the disadvantaged and rural poor and the marginalized, an enabling environment needs to be created.

CONSTRAINTS

1. So far no hardware is manufactured or assembled in Namibia. All hardware and software are imported with South Africa being the main supplier. Microsoft software products dominate the market with Novel and UNIX following.

2. The cost of introducing and establishing computer laboratories with Internet connections accessible to the majority is high, even with the "Open Source" access. Monthly expenditure including telephone charges is beyond most communities, schools, and individuals.

3. Lack of qualified ICT professionals to keep up the maintenance of equipment is a problem. In addition, lack of adept teachers severely affects effectiveness in imparting proper ICT knowledge and skills to significantly contribute to the achievement of national development goals.

4. Fiber optics cabling and lack of telephone services affect access to technology in some areas.

RECOMMENDATIONS

1. Research into access and the use of ICTs in Namibia at present is of imperative importance. This will give data on the situation and the needs of the people and can guide on strategies to contribute to the improvement of current teaching and learning processes.

2. Training and the promotion of ICT, enhanced learning, and awareness raising about the importance of ICT literacy at all levels of Namibian institutions and education need to be emphasized.

3. Associated skill with ICT infrastructure and applications should become more available and widely used, in order to utilize, diffuse, and maintain the equipment. Empowering people in ICTs is a crucial prerequisite for harnessing ICTs for education. ICT literacy enhances the pursuit of knowledge by equipping individuals with the skills and capabilities of crucial reception, assessment, and use of the information they access.

4. There must be awareness of the need for accessing and using ICTs in education and other development programs, how much knowledge is currently

possessed, and the gap between what is known and what still needs to be known.

5. The improvement of infrastructures is a necessity for development.

CONCLUSION

Namibia as part of the developing countries is still in its infant stage to becoming a full technological innovator in Africa. The government, the private sectors and international organizations have provided basic infrastructure, but still more needs to be done. Training in technology skills and educating people how to handle the bombardment of information and knowledge presented by ICTs remain a critical issue. Full utilization of ICTs can also be strengthened by equipping technical staff with the necessary skills for maintenance. If not properly utilized, ICTs can invade privacy and reduce employment instead of making people more productive. It is therefore recommended by the UN Commission on Science and Technology for Development that each developing country should establish a national ICT strategy. (Oxford University Press, 1998).

Development and democratic participation needs more than just open access to ICTs. Paradoxically, the question of balance between the cost and the advantages of ICTs will remain unanswered.

However, one wonders if the absence of ICTs (radio, telephone, mobile phone, television, CD/DVD players, computers, the Internet, and the like) in the 20th and 21st centuries can lead a society to collapse and the old communities (family, village, parish) to disappear in the sweeping change of information, knowledge, and the way of learning. Shalyefu & Carr-Chellman (2003) assert this paradox when they state that "even though there are concerns in the use of ICTs, we still cannot disregard it, because its value cannot be denied" (p. 55).

REFERENCES

Foster, S. S. M. (2003). *Capacity and utilization of information and communication technologies within sub-national structures of government.* (E-Government Baseline Survey), Namibia.

Gergen, K. J. (1999). *An invitation to social construction.* London: Sage Publications.

Government of the Republic of Namibia. (2003). *National policy on adult learning* (Draft).

Government of the Republic of Namibia. (2002). *Second National Development Plan (NDP2), 2001/2002–2005/2006. Volume One: Macroeconomic, Sectoral and Cross-Sectoral Policies: 2* (Chapters 24–47). Windhoek, Namibia: National Planning Commission.

Hammond, A. S. (1997). The telecommunications act of 1996: Codifying the digital divide. *Federal Communication Law Journal, 50*(1), 179–214.

Mansell, R., & Wehn, U. (Eds.). (1998). *Knowledge societies: Information technology for sustainable development.* Oxford, UK: Oxford University Press.

Management Board Environmental Steering Committee (MBESC)/National Institute for Educational Development (NIED). (1995). *Policy for information technology in education in Namibia.* Retrieved November 16, 2004, from http://www.eskom.co.za/enviroreport01/MBESC.htm

Ministry of Higher Education, Vocational Training, Science and Technology (MHEVTST). (1998). *Developing a country: Higher education for development in Namibia* (White Paper on Education). Windhoek, Namibia. Retrieved November 10, 2004, from http://www.fire.uni-freiburg.de/iffn/country/na/na_7c.htm

Ministry of Information and Broadcasting (MIB). (2001). *Information and communication policy for the Republic of Namibia, 2001.* Windhoek, Namibia: Author.

Ministry of Information and Broadcasting (MIB). (2003). *Information and communication policy for the Republic of Namibia.* Windhoek, Namibia: Author.

National Planning Commission. (2003, July). *The Republic of Namibia 2001 Population and Housing Census.* Windhoek, Namibia: Author.

Southern African Transport Communications Commission-Technical Unit (SATCC-TU). (1998). *SADC protocol on transport, communications and meteorology.* Retrieved November 10, 2004, from http://www.transport.gov.za/library/docs/misc/sadc.html

Shalyefu, R. K., & Carr-Chellman, A. A. (2003, Spring). Exploring Web-based education in South Africa. *Academic Exchange Quarterly, 7*(1), 53–56.

UNESCO. (2002). *Medium-term strategy for 2002–2007.* Retrieved November 10, 2004, from http://unescodoc.unesco.org/images/0012/001254/125434e.pdf

⁂ THIRTEEN ⁂

CAN YOU LEAD FROM BEHIND?

Critical Reflections on the Rhetoric of E-Learning, Open Distance Learning, and ICTs for Development in Sub-Saharan Africa (SSA)

Wayne Mackintosh

> *You cannot be part of the global village by just sitting and waiting to be 'globalized'... We want to be the globalizers.*
>
> —Massingue, cited in Useem, 1999, p. A52

Africa faces challenges of immense proportion and complexity when moving into technology-mediated learning. Paradoxically, however, the potential of digital information and communication technologies (ICTs) offers unprecedented opportunities to begin confronting the challenges of access, cost, and quality associated with the higher education crisis on the Continent. The aim of this chapter is to explore whether contemporary rhetoric associated with e-learning may provide insights into tackling the higher education crisis in Sub-Saharan Africa (SSA). While rhetoric does not necessarily represent reality, the spaces and contradictions in different rhetorics enable new opportunities to be perceived.

The opening citation encapsulates the spirit of the African Renaissance. The significance of a new economy that is global and informational (Castells, 1996) is recognized and there is an appreciation that this new social order offers opportunities to participate in a meaningful way on a global scale. In the world of sociological discourse, Africa's aspiration to play a part in this technologically enabled economy is plausible. Giddens (1990), for example, describes globalization as "the intensification of worldwide social relations which link distant localities in such a way that local happenings are shaped by the events occurring many miles away and *vice versa*" [my emphasis]. Clearly the dialectical nature of globalization suggests that events and innovations in Africa could arguably have an impact on happenings elsewhere. This raises the interesting question whether because of a conjunction between conditions in Africa and convergences in technology, SSA could potentially lead innovations that have a global impact in the sphere of technology-enhanced distance education. The following questions provide a framework for thinking about such a possibility:

- In what ways will the global-local relationship influence the evolution of e-learning in SSA and your own country?
- What are the foundational similarities and differences between the higher education challenges in SSA and your own country?
- What can we learn from the challenges facing higher education in SSA concerning the opportunities and risks associated with the survival of the traditional university in the light of the pervasive advances of online learning?
- What is the significance of the distance education experience with regard to the future of e-learning?
- What possibility is there for SSA to develop strategies to "lead from behind" by applying the techniques of conceptual modeling?

This chapter posits that the magnitude and complexity of the imperative to radically expand higher education provision in SSA are unique. This challenge is amplified when the absence of universal access to basic ICT infrastructure is taken into account. However, crisis is a powerful catalyst for innovation.

Analyzing successful corporate innovators, Hargadon and Sutton (2000) have found that successful innovators very often take good ideas in one area and successfully move, adapt and apply these ideas in other areas where they are not commonplace. This is well aligned with Drucker's (1995) strategic thinking on conceptual modeling:

It is commonly believed that innovations create changes—but very few do. Successful innovations exploit changes that have already happened. They exploit the time lag—in science, often twenty-five or thirty years—between the change itself and its perception and acceptance. (1995, p. 40).

Perhaps ICTs present changes that can be exploited in response to the higher education crisis in SSA. In turn, Africa's unique context could conceivably give rise to innovations regarding the future of e-learning that are unlikely to evolve within highly industrialized countries.

Contemporary advances in technology have triggered a global trend where conventional campus-based institutions increasingly utilize flexible and distance methods of delivery—often referred to as the convergence of distance and conventional education (see, for example, Tait, 1999, p. 141). Similarly there are multiple emerging discourses associated with the notions of e-learning, open access, and distance education. Critical reflections on nuances within these discourses and their associated "rhetorics" may provide valuable insights into the future, because, very often, discourses construct our perceptions and rhetoric inspires much of our practice.

This chapter begins with a brief summary of the higher education crisis in SSA. International rhetoric associated with, first, e-learning; second, open distance learning; and third, ICTs for development follows. This analysis draws on the global-local relationship as an aspect of the concept of globalization. Finally, the implications of the "rhetorics" in these three areas for the future of higher education in SSA and whether Africa can "lead from behind" are considered.

A SUMMARY OF THE HIGHER EDUCATION CRISIS IN SSA

The future of e-learning in SSA represents a unique context, comprised of the interaction among a number of factors that are not replicated in the same mix or proportions elsewhere in the industrial world. The following points are indicative:

- The gross enrollment ratio for tertiary education in SSA is below 3% for many countries and is the lowest average participation rate when compared to other regions of the world (Saint, 1999)—for instance, many of the highly industrialized countries report ratios in excess of 90%.

- The majority of Africa's population resides in remote rural areas where basic services and infrastructure are virtually nonexistent (UNESCO, 1999).
- While Africa has a long history of distance education provision, the Continent has only one mega distance teaching university (see Daniel, 1999). Furthermore, most of Africa's distance education initiatives have focused on training for teachers as opposed to offering a comprehensive curriculum at a distance.
- Distance education provision in Africa relies heavily on older technologies and is predominantly text-based.
- The majority of university students in Africa are required to study through the medium of a second, third, or fourth language.
- As an economic region, SSA has one of the lowest per capita incomes in the world.

The magnitude of the education crisis in SSA is disturbing. UNESCO (2001) claims that a "massive effort is required in SSA, which will have to increase its 1990s pace of enrollment by between 2 and 3 times in order to achieve universal primary education by 2015." Saint (1999, p. 2), using demographic population projections, points out that many of the countries in Africa will need to *double* current enrollments in the tertiary sector within the next decade simply to *maintain* the existing gross enrollment ratio. It is simply not possible for Africa, for example, to double the number of universities within the next decade let alone bring the gross enrollment ratio up to the current average for developing societies.

Daniel (1999a) points out that it will be necessary to create a sizable new university every week simply to sustain current higher education participation rates in the developing world when taking population growth into account. This is why Daniel and Mackintosh (2003) conclude that "harnessing the forces of the global knowledge economy to ensure that all people of the world get a decent education is the greatest moral challenge of our age" (2003: 812).

Figures quantifying access to telecommunications infrastructure in SSA show a similarly bleak picture. For example, approximately 42% of the inhabitants in the industrialized countries have a mainline telephone connection compared with the 4.5% average for developing countries and a disturbing 1.4% for SSA (UNESCO, 1999). The extent of the digital divide in Africa is well illustrated by the fact that "New York has more Internet hosts than the rest of Africa and Manhattan has more telephone lines than the rest of Sub-Saharan Africa" (Mbeki, 1999). Although indicators like these do not take into account how single telephone lines are creatively shared within communities in less developed countries, it is not surprising that many advisers recommend older technologies that do not rely on access to telecommunications infrastructure for expanding higher education access.

Clearly Africa will need to find innovative solutions to expand access to tertiary education. It is unlikely that countries in SSA will have adequate funds to expand access using the conventional campus-based model. Therefore, the Continent will need to explore the potential of technology-mediated education notwithstanding the challenges associated with overcoming the infrastructure problems. With this in mind, the next section of the chapter will explore the growing international rhetoric associated with technology-mediated learning.

THE RHETORIC OF TECHNOLOGY-MEDIATED LEARNING

In this section, the international rhetoric associated with technology-mediated learning will be analyzed for clues concerning how Africa might begin to tackle its educational crisis. Rhetoric in three areas is considered: technological change and the university, open distance learning, and ICTs for development.

The Rhetoric of e-Learning and Corresponding Changes to the University as Institution

The essence of the e-learning rhetoric suggests that the implementation of digital ICTs in education will change the university in fundamental ways. Universities in SSA are largely based on the traditional universities of the West. After all, this model has contributed to the economic prosperity of industrialized nations, and it seems reasonable that this model should be replicated for SSA. However, if e-learning is about to change the university in fundamental ways—as expressed in some of the e-learning rhetoric—should SSA continue to expand access to tertiary education based on the traditional idea of the university?

For some time, a few management strategists have speculated about the potential shortcomings of the classical university in the digital age. For example, Peter Drucker (1997)—icon of strategic management—has suggested that "thirty years from now the big university campuses will be relics.

Universities won't survive." SSA would need large universities to expand access. What is to replace this institution in SSA if the university model does not survive? While these assertions may be disconcerting for some, John Chambers, CEO of Cisco Systems, sees great opportunities. He claims that "the next big killer application for the Internet is going to be education. Education over the Internet is going to be so big it is going to make e-mail usage look like a rounding error" (Chambers, cited by Irvine, 2001). How will SSA participate in education over the Internet in the absence of universal ICT infrastructure?

Although such rhetoric has gained cliché status, there is a need to reflect on whether fundamental change is upon us. In addition, SSA should reflect on the meaning of the contemporary university for its own context. If the ethos and tradition of the university is something that is worth preserving, we should consider how these traditional values could be conserved and perhaps reconfigured for the rapidly accelerating e-world.

The imperative driving change in the university as institution involves considerably more than the question of how technology can facilitate or augment existing models of delivery. Digital ICTs and how they have been "deployed by business, government, and other institutions have yielded significant, and sometimes fundamental, changes to the way work and society operates" (Evans & Nation, 2003, p. 785). There is a strong reciprocal relationship between society and the university. Thus fundamental change in the university could be the consequence of broader societal trends but also involves the question of how the university itself contributes to ongoing changes in society through its teaching and research.

Contemporary advances in digital ICTs are important for the university because they have the potential "to change the ways in which we can impart skills and knowledge" (Dhanarajan, 2000, p. 13)—more than previous universal communication technologies. Tony Bates (1997) contends that "the widespread introduction of technology-based teaching will require such fundamental changes to an institution that its use should not be embarked upon lightly." Daniel (1999b), for example, suggests that "the knowledge media are such a quantitative advance, such a quantum leap, that they represent a qualitative change ... Complacency is not in order. This is going to change universities" (p. 13).

There are claims that epistemological shifts are taking place—supported and fuelled by ubiquitous and instantaneous access to global knowledge—from traditional "scientific" knowledge production by the university as custodian of this process (Mode 1) to a distributed knowledge production system motivated by application to real world problems, typically involving a wide range of knowledge workers in industry (Mode 2). In this regard, Gibbons (1998) suggests that universities

> have been far more adept at producing knowledge than at drawing creatively (re-configuring) knowledge that is being produced in the distributed knowledge production system. It remains an open question at this time whether they can make the necessary institutional adjustments to become as competent in the latter as they have been in the former. (p. i)

Gibbons (1998) also cautions universities that their "existing structures are too inflexible to accommodate emerging modes of knowledge production or the demands that a greater variety of 'students' will make" (p. ii). Thus the forces underpinning change in the traditional functions and methods of the university are not simply the result of ICT-enabled opportunities of delivery anywhere and anytime. They also correspond with deep-seated epistemological shifts combined with changes in the socio-institutional roles associated with the responsibilities for knowledge generation in society. It is a complex relationship because digital ICTs facilitate distributed knowledge production systems on a global scale, but at the same time enable universal access to the knowledge that is produced. Therefore, it will become increasingly difficult for the university as institution to claim sole custodianship of knowledge or its production.

What then is the meaning for the continued existence of the university in a world that is changing amid the pervasive advances of digital technology? What do these changes mean for the higher education crisis in SSA?

In answering these questions, we should consider the societal value of the university. Some commentators suggest that a managerial and business-like strategy will ensure its survival. McNay (1995) argues that if "the entrepreneurial academy can do better than its ivory-towered predecessor . . . the university may well continue its long historical record of adaptive genius which has allowed it to outlive most institutions" (p. 114). The rationale is that if the university is able to offer something of value at the "right" price then it should continue to exist. While this is a compelling argument, universities are complex organs of society and ensuring their future would understandably involve more than the mere dynamics of supply and demand.

Universities represent one of society's most important social spaces for fostering open debate and transparency (Klein, 2000) and these values should be protected. Unfortunately, the validation for technology-induced change in the university sector is, very often, a camouflage for the commercialization of higher education. As Noble (1998) predicts:

> Quality higher education will not disappear entirely, but it will soon become the exclusive preserve of the privileged, available to children of the rich and powerful. For the rest of us a dismal new era of higher education has dawned. In ten years, we will look upon the wired remains of our once great democratic higher education system and wonder how we let it happen. (p. 12)

In their seminal essay, *Universities in the Digital Age,* Brown and Duguid (1995) observe that universities offer something of value that is difficult to measure, yet it contributes to the continued success of the institution. They refer to the exchange value that society places on a university degree. The university, as a community of scholars, is able to validate the learning experience and provide a credential that is respected by society. While universities are frequently criticized for curricula that are too far removed from the market place and that its students lack relevant experience, Brown and Duguid remind us of the social value of the credential:

> Those who have the label but not the experience present one problem. But those who have the experience but not the label face another. Experience without a formal representation has very limited exchange value—as those whose only degree is from the university of life well know. (p. 10)

Deserving particular mention is the fact that the exchange value of a university degree has more to do with the validation that a community of scholars can provide than it has to do with the modes of delivery. Consequently, the exchange value of a university degree offered by distance should not differ from a degree obtained through a conventional university assuming that a community of scholars conducts the validation of the learning experience. This is evidenced, for example, by the achievements of the British Open University—a single-mode distance education institution—which is ranked within the top 10% of universities in the United Kingdom by the independent state-run system of quality assessment (Daniel, 2001, p. 6). This suggests that the mode of delivery is not the primary determinant of the quality of a university credential if it is supported by respected scholars, robust course design, and student support.

Drawing on the discussion above, universities are likely to experience increasing pressure for fundamental change given the advances in digital communication technologies in a global knowledge society. For the majority of people, a university education in SSA is still the preserve of a very small elite group, especially when considering the distressingly low participation rates for higher education in SSA. Paradoxically, the expansion of "off-shore" provision on the Continent could result in the university system becoming even more elitist for the majority of Africans. Assuming that the university is a valuable organ of society for promoting indigenous development, Africa will have to widen access to university education at an exponential rate of growth in ways that succeed in maintaining the core values of the university as institution.

It would appear that SSA should avoid e-learning strategies that are based on the commercialization of knowledge given the risks associated with higher education becoming more elitist. As the mode of delivery is not the primary determinant of the value of a university credential, there are opportunities for SSA to focus on how ICTs can be used creatively to extend access to an African community of scholars. In many remote, rural areas access to this community of scholars is constrained. However, it is possible to develop an African virtual network of scholars to assist with the credentializing of the learning experience for remote students. There are also opportunities to leverage the assistance of the larger academic community associated with the African diaspora.

In conclusion, the rhetoric of e-learning with regard to the prospects of fundamental change in higher education is certainly plausible. However, how the university will sustain its core values when facing the onslaught of electronic forms of delivery is an entirely different matter. For SSA, this challenge is particularly acute, as the Continent cannot afford any regressions back to an elitist higher education system as inferred by Noble (1997) above. What is clear is the obligation for the university sector in SSA to play an active role in the determination of its own future; otherwise the leaders of the international business sector may assume this "responsibility" on their behalf.

The Rhetoric of Distance Learning and Open Access

There is an emerging rhetoric associated with distance learning and open access that corresponds with the growing deployment of digital ICTs in the delivery of higher education at traditional campus-based institutions. In particular, asynchronous forms of online learning are heralded as the geneses of a new democracy in higher education. Certainly digital ICTs have enhanced the capacity of traditional universities to widen access by providing education anywhere and anytime. However, many conventional universities that have embraced the new technologies for distance delivery, have often done so "without the benefit of the expertise and understanding that decades of research, theory and practice in distance education could provide" (Evans & Nation, 2003, p. 785).

In spite of the newness of the rhetoric, distance education is not a new phenomenon. The institutionalized practice of deploying technology to mediate the teaching-learning transaction over time and space can be traced back to the turn of the 20th century. There are references to correspondence study as early as the 1720s (see, for example, Holmberg, 1989). It is also interesting to note—not unlike the current corporate interest in e-education—that the first examples of institutionalized distance education were commercial providers (Peters, 1998, p. 110). These organizations were created for the commodification of knowledge and were prepared to use new methods and technologies previously frowned upon by the traditional state-funded education providers. The early institutionalized practice of correspondence education was not primarily concerned with the democratic ideals of widening access. The point being that the democratization of education through technology is unlikely unless underpinned by a philosophy aimed at promoting these ideals.

It was not until the early 1960s that the democratic ideals of open access began to influence the mainstream state-funded practice of distance education. This is not surprising, given the student unrest of the 1960s, particularly in Europe where questions of equitable access to higher education began to receive greater priority for decision-making among politicians of the time. The most notable distance education example was the inception of the British Open University in 1969. The foundation of the British Open University was a political decision aimed at increasing access to higher education for working adults in Britain. Walter Perry, the founding vice-chancellor of the British Open University, attests to the vision of openness in his inaugural ceremony referring to the institution as being "open as to people, open as to places, open as to methods and finally open as to ideas" (cited by Daniel, 1995, p. 400).

At this time, there was also a growing educational focus on the relationship between openness and technology-mediated learning systems. Deserving particular mention is the work of Charles Wedemeyer and the Articulated Instructional Media (AIM) project conducted during the late 1960s at the University of Wisconsin (see Moore & Kearsley, 1996, pp. 25–27). Wedemeyer's interest in education was driven by the humanistic ideals of promoting the fundamental right of learning for every adult. Wedemeyer recognized that it would not be possible to expand access to education to large numbers of adults unless the acts of teaching and learning could be separated in time and space. Hence the AIM project focused on the pedagogical and systemic implications of connecting (i.e., articulating) teaching and learning through a variety of communication media. Wedemeyer's work was "not a whimsical curiosity into the use of technology in education" (Daniel & Mackintosh, 2003, p. 816), rather it was driven by the ideal of promoting the fundamental right of learning. Wedemeyer was closely involved in the early planning phase of the British Open University, and there are strong relationships between his work and the philosophy of open learning.

The concept of open learning has developed into a philosophy of education that strives to promote open access to learning as well as the development of student autonomy (Lewis, 1997). There is a close relationship between distance education and open learning because distance methods can facilitate increased access and autonomy. Open learning, however, is not necessarily synonymous with distance education or e-learning. It can refer to a philosophy underpinning all forms of educational practice.

Open access, on the other hand, is the conceptual foundation of large-scale distance education systems. The large-scale, single-mode distance education providers were conceived with the prime purpose of widening access by applying an operational model based on economies of scale. While most definitions of distance education are based on the separation of teaching and learning in terms of time and space ("anywhere-anytime"), they do not necessarily consider the emergence of distance education in relation to the broader societal trend of the industrial revolution.

The large-scale, single-mode distance education systems were purposefully designed for mass education. By applying the principles of mass standardization, rationalization, and division of labor, these systems are able to provide mass education to large numbers of students in a cost-effective way. It can be argued that this form of distance education was a consequence of the industrialization of society but at the same time was simultaneously enabled by the industrial technologies of the time, namely print and universal postal services. On the basis of extensive pedagogical and sociological analysis, Peters (1989) concludes that distance education "is the most industrialized form of teaching and learning" (p. 7).

Drawing on this international history of open distance learning, SSA will need to consider two issues:

- The future of technology-mediated learning is more likely to succeed if it is underpinned by a philosophy of promoting the fundamental right of every adult to have reasonable access to a tertiary education;
- On the assumption that the knowledge society constitutes a new societal trend, then SSA will need to think critically about whether ICTs should be used to replicate previous models of provision that have worked in the West or whether Africa will be required to build a new model of tertiary education provision.

Clearly, these are not easy questions to answer, but they demonstrate the value of reflective analysis of the "rhetorics" for thinking strategically about higher education provision in SSA.

The Rhetoric of ICTs for Development in Distance Education

The discussion of ICTs, development, and distance education is perplexing because of two conflicting rhetorics.

The first dominant rhetoric concerns the problem of the lack of universal access to ICT infrastructure. It suggests that distance education strategy and corresponding democratizations of education should prioritize older and more accessible technologies like print.

The opposing rhetoric argues that it is not possible to tackle the education crisis in Africa without the smart implementation of digital technologies, notwithstanding the disconcerting access statistics. In fact, many argue that a legacy technology focus would widen the digital divide between developed and developing societies.

The ICTs for development discussion—insofar as educational provision for SSA is concerned—cannot be divorced from discussion on the impact of globalization. The emergence of a global informational economy combined with innovations in digital ICTs will not leave Africa untouched. The seductive allure of the opportunities associated with generating income for universities in the West through borderless education—supposedly assisting with the development agenda—is tempered by the tangible risks of widening the digital and educational divide in Africa.

Decreased funding for higher education, combined with the inability of governments to regulate foreign higher education provision because, for instance, of political instability, poses significant threats for higher education provision in SSA. Among policy makers, there is a growing "concern that the decreasing state funding for higher education will decrease even further and that students will be targeted by private and often expensive providers which will further favor the rich and further disadvantage the poor" (UNESCO, 2003, p. 7). Moreover, questions relating to the cultural relevance of foreign content and the inherent threat of the digital "diploma mills" are matters of grave concern for the Continent. Consequently, Africa must deal with a difficult paradox. Technology-mediated delivery can expand the capacity of the higher education system while simultaneously expensive offshore provision enabled through virtual delivery could further disenfranchise the poor.

The risks associated with ICTs for development in Africa are huge and "[t]hose who do not have some mechanisms to monitor and understand the internationalization of knowledge are likely to be left out of important spheres of discovery, and they may find themselves less competitive in ways that have major economic and political consequences" (Green & Hayward, 1997, p. 17).

With regard to ICT, enabled futures in education, SSA will need to manage a difficult strategic balance. On the one hand, creative solutions for providing reasonable access to ICT infrastructure must be found. Yet at the same time, there is a dangerous feedback loop where the constraints of existing practice (for instance, the absence of basic ICT infrastructure) and immediate operational needs (for instance, the need for rapid expansion of higher education delivery) dictate the formulation of strategy at the expense of opportunities for sustainable innovation in the sector. In many instances, this feedback loop can be observed when technology is applied in ways that effectively replicate the past. A prime example is when digital ICTs are used to relay conventional classroom lectures to remote locations. While this may widen access in terms of geographical location of students, essentially the technologies are being used to replicate existing pedagogy.

An alternative approach would be to innovate knowledge strategies and systems based on a vision or "conceptual image" of the future, but capable of carrying current operational priorities. This concerns the question of whether it is possible to lead from behind.

PERSPECTIVES ON LEADING FROM BEHIND IN THE EMERGING E-LEARNING WORLD

Africa's ideals to lead from behind in the field of technology-mediated learning, when viewed historically, are arguably more than wishful thinking. Consider for example that the foundation of large-scale, single-mode distance education provision at university level was pioneered by Africa. In 1946, the University of South Africa (UNISA) began offering all its qualifications by distance and is the oldest single-mode distance teaching university. Peters (1998) recognizes that UNISA is an important prototype because

> nowhere else was it possible to let correspondence studies mature over the years into an accepted method of university teaching. Nowhere else was it possible for distance-teaching pedagogical routine to be developed so early from a university-based pedagogical experiment. (p. 158)

SSA's mission to expand tertiary education provision will need to find solutions that will take education to the remote rural regions despite the hopelessly inadequate ICT infrastructure and find innovative ways to roll out quality distance education provision covering the full curriculum, notwithstanding desperately insufficient funds to finance potential solutions. It is unlikely that industrialized nations will be able to find sustainable solutions for the Continent simply because they are not faced with the same challenges. For example, how do you provide access to digital learning resources in remote rural regions where telecommunications infrastructure is nonexistent?

There are two compelling enablers that could conceivably facilitate the idea of "leading from behind" in SSA:

- advances in digital ICTs now enable education systems to do things that were not possible before, and
- the emergence of a "new" networked pedagogy that spans across traditional organizational arrangements.

With regard to advances in digital ICTs, it is important to recognize that the cost of communication has decreased by a factor of 10,000 since 1975, while the power of computing measured against cost has also increased by a factor of 10,000 (Bond, 1997). Few technologies in the history of social evolution have demonstrated this magnitude of change over such a relatively short period of time.

Arguably, the most significant feature of digital ICTs relevant to developments in SSA concerns the convergence of technology. This refers to the convergence among telecommunications, computing, and what we are learning from the cognitive sciences and contemporary brain research.

Convergence demonstrates powerful advances. First, different modes of communication, for example, voice, video and data can be carried over the same carrier technology without requiring a dedicated carrier technology for each separate mode of communication. Second, the distribution of digital resources is independent of the specific carrier technology. This means that the same digital resources can be distributed using a variety of technologies, for instance optic fiber, satellite data broadcast, copper wire, and CD-ROM via conventional postal delivery, thus increasing the range of potential solutions for SSA in different local contexts. Finally, the convergence of technology means that audio, static and dynamic images, video, and text can be delivered using a single delivery platform like a Web browser.

The strategic advantage for developing societies is that multimode, multimedia learning resources can be distributed to remote locations without fixed-line infrastructure. In many instances, these contexts do not have to deal with problems associated with overcoming the legacy of existing infrastructure that is outdated, largely because it does not exist. For example, in South Africa, the number of cell phone subscribers recently exceeded the number of fixed-line subscribers (see Nash, 2000, p. 11) suggesting that new technologies provide a vehicle to "leapfrog" legacy communication infrastructure, particularly where rollout requires new infrastructure instead of replacing old networks. Building on the design experience of asynchronous distance education, it is now possible to provide access to broadband learning resources in remote rural regions. For example, using a spoke-and-hub model, asynchronous digital content can be broadcast via satellite to a number of hubs. Last-mile delivery could utilize wireless or more humble forms of distributing content on CD-ROM. With a generator and data projector, alternatively a multipurpose community center equipped with appropriate computer technologies could bring high-quality learning resources to remote regions. Fontaine (2000) has argued that digital ICTs could deliver a higher quality of teaching and support and suggests that the "improvement may even be more pronounced in poor, isolated schools in developing countries, where infrastructure challenges might suggest otherwise" (p. 14). A holistic strategy would be required where education, government services (like e-health), and local business work together to promote shared use of the infrastructure.

The second enabler concerns the emergence of a "new" pedagogy now possible because of the advances in digital ICTs. Reflecting back on the analysis of the evolution of education, Peters (1989, 1994) concluded that distance education is a consequence of the industrialization of society. He has also demonstrated that distance education is structurally different from face-to-face teaching. Similarly, Peters contends that the global knowledge society—as a distinct phase in the evolution of society—will result in a new pedagogy that is structurally different from that which preceded it. In the absence of an extensive research base on the distinctive elements of a new pedagogy, it is premature to accept these claims as definitive. However, Peters has begun analyzing these differences and suggests that the university of the future will be "an institution that looks completely different to a traditional university" (2002, p. 167). He suggests that a new pedagogy is plausible and that its delivery may result in new organizational arrangements that capitalize on the advantages of a distributed but connected society. The implicit assertion is that it may not be necessary or feasible for Africa to replicate the conventional campus-based or mega-university model to widen access in a sustainable way. New organizational arrangements will be required that foster the values associated with a university education. A tapestry of societal networks building on the capabilities and potential of digital ICTs to deliver this new pedagogy would need to be established.

In conclusion, I argue that it is conceivable for Africa to innovate new pedagogical modalities as a result of the uniqueness of its current educational challenges. Business strategists point out that strategy innovation is conceptual and requires the ability to see patterns from which future paths can be determined (Hamel, 2000, p. 17). This is not a superficial process relying on historical data to forecast future planning but is more akin to deep conceptual modeling. In many respects, critical reflection on the rhetorics of e-learning, open distance learning, and ICTs for development may provide a framework to begin developing strategy for the future of e-learning in Africa. Moreover, encouraged by the catalyst of a material educational crisis, SSA may choose to use conceptual modeling as a tool to generate sustainable futures. In the words of Prahalad (1998), "The future belongs to the imaginative, those that have the courage to overcome the discontinuities and reshape their firms to meet the challenges of the New Economy" (p. 23).

REFERENCES

Bates, A. W. (1997, June 18–20). *Restructuring the university for technological change.* The Carnegie Foundation for the Advancement of Teaching: What kind of Teaching; What Kind of University? London, England. Retrieved January 2003, from http://bates.cstudies.ubc.ca/carnegie/carnegie.html

Bond, J. (1997, July). The drivers of the information revolution—cost, computing power and convergence. *Public policy for the private sector.* The World Bank Group. Retrieved November 11, 2004, from http://www.worldbank.org/html/fpd/lelecoms/it.pdf

Brown, J. S., & Duguid, P. (1995). *Universities in the digital age.* [Work in progress.] Retrieved February 5, 2002, from http://www.parc.xerox.com/ops/members/brown/papers/university.htm

Castells, M. (1996). The rise of the network society. In M. Castells, *The information age: Economy, society and culture, Vol. I.* Oxford: Blackwell.

Chambers, J. (1999). *Comdex keynote address.* Cited by M. Irvine, 2001. Net knowledge: The coming revolution in higher education. Retrieved January 22, 2002, from http://www.georgetown.edu/faculty/irvinem/articles/netknowledge.html

Daniel, J. S. (1995). What has the Open University achieved in 25 years? In D. Sewart (Ed.), *One world many voices: Quality in open and distance learning* (Vol. 1; pp. 400–403). ICDE and The Open University: Milton Keynes.

Daniel, J. S. (1999a). *Mega-universities and knowledge media. Technology strategies for higher education* (rev. ed.). London: Kogan Page.

Daniel, J. S. (1999b, November 10). *Distance learning and academic values.* Teaching and learning with technology conference, Indianapolis. Retrieved June 21, 2001, from http://www.open.ac.uk/vcs-speeches/edin-admin.htm

Daniel, J. S. (2001, January 30). *Life in the eternal triangle: Access, quality and cost.* Presentation at the annual meeting of the National Association of Independent Colleges and Universities, Washington, DC. Retrieved June 26, 2001, from http://www.open.ac.uk/vcs-speeches/edin-admin.htm

Daniel, J. S., & Mackintosh, W. G. (2003). Leading ODL futures in the eternal triangle: The mega-university response to the greatest moral challenge of our age. In M. G. Moore & W. G. Anderson (Eds.), *Handbook of distance education.* Mahwah, NJ: Erlbaum.

Dhanarajan, G. (2000). Technologies. A window for transforming higher education. *Techknowlogia, 2*(1), 11–13. Retrieved April 18, 2001, from www.techknowlogia.org

Drucker, P. F. (1995). *Managing in a time of great change.* New York: Truman Talley Books/Plume.

Drucker, P. F. (1997, March 10). *Forbes.* [Untitled].

Evans, T., & Nation, D. (2003). Globalization and the reinvention of distance education. In M. G. Moore & W. G. Anderson (Eds.), *Handbook of distance education.* Mahwah, NJ: Erlbaum.

Fontaine, M. (2000). Supporting teachers with technology: Don't do today's jobs with yesterday's tools. *Technologia*, 2(6), 14–16. Retrieved May 8, 2001, from www.technowlogia.org

Gibbons, M. (1998). *Higher education relevance in the 21st century*. Paper presented at the UNESCO World Conference on Higher Education, Paris, October 5–9, 1998. Retrieved January 16, 2003, from http://www.worldbank.org/education/tertiary/publications.asp

Giddens, A. (1990). *The consequences of modernity*. Stanford: Stanford University Press.

Green, M. F. & Hayward, F. M. (1997). Forces for change. In, M. F. Green (Ed.), *Transforming higher education: Views from leaders around the world*. Phoenix: American Council on Education and Oryx Press.

Hamel, G. (2000). Conceptual thinking. *Executive Excellence*, 17(4), 17–18.

Hargadon, A., & Sutton, R. (2000). Building an innovation factory. *Harvard Business Review*, 78(3), 157–167.

Holmberg, B. (1989). *Theory and practice of distance education* (2nd ed.). London: Routledge.

Klein, N. (2000). *No logo: Taking aim at the brand bullies*. London: Flamingo Press.

Lewis, R. (1997). Open learning in higher education. *Open Learning*, 12(3), 3–13.

Mbeki, T. (1999, November 9). The global information infrastructure—What is at stake for the developing world? Address to the Worldbank Infodev Symposium. Retrieved April 17, 2004 from http://www.anc.org.za/ancdocs/history/mbeki/1999/tm1109a.html

McNay, I. (1995). From the collegial academy to corporate enterprise: The changing cultures of universities. In T. Schuller (Ed.), *The changing university?* Buckingham: The Society for Research into Higher Education and Open University Press.

Moore, M. G., & Kearsley, G. (1996). *Distance education. A systems view*. Belmont: Wadsworth.

Nash, P. (2000). *Unisa's vision for the future. Information and computer technology implications*. Unpublished consultant report. Unisa: Pretoria.

Noble, D. F. (1998). Digital diploma mills: The automation of higher education. *First Monday* 3(1). Retrieved February 10, 2003, from http://firstmonday.org/issue3_1/noble/index.html

Peters, O. (1989). The iceberg has not melted: Further reflections on the concept of industrialisation and distance teaching. *Open learning*, 4(3), 3–8.

Peters, O. (1994). *Otto Peters on distance education. The industrialisation of teaching and learning* (D. Keegan, Trans.). London: Routledge.

Peters, O. (1998). *Learning and teaching in distance education. Analyses and interpretations from an international perspective*. London: Kogan Page.

Peters, O. (2002). *Distance education in transitition new trends and challenges* (2nd ed.). Oldenburg: Carl von Ossietsky University of Oldenburg, Centre for Distance Education.

Prahalad, C. K. (1998). Managing discontinuities: The emerging challenges. *Research Technology Management, 41*(3), 14–23.

Tait, A. (1994). The end of innocence: critical approaches to open and distance learning. *Open Learning, 9*(3), 221–238.

Tait, A. (1999). The convergence of distance and conventional education. Some implications for policy. In A. Tait & R. Mills (Eds.), *The convergence of distance and conventional education.* New York: Routledge.

UNESCO. (1999). *World communication and information report, 1999–2000.* Paris: UNESCO.

UNESCO. (2001, October 26). *32 countries risk failing education pledge* (Press Release, Paris). Retrieved February 5, 2004, from http://www.unesco.org/education/efa/global_co/policy_group/paris_No_26_10_2001.shtml

Useem, A. (1999, April 2). Wiring African universities proves a formidable challenge. *The Chronicle of Higher Education,* p. A51–A53.

FOURTEEN

STALLED:

E-Learning as Thwarted Innovation

Robert Zemsky and William F. Massy

Given our interest in e-learning as a global phenomenon, we were struck by what we had come to see as a truly dangerous irony: The sense of disappointment now pervading the market for e-learning is as misplaced today as the euphoria that once celebrated e-learning as an invincible revolution. The fact of the matter is that e-learning is alive and well. Money is being spent, smart classrooms are being built everywhere, and collegiate faculty and corporate trainers are successfully integrating electronically mediated learning into literally thousands of courses focusing on both traditional and nontraditional subjects. That said, it is also the case that e-learning is evolving in ways few predicted and with economic consequences that even its most ardent supporters are still struggling to understand.

There is a larger lesson in the uncertainty, even confusion, that surrounds the market for e-learning today: namely, if educational institutions are to be serious about e-learning and its market, they require a data collection strategy and set of measuring instruments that can track not so much current usage and sales as the dynamic rhythms of e-learning's competing adoption cycles. That, at least, was the premise with which we conceived of the Weatherstation Project—a joint undertaking of the University of Pennsylvania, one of the United States' major research universities, and the Thomson Corporation, a leading supplier worldwide of e-learning and traditional print materials to the education market. The project's measuring and tracking strategies are reflected in its name. Given the absence of standard institutional data reflecting e-learning usage or supplier-provided data on e-learning sales, the Weatherstation Project established observation posts (the metaphorical weatherstations in the project's title) on six college campuses in the United States consisting of faculty and administrator panels that reported quarterly on their attitudes toward, expectations of, and uses of e-learning.

As you think about the trends the Weatherstation Project and its ability to document e-learning's uncertain future, you might ask yourself the following questions:

- Would parallel studies of the market for e-learning in other countries likely document similar or different trends?
- What other measurement strategies might prove fruitful?
- Is it fair to say that e-learning is generally stalled—if not, where is the market for e-learning now thriving, and what lessons might those successes teach e-learning's early adopters elsewhere?
- Is a robust market capable of supporting a wide variety of e-learning ventures a fair test of its potential now and into the future?

THE CAMPUS PROTOCOL

The Weatherstation data collection process began with an interview, either in person or via the telephone, that explained the nature of the project and asked panel members a set of standardized questions about their own use of e-learning, their sense of e-learning's likely rate of growth and its principal benefits, the forms of support it was receiving on campus, the products and services actually being used, and any new developments or hot prospects they had spotted. Each quarter thereafter, respondents were sent follow-up e-mails, which included a customized URL, asking them to check previous answers and tell us, via the Web site, how their attitudes and experiences had changed.

What the measurement strategy embedded in our use of campus weatherstations resembled most was that used by the Nielsen Ratings to track TV viewing through a sample of households. In the Weatherstation Project, the sample of institutions reflected both the experimental nature of the project—just six campus weatherstations—and our desire to have as broad a mix of institutions as possible. All six institutions participating in the project had reputations for having well-developed strategies for deploying learning technologies and chief information officers on whom we could rely to help us recruit and motivate survey respondents. Thus we knew in advance that our sample of institutions was biased. We also understood that the respondents in our faculty and administrator panels would themselves most likely be among e-learning's early adopters.

In one important respect, our sample of institutions was representative of the larger population of degree-granting institutions of postsecondary education in the United States. Among the six were a community college, a public comprehensive university, a public land grant university, a major public research university, a private liberal arts college, and a major private research university.

TRACKING E-LEARNING ON THE WEB

There was a second element to the Weatherstation Project that involved tracking e-learning on the Web. On a weekly basis, we "Googled," that is, we used Google's advanced search features to input "e-learning" plus a specific product category—for example, "education" or "business and investing" or "humanities." For each category, for each week, the probe produced a total number of "pages" that then became an entry in the Weatherstation database. On a weekly basis, that database made two calculations for each category—the category's share of the total number of pages for that week, and the week-to-week change in the category's number of pages.

From the data produced by the campus weatherstations, we could deduce a strategic story of changing attitudes and expectations being shaped, on the one hand, by the budget chill creeping across higher education and, on the other, by e-learning's failure to promote a fundamental pedagogical change in the classroom. The data from the Google tracker largely reflected more of the same for the corporate market—not currents or directions, but rather ripples in a pond that was being drained by an economic recession centered in manufacturing and technology.

We also used the Web to track the course objects—e-learning's most creative building blocks—posted to MERLOT (an acronym that stands for Multimedia Educational Resource for Learning and Online Teaching). What

MERLOT has become is a readily available, low-cost, Web-based service to which individual experimenters could post their learning objects and from which interested practitioners could download objects to use in their courses. MERLOT itself is a marvel of careful documentation and reliable programming—features that allowed us to ask a series of critical questions: Who were MERLOT's members? Which fields of study were best represented? Which disciplinary communities? How fast was MERLOT both growing and changing?

Problematic Assumptions

The most productive way to mine the rich mix of data supplied by the six campus weatherstations plus our Google and MERLOT probes is to explore why the three basic assumptions that defined e-learning's initial promise have proved to be particularly problematic.

Assumption 1: If we build it, they will come.

As with most innovations, e-learning's advocates and first adopters simply assumed, "If we build it, they will come." Almost all of e-learning's first applications began as individual experiments whose interesting results led e-learning's champions to believe that they would attract the attention of other experimenters and eventually the interest of the practice community. Not surprisingly, then, most descriptions of both the spread and the potential of e-learning derive either from catalogs of interesting experiments or from collections of successful applications.

It was MERLOT augmented by the results of our campus weatherstations that helped us make sense of e-learning's initial appeal. From June 2001 through January 2003, MERLOT's registered members nearly tripled, growing from just over 4,500 to just over 11,600. Faculty members were the largest group, growing from more than 2,700 to more than 8,000.

However impressive that rate of growth, the fact remains that MERLOT's registered faculty users numbered less than 10,000 meant that MERLOT's total market share amounted to less than 1% of collegiate faculty in the United States. Like our own weatherstation panels, MERLOT primarily tapped the opinions and interests of e-learning's innovators and early adopters.

Tracking MERLOT helps to document the degree to which the most complex of e-learning's adoption cycles—the one focusing on learning objects—has yet to take off. In general, the learning objects posted to MERLOT are not becoming more sophisticated, and, while the number of MERLOT's visitors and members continues to grow, collectively they represent only a small portion of e-learning's potential adopters. Users continue to share what they have produced themselves without exhibiting much interest in rating or evaluating what others are offering. There is no feedback loop, no evident connection between the suppliers and consumers of learning objects. Indeed, if one follows MERLOT's postings as we did, one comes away with the feeling that there really are no e-learning consumers at all—only innovators and inventors eager to showcase what they have accomplished.

Assumption 2: The kids will take to e-learning like ducks to water.

Two years ago, most faculty or staff members within a university community would have been nearly unanimous in their assessment of whether students would be able to utilize computer-based learning as part of a course either on the Internet or in a classroom using an electronic course management system or learning objects. Indeed, they would be incredulous that you would even question it. When Weatherstation interviewers posed this question in the fall of 2001, they were regularly told: "Not a problem—the kids take to e-learning like ducks take to water. After all, they love games and technology, are dismissive of professors who seem to have trouble navigating Blackboard and WebCT, and think that PowerPoint is state of the art."

When asked, however, how comfortable students would be if, for a particular course or program, e-learning were substituted for in-class instruction, the members of our Weatherstation campus panels were less sure. Eighteen months ago, just over half of the administrative staff surveyed—for the most part administrators with responsibility for supporting faculty in their role as teachers—said students would have little or no trouble if e-learning were substituted for in-class instruction. One-third of the group said students would have some, but not a great deal of trouble; only 15% said most students would likely have a lot of trouble. A year later the distribution of opinion among administrative staff in the Weatherstation panels was roughly the same: 46% said there would be no problem; 41% said most students would have some but not a lot of trouble substituting e-learning for in-class instruction; and 11% said most students would have difficulty.

The similarity of the two distributions, however, obscures the fact that one of every four administrators in the panels changed their opinion over the course of a single year—with 15% saying they now believed students would have more trouble, and another 10% saying that students would actually have less trouble. What is important to note here is the volatility of the responses. Among administrators, only the questions about e-learning's market position and institutional priority generated a greater degree of change over the course of a year.

Faculty responses generally mirrored those of their administrative colleagues, though in more muted tones. When first asked if they thought most students would have trouble substituting e-learning for in-class instruction, the faculty members who were part of the campus Weatherstation panel broke nearly into thirds: 37% said students would have little or no trouble; 32% said most students would have some, but not a lot of trouble; and 31% said most students could have a lot of trouble with the substitution. As with their administrative colleagues, faculty opinion on this issue was noticeably volatile. How many faculty changed their mind over the course of the year? The answer is nearly one in five, although again the overall distribution of opinions remained roughly the same.

What was being questioned was that early assumption that students would see in the computer a tool for problem solving and hence would see in e-learning a new, exciting way of mastering course material. To be sure, there are some students just like that, though, for the most part, they are concentrated in engineering schools. The most successful e-learning experiment was Studio Physics developed by Jack Wilson, then at the Rensselaer Polytechnic Institute (RPI). Studio Physics is **(or was ??)** taught wholly on the computer in specially designed "studios" where students work in two-person teams on upwards of 25 computers. Faculty circulate throughout the studio, providing help and instruction as needed, as each student pair works through a complex set of problems and computer simulations designed to teach the basics of introductory physics.

The program worked at RPI because the curriculum itself was problem-based, because simple graphics could be used to simulate physical properties and rates of change, and because the students themselves saw Studio Physics as an example of the kind of system they had come to this engineering school to learn to develop. Yet, this set of characteristics is hard to match for other curricula. It is also important to point out that Studio Physics remained a group activity. The students came to class, and they worked directly with their partners and the faculty assigned to the Studio. No one was isolated—no one was off in a room by him- or herself with just a computer and a set of e-learning exercises.

The importance of an actual, physically intact learning community can be demonstrated in another way. Three of the universities participating in the Weatherstation Project had launched extensive programs of distributive instruction that used Web-based e-learning modules as the principal means of instruction. By intention and design, they were to be programs of outreach capable of enrolling part-time adult learners who were distant from campus. What each of these universities discovered, however, was that more than 80% of those enrolling in the e-learning courses were full-time students living on campus. Some apparently took these e-learning courses because they were interested in or curious about computer-based instruction. Most students, however, enrolled in these e-learning courses because they were "convenient." Because they were on campus, the e-learning experience was neither remote nor detached, but simply there.

Assumption 3: E-learning will force a change in how we teach.

One of the more hopeful assumptions guiding the push for e-learning was the belief that the use of electronic technologies would force a change in how university students are taught. Only bureaucratic processes have proven to be more immutable to fundamental change than the basic production function of higher education. Most faculty today teach as they were taught—that is, they stand in the front of a classroom providing lectures intended to supply the basic knowledge students need. Those who envision a changed, more responsive learning environment have argued that the most effective instructor is not the "sage on the stage," but rather the "guide on the side." Learning, they have argued, works best when it is participatory. Students can become effective problem-solvers only when they have mastered the art of critical thinking and have acquired the discipline necessary to be self-paced learners. Constant assessment and feedback are critical so that both student and instructor can determine, before it is too late, whether the student is mastering the necessary material.

E-learning seemed more than ready to satisfy each of these goals. As Studio Physics at RPI demonstrated, within fully integrated e-learning courses, faculty are in fact guides—and designers and mentors and conveners. They are not presenters, unless they happen to have filmed themselves performing an experiment or conducting a simulation and then made those images available on their students' computers. The student pairs represented exactly the kind of interactive learning groups that educational reformers envisioned. The feedback was immediate and continuous. Students knew if they had the right answer or were at least proceeding in the right direction as soon as they submitted answers to the problem sets on which they were working. What the designers of Studio Physics also learned is that there could be no hidden assumptions—no relying on one's intuition or past experience to know when and how to introduce new topics. For the first time, many of the faculty involved in Studio Physics had to spell out their teaching strategy as well as think through what kinds of learning strategies their students were likely to bring into the Studio.

Alas, Studio Physics is the exception, not the rule. For the most part, faculty who make e-learning a part of their teaching do so by having the electronics simplify tasks, not by fundamentally changing how the subject is taught. Lecture notes are readily translated into PowerPoint presentations. Course management tools like Blackboard and WebCT are used to distribute course materials, grades, and assignments—but the course materials are simply scanned bulk packs, and the assignments neither look nor feel different. Even when the textbook comes with an interactive CD-ROM or when the publisher makes the same material available on a proprietary Web site, most faculty do not assign those materials. Only modest breakthroughs have occurred—in the use of e-mail to communicate rapidly and directly with students and in the adoption of computerized testing materials, many of which provide a more robust, but still static, means of evaluation.

A number of people are coming to believe that the rapid introduction of course management tools has actually reduced e-learning's impact on the way most faculty teach. Blackboard and WebCT make it almost too easy for faculty to transfer their standard teaching materials to the Web. While Blackboard's promotional materials talk about enabling faculty to use a host of new applications, what the software promises upfront is less dramatic: the ability for them "to manage their own Internet-based file space on a central system and to collect, share, discover and manage important materials from articles and research papers to presentations and multimedia files." All faculty really need are the rudimentary electronic library skills that most have already mastered. Blackboard and WebCT allow the faculty users to respond, when asked, "Are you involved in e-learning?" by saying, "Yes, my courses are already online!"

The rapid introduction of PowerPoint as e-learning's principal course enhancement tells much the same story. PowerPoint is essentially clipart e-learning—in the sense that it allows the instructor to import graphics and graphs from other mediums, including the instructor's old lecture notes. Illustrated lectures do not constitute electronically mediated learning any more than courses that use Blackboard or WebCT to distribute learning materials without introducing learning objects.

Even the most adventurous and committed faculty members often approach the use of e-learning in ways that lessen its general impact on the curriculum. On each of the campuses participating in the Weatherstation Project, faculty were initially recruited to experiment with e-learning, supported by dedicated technical support, summer salaries, and the ability to make their e-learning course on any subject of interest to them. With this level of support, most of the courses were well designed, technically sophisticated, and, given the faculty members' freedom to teach what they wanted, idiosyncratic. Once the course had been offered for two or three years, the faculty member often moved on to other topics and different experiments, having satisfied his or her own interests and curiosity. Then their courses died—simply because no one wanted to teach someone else's e-learning syllabus. What these universities began to discover is that they constantly had to make extra incentives available to faculty in order to involve them in e-learning. When the expenditures of those funds became too great, the institutions dropped the incentive programs and witnessed a general flattening of e-learning adoptions and experiments. All but forgotten, by then, was the idea that e-learning might lead to a more general reformation of both teaching and learning styles.

An International Perspective

This volume builds on the hope and anticipation that e-learning will lead to the development of international networks linking both scholars and learners. On the scholarly side, many of those networks now exist, leading to lively exchanges, shared research, and cooperative investigations. On the e-learning side, however, the big news at any moment concerns what is about to happen rather than what has actually been accomplished.

What is better understood now is that most e-learning takes place within national borders and contexts, reinforcing the fact that place remains of paramount importance. Little is actually known in one country about the e-learning capacities of other nations unless those products are advertised on the Web in English. Over the last two years, Professor Motohisa Kaneko of Tokyo University and his colleagues, principally Naoki Ottawa of Todai and Fujie Yuan at the National Institute of Multimedia Education (NIME), have employed probes to analyze Japanese e-learning Web sites that are similar to those used by the Weatherstation Project. Two conclusions are evident. First, Japanese Web-based e-learning is in its infancy, and the products remain both limited in variety and rudimentary in style and design. At the same time, the Japanese Web probes make clear that what has market appeal in Japan can be of little interest to the American market. For example, one of the largest product categories among the Japanese Web sites is language instruction and acquisition—a subject that is simply not present on U.S. e-learning Web sites. When e-learning products begin to penetrate the market, they usually do so by appealing to immediate, often very local, needs. Eventually, no doubt, there can be a merging of interests and products. In the beginning, however, it is differentiation and specialization along lines defined by national cultures and local proclivities that matter most.

There are two important exceptions to this generalization. The first involves tests and examinations that students must take if they seek admission to an American or international university, principally the SAT and TOEFL. Prometric **(explain what it is?)** and its Japanese affiliate R-Prometric do have internationally configured networks spawned by the need to ensure the fair and efficient administration of these exams. But Prometric—and similar electronic-based testing organizations—serve rather than link their customers. To the extent that there is a network, it is of providers rather than learners.

The second exception is the development of a variety of high-cost, high-prestige programs of business education, usually leading to the MBA, involving some of the western world's best known universities and business schools. Initially, the most visible as well as the first to launch a well-conceived and well-financed set of products designed to serve a worldwide market for business education was Cardean University, a joint venture of five major business schools—Stanford, Columbia, Carnegie Mellon, Chicago, and the London School of Economics—and UNext, a major Internet education company. The problem was that the web-based products, despite the prestige and visibility of Cardean's sponsors, never attracted the volume of students required to be a successful business enterprise.

More recently, Universitas 21 has sought to make a web-based, but nonetheless top-end, business education available to students in developing countries, offering MBAs at roughly 20% of the price of the in-residence programs that the sponsoring universities offer. A different set of institutions—for the most part either present or former British Commonwealth universities—forged a joint venture with the Thomson Corporation, the single largest economic enterprise with major investments in programs of e-learning. Launched in August 2003, it is too early to tell if Universitas 21's educational offerings will attract students in sufficient numbers to sustain the enterprise.

The promise of an international community of learners accessing a common set of educational products and thus becoming a true network without borders is not less appealing—but fulfilling that promise remains a somewhat distant goal.

What's the Answer?

Why then, did the boom go bust? E-learning, particularly in the United States, attracted a host of skilled entrepreneurs and innovators who sought, as their most immediate goal, to establish early prominence in an industry that had yet to be defined. They sought to achieve market position quickly, lest others get there sooner and close the door behind them. In seeking that advantage, they were aided by two phenomena particular to postsecondary education and to the times. First, the boom in commercial investments in e-learning enterprises followed more than a decade of experimentation by faculty with the use of computers in teaching. A few experiments even flowered into commercially successful products such as Maple and Mathematica, applications designed to teach students calculus using electronically mediated instruction.

The dot-com boom provided a second major impetus. It spawned rosy estimates of the market for Internet-based services. Assured by the technology's advocates that the necessary expertise was in hand or soon would be, entrepreneurs both inside and outside traditional postsecondary education rushed to market with e-learning ventures. A veritable feeding frenzy ensued, with large amounts of time, effort, and capital committed to e-learning development and marketing.

In retrospect, the rush to e-learning produced more capacity than any rational analysis would have said was needed. In a fundamental way, the boom-bust cycle in e-learning stemmed from an attempt to compress the process of innovation itself. The entrepreneurs' enthusiasm produced too many new ventures pushing too many untested products—products that, in their initial form, turned out not to deliver as much value as promised. Some successes were recorded and certain market segments appear to remain robust and growing, particularly the transactional segment dominated by course management systems like Blackboard and WebCT and more recently receptive to computerized testing routines like those developed by Prometric. But overall, the experience with e-learning has been disappointing.

There were many aftereffects to e-learning's inevitable crash, though perhaps the most dangerous was that the experience jaundiced the academy's view concerning the actual value of technologies promising electronically mediated instruction and the market's willingness to accept new learning modalities. The hard fact is that e-learning took off before people really knew how to use it—before anything like a dominant design was even on the horizon. Missing, in the first instance, was a proven knowledge base of sufficient breadth to persuade faculty that adaptation was necessary. As a result, e-learning entrepreneurs assumed a much higher level of risk than they bargained for—and not surprisingly, most ended up paying the price.

Necessary Conditions

We believe now is the time for e-learning to get real—in a dual sense. Those who promote, fund, and ultimately depend on e-learning need to talk less and succeed more. And those early adopters need to understand that their success depends as much on the context in which they operate as on the power of the technologies they employ.

The first set of necessary conditions involve changes within the academy itself. The future of e-learning—particularly for full-time, residential students—is now and for the foreseeable future linked to the pace of educational change and reform. The full potential of e-learning and electronically mediated instruction will not be realized unless there is an acknowledgment, on the part of a large number of faculty, that there is need to substantially improve educational quality, especially for undergraduates. What is required is a commitment to organized quality processes that transcend curricular innovation, stress technology as an important tool for improvement, and do not assume things are going well, absent evidence to the contrary.

- *A methodology for calculating costs and efficiencies.* Once a significant number of institutions, including a fair share of market leaders, have determined they need to improve the quality of their educational programs and that e-learning can serve as a means to that end, these institutions will find themselves addressing questions of costs and efficiencies. What adopting institutions will require is a methodology that allows the calculation of the economic contributions as well as the costs of on-campus e-learning—and how those contributions and costs compare to those of more traditional forms of on-campus instruction.

- *Less rigid trade-offs between costs and quality.* With the necessary educational incentives and costs analyses in place, the final step in this on-campus process will be for institutions to better understand—and hence be able to articulate and make a central feature of their strategies and plans—how e-learning can allow for a less rigid set of trade-offs between costs and quality. It requires a fundamental change in a mind-set which heretofore assumed that education's production functions are largely fixed—that is, a change to one part requires corresponding changes to all other parts, because the relationship between inputs and outputs is fixed. In the final analysis, what the widespread adoption of e-learning requires is a broad willingness on the part of adopting institutions to search for more flexible combinations of inputs: people, facilities, and technology.

- *A technological focus on what students really want.* At the same time, it is important for e-learning designers to resolve questions regarding what students expect from e-learning, as an extension of their interest in other technologies. Here, we require ways to motivate students to learn how to use the technologies and to bring human interaction into the equation in optimal ways.

- *More market successes.* More specifically, e-learning needs a substantial number of showcase ventures that generate revenue growth sufficient to sustain continuing innovation without continuous infusions of capital. In this arena, nothing will succeed like success.

- *A real market for learning objects.* At the same time, there needs to develop a robust and growing "market" for e-learning objects. Economies of scale in e-learning depend critically on the ready importation of learning objects. Finding, acquiring, and using such objects in courses needs to become an accepted element of faculty effort.

We believe electronically mediated instruction will become a standard, perhaps even dominant, mode of instruction. But we also understand that progress over the next decade is likely to be slow, probably best described as plodding. The technology's skeptics, emboldened by the fact that, to date, e-learning's failures have been much more prominent than its limited successes, will challenge each new product and innovation. Ultimately, however, the lure of anywhere-anytime learning will prove irresistible—educationally as well as financially.

BUILDING AN INTERNATIONAL WEATHERSTATION

The challenge at hand involves the acceleration of e-learning's adoption. Three practical steps are required before e-learning and electronically mediated instruction can achieve its full potential.

- *Develop a catalog of lessons learned.* First and foremost, the industry needs a catalog of lessons learned.

- *Map the obstacles still to be overcome.* Second, we will need a more realistic mapping of the obstacles that must be overcome—in terms of the technology itself; in terms of assuring that universities in particular become platforms of adoption as well as sources of innovation and invention; and in terms of achieving the market conditions necessary for growth.

- Move ahead in developing dominant designs and global networks. Finally, e-learning in all four of its innovation cycles requires a set of realistic strategies for developing the dominant designs and the global networks that will make it possible for e-learning to come of age—and to signal its broad adoption.

We want to suggest one final strategy to promote change, particularly on an international scale. We launched the Weatherstation Project believing that what was required for the American market was a healthy dose of reality. The dominant measurement strategies then being employed to estimate market demand for e-learning and e-learning products were leading respected institutions and corporations to project and then invest in what they believed would shortly become a multibillion dollar market. For the most part, what passed for measurement involved collecting evidence from early successes—principally, the stories innovators like to tell one another and anybody else who will listen.

It is crucial that those who pursue e-learning's international potential do not repeat this mistake. What is required, from the outset, is a measurement strategy that establishes and then consistently tracks changes to an accepted baseline. What worked for the Weatherstation Project in the United States ought to work for those interested in tracking the emerging international market for e-learning. There needs to be an international network of listening posts that can regularly and consistently sample both faculty and staff attitudes and practices—asking roughly the same set of questions we used to track faculty and administrative responses in the Weatherstation Project. The key to such a strategy lies in identifying both a sponsoring agency and a funding source capable of organizing and supporting a dozen or more listening posts in 25 or more countries. At the same time—and requiring considerably less in terms of resources and personnel—there needs to be one or more organizations charged with building and then executing the kind of Web probes that provided a useful set of complementary data to that supplied by the Weatherstation's outposts. Here, perhaps a coalition of organizations might be appropriate—linking, for example, MERLOT in the United States, Japan's National Institute of Multimedia Education (NIME), and ARIADNE in Europe.

Despite the travails of the last several years, e-learning has retained a core of true believers who argue, still forcefully and occasionally persuasively, that a revolution is at hand—that the computer will do for learning today what printing did for scholarship in the 15th century. Don't be fooled by the failures and false steps, they proclaim. The best is yet to come.

More quiet, and also more numerous, are the pragmatists who point out that e-learning is alive and has in fact spurred a host of important educational changes, probably best symbolized by the widespread adoption of course management tools such as BlackBoard and WebCT. Money is being spent.

Smart classrooms are being built both on campuses and businesses. Collegiate faculty and corporate trainers are successfully integrating electronically delivered learning materials into literally thousands of courses focusing on both traditional and non-traditional subjects. What these pragmatists have come to understand is that e-learning is evolving in ways that few had predicted.

We count ourselves among the pragmatists. We believe the story of e-learning is still unfolding—no one really knows what tomorrow will bring, although we suspect that computer-based learning technologies will continue to serve as a major catalyst for innovation. The underlying information technologies on which e-learning depends are themselves too ubiquitous, and the people attracted to having them serve as learning platforms too smart, for us not to take seriously the prospect that major changes will flow from their efforts.

CONCLUSIONS

Alison A. Carr-Chellman

Consider the following (admittedly ethnocentric) events . . .

- The U.S. Department of Education, in September 1999, set aside $10 million in grants for teams of colleges, universities, companies, and nonprofit organizations to develop *products* that will help adults gain access to distance-learning opportunities. (Ganley, 1999).

- The National Association of State Universities and Land-Grant Colleges released a survey report, *Connecting with the Future,* that indicates that millions of dollars (approximately 5% of total budgets) are spent annually by state universities to add and upgrade computers. The average student at state universities now pays $83 per year for technology fees, with students at SUNY Buffalo paying the highest fees at $400 per year.

- A Penn State student, writing about his experiences with online learning at Penn State's World Campus wrote, "I took the [online] course last semester and it was very easy. I took the class for all the same reasons that almost every other student takes the class—because I can finish it in six weeks and receive an A for putting forth little effort. Here is why I think the class is not good for learning and why we need to stop and think before we incorporate more of these classes into school." (Panczk, 1999)

- A recent report from the *Chronicle of Higher Education* indicates that Harvard's Extension School is carefully considering its future. The previously correspondence-oriented program is rapidly moving to online venues, but its dropout rate when entire degree programs are considered is a very high 98.5%.

- The Commission on the Future of State and Land Grant Universities released a report indicating that all universities need to strive to create a "learning society" in which education would be "universally accessible and lifelong learning would be promoted. . . . Information technology, particularly distance education makes such universal access possible." (McCollum, 1999)

These events, admittedly anecdotal and restricted to the United States are indicative of events occurring daily all over the world. The global economy has made education a commodity to be sold via advertising to anyone with the funds to buy it (Noble, 2002). It is a premise based on possession of a liberal education in exchange for the purchasers money that has nothing to do with democratizing higher education. Open access has not proved out over the course of all of the cases presented in this series paper. In China, the online world will be open far more widely to those in urban centers than those populating the poor, rural countryside. Among workers' groups, participants still need to speak English to participate. In Ireland, the "inevitable" advance of technology is aimed at adults seeking career advancement. In South Africa, online education may be a way to perpetuate distance (physical and psychic) between races; in the United States, the gap between haves and have-nots continues to grow.

The essential point of this critique of online education is not merely to point out the fallacy of overreliance on technology to produce democratic forms of adult education. Indeed, a balance is what we seek—balance in public policies surrounding the introduction and development of technology to education, balance in public funding for technological infrastructures, and balance in our zeal for technology as a form of open access. We ought to balance these hopes with more traditional solutions and proactive attempts to redress the elitism of the university. We must seek ways to use technology for democratic ends that are sincere not only in their rhetoric but in their implementation. Such systems need to recognize the inherently mediated nature of online education, the inequities that are too often perpetuated rather than redressed by their use, and the homogenization of the culture that results from monolithic online education solutions. We fear that balance is impossible to reach when, as David Noble (2002) points out, we have created "a technological tapeworm in the guts of higher education feeding off its host" (p. vii). The fear now is that we've introduced the virus worldwide—that the technological feeding frenzy is far from over but rather just beginning on an international rampage. The needs of the poor, underserved, and disenfranchised stand little chance in the face of international capitalist e-learning.

REFERENCE

Noble, D. F. (2002). *Digital diploma mills.* New York: Monthly Review Press.

INDEX

ABC News 20/20 program, 152
Academy for Educational Development, United States, 187
Access:
  cross-border, 181
  in Africa, 201
  in Burkina Faso, 96
  in China, 28–29, 96
  in India, 59–60, 96
  in Ireland, 75, 79, 83
  in Korea, 96
  in Namibia, 214–219
  in New Zealand, 172–173
  in Niger, 96
  in Sub-Saharan Africa, 225–226, 230–233
  in Taiwan, 37–38, 45–47
  in United Kingdom, 93–96
  in United States, 96, 155–156
  issues of, 2–8
Access Rainbow, Canada, 138–139
Accreditation bodies, 146–147
Addiction to Internet, 150
Adoption cycles, e-learning, 241–242, 244
ADSL access, 38. *See also* Broadband Internet access
Adult education. *See* International study circles
Afele, J. S. C., 190, 195
Africa. *See* Namibia; Sub-Saharan Africa
African Diaspora, 230
African Renaissance, 223
African Virtual University, 188
Agre, Phil, 3

Aliant Corp., 135
"All Schools Connected Project," China, 26
Ambedkar Open University, India, 60
American Association of University Professors (AAUP), 147
American Federation of Teachers, 11
American Psychological Association (APA), 150
America Online (AOL), 135
Anadolu University (AU), Turkey, 116–117, 120
Annan, Kofi, 199, 208
Anthropocentrism, 9
Aotearoa. *See* New Zealand
Apartheid, 207
ARIADNE project, Europe, 181, 255
Articulated Instructional Media (AIM) project, University of Wisconsin, United States, 232
Asia, 17–20. *See also* China; India; Taiwan
Asian Association of Open Universities (AAOU), 185
Association for Progressive Communication, 102
Asynchronous discussion, 98, 176
Audioconferencing, 186
AusAID, Australia, 185–186
Australia, 161–162, 179–197
  borderless virtual learning in, 194–195
  consortia in, 191–193
  culture and pedagogy in, 189–190
  development programs in, 185–188
  distance education in, 180–184

free trade in education in, 184–185
sustainability of distance education in, 189
Australian Federal Government, 194
Australian National Board of Employment, Education, and Training, 180
Australian University Quality Agency, 183
Automatized e-learning, 148
Autonomy, individual, 9

"Back to basics" curricula, 141
Bang, J., 78
Barlow, M., 9
Bates, A. W., 189, 195, 227
Beeby, Clarence, 167
Berry, W., 148
Bilkent University, Turkey, 116
Birla Institute of Technology, India, 57
Blackboard course management tool, 248
Blight, D., 179
Blueprint for the Future of ICT in Irish Education, A (Department of Education and Science), 74
Boisjoly, Élise, 135
Borderless virtual learning, 194–195, 233–234
Bottom-up learning networks, 190
Bowers, C. A., 9, 176, 177
Boycotts, 102. *See also* Unions
Boyer, E., 80
Brand loyalty, 18
Bridgestone/Firestone campaign, 102
British Columbia Task Force on Internationalization, Canada, 180
Broadband Internet access:
 in India, 61
 in Ireland, 75
 in New Zealand, 169–170, 173
 in Taiwan, 37, 39–40
 multimedia and, 195
Brown, J. S., 229
Bruce, B. C., 72–73
Bureaucracy, streamlining, 147
Burkina Faso, Africa, 96

Bush, George W., 154
Buyukseren, Y., 123

Cain, J., 182–183
Caldwell Partners, Canada, 132
Canada's Schoolnet, 131–144
 connectivity in, 137–140
 First Peoples and, 127–129
 public screen of, 140–142
 stakeholders of, 132–137
Canadian International Development Research Center (IDRC), 185
Canadian Teachers Federation, 138
CANDLE project, Europe, 181
Capitalism, virtual, 8
Cardean University, United States and United Kingdom, 250
Carleton University, Canada, 132
Cellular telephone networks, 207
Center for Development of Advanced Computing, India, 57
Central Committee of the Chinese Communist Party, 22, 46
Centre for Flexible and Distance Learning, University of Aukland, New Zealand, 262
Centre for Māori Innovation and Development, New Zealand, 171
Chambers, John, 227
Chatelaine magazine, Canada, 132
"Chat" mechanisms, 110
Chi, Chiang Chia, 35
Children, e-learning impact on, 43
China, 21–34
 access in, 28–29, 96
 demand for distance education in, 27–28
 distance *versus* traditional degrees in, 29–31
 educational funding in, 31–32
 foreign educational offerings in, 30–31
 open access in, 258
 rural areas in, 25–27
China Central Radio TC University (CRTVU), 28
China Education and Research Network, 25–26, 28
Chomsky, Noam, 10

Chrétien, Aline, 141
Chronicle of Higher Education,
  11, 147, 257
Cisco Systems, Inc., 135, 227
Clark, H. F., 9
Clarke, A., 95, 97
Class (economic), e-learning and,
  18–19
Clinton, Hillary, 141
"Clip art" e-learning, 249
Collective bargaining, 138
Colonialism, 207
Commercialization of education, 141,
  182–183, 229
Commission on the Future of State and
  Land-Grant Universities, United
  States, 258
Commodification of e-learning,
  182–183, 185, 231
Commonwealth of Learning, India,
  56, 185, 194
Commonwealth Secretariat, Australia,
  180, 193
Communism, 18, 46. *See also* China
Community Access (CAP) program,
  Canada, 131
Community building, on Internet,
  150, 157
Community Learning Centers,
  LearnLink, United States, 187
Competitiveness. *See* Economic
  competitiveness; Market
  competition in e-learning
Computer Assisted Telephone
  Interviews (CATI), 37
Computer games, 95
Computer literacy, 119–120
Computers, international study circles
  and, 106, 111–112
Computers for Schools Program,
  Canada, 133
Concordia University, Canada,
  261, 263
Concord University, United States, 153
Conduit view of language, 9
Confederation of Indian Industry, 61
"Connectedness Strategy," Canada, 134
"Connecting Canadians" agenda,
  131, 133, 136

Connectivity, 70
  in Canada's Schoolnet, 133, 135,
    137–140
  in Ireland, 75, 83
Consortia for distance education,
  191–193
Consumer Protection Act,
  United States, 147
Context-free knowledge, 9
Convergence, 236
Cooke, Sir Robin, 166
Coopers & Lybrand accounting
  firm, 148
Copyrights, 185
Corporate University Xchange,
  Inc., UK, 97
Corporations, e-learning and, 154, 156,
  182–183
Correspondence courses, 52, 231
Correspondence School, New Zealand,
  166–167
Cost of education. *See* Funding
  e-learning
Credentials, of learners, 185, 229
Crump, B., 174–175
Cuban, L., 136, 142
Cultural sensitivity:
  globalization and, 217–218
  in Africa, 202
  in Australia, 161, 189–190
  in Europe, 69
  in Turkey, 117, 123–124
Cunningham, S., 194
Currie Report of 1962,
  New Zealand, 165
Curtin University of Technology,
  Australia, 182, 262
Customization, 8–10

Daniel, J. S., 225, 227
Davis, D., 179
Dawson, M., 7
*Decisions on Improving Education
  in Rural China* (State
  Council, 2003), 25
Degrees, distance *versus* traditional,
  18, 29–31
Delivery systems, 148, 229–230
DeLuca, K. M., 140

Department of Adult Education, Ministry of Basic Education, Sport and Culture, Namibia, 218
Department of Education and Science, Ireland, 74
Department of Information Technology, India, 61
Department of Telecommunications, India, 61
Deregulation, in United States, 157
de Wit, H., 180
Dhanarajan, G., 195
Dial-up modem access:
　in New Zealand, 173–174
　in Taiwan, 38
　in Turkey, 119–120
Dianda distance education system, China, 21
Diffusion of innovations, 8
Digital Access Index 2002, International Telecommunications Union (ITU), 38
Digital Culture Development and Training Centers, Taiwan, 49
Digital divide:
　in Canada, 131, 137
　in India, 63–65
　in international distance education, 190
　in New Zealand, 175
　in Taiwan, 37–40
　in United States, 127
Digital Horizons (Ministry of Education, New Zealand), 165, 167–168
Digital Women of the Year program, 132
"Diploma mills," 147, 234
DirecPC™, Canada, 133
Disenfranchised populations, 18
　in India, 52
　in Ireland, 72, 79, 86
　in Taiwan, 36, 43
　language to describe, 69
Distance education, 18
　accountability of, 162
　as borderless virtual learning, 194–195
　as "second-rate," 18–19, 52, 121–122

　boom and bust of, 251–252
　changes in universities from, 226–230
　conditions for, 252–254
　face-to-face teaching *versus,* 237
　for Māori in New Zealand, 164, 176–177
　in Africa, 225
　in Australia, 180–184, 188
　in China, 21, 23–24, 27–28
　in India, 55–58
　in Ireland, 77–79
　in Namibia, 211
　in New Zealand, 163, 166–167, 172–173
　in Sub-Saharan Africa, 230–234
　in Taiwan, 36
　in United Kingdom, 90–91, 93
　in United States, 145, 147
　open distance learning model of, 78
　quality of, 2
　sustainability of, 189
　synchronous, 176
　Turkish attitudes toward, 122, 125
　See also Turkey, distance education in
Distance education *versus* traditional degrees:
　in China, 29–30
　in India, 52
　in Ireland, 85
　in Turkey, 121–122
Distance Open Higher Education, China, 22
Distributed knowledge production system, 228
Diversity, 115, 157, 189. *See also* Cultural sensitivity
Dong Hwa University, Taiwan, 49
Dot.com boom, 251
Dotterweich, 47
Dropout rates, from online courses, 97–98
Drucker, P. F., 223, 226
Dual open distance learning model, 78
Duguid, P., 229
Duke, C., 182

Earnings, distance education and, 93, 121
E-banking, 209
Ebeling, A., 3
E-commerce, 185
E-conferencing, 35
Economic competitiveness from e-learning:
 knowledge economy and, 35, 42, 140, 165, 177
 of Canada, 137
 of Ireland, 71, 83
 of Taiwan, 40–42
 of United States, 154
Economies of scale, 145, 253–254
Education, adult. *See* International study circles
Education Act of 1877, New Zealand, 164
Educationally disadvantaged populations. *See* Disenfranchised populations
Educational opportunity, 3
Educational television (ETV):
 in China, 23–24
 in Namibia, 211
 in United Kingdom, 90
Education Review Office, New Zealand, 167
Educators, Internet use by:
 in Ireland, 75, 81–82
 in Namibia, 210
 in New Zealand, 173
Efficiency of e-learning:
 calculating, 253
 diversity and individuality *versus*, 115
 in United Kingdom, 90–91
 in United States, 147–149, 157
Egalitarianism, 165, 177
e-Generation Manpower Cultivation Plan, Taiwan, 49
E-governance, 185
Elderly populations, Internet usage by, 39
E-learning. *See* Distance education
E-learning Advisory Group, New Zealand, 171

E-learning Collaborative Development, and Innovation and Development Funds, New Zealand, 171
E-learning Industry Research and Development Alliance, Taiwan, 44
E-learning Public Network Access Solution provider market, Taiwan, 43–45
Electrification, 62, 64
Electronic-based testing organizations, 250
Elitism, computers and, 3, 68, 106
Empowerment, 213
England. *See* United Kingdom
English, as technology language, 109, 190, 258
Entrepreneurial academy, 228
Equity. *See* Social equity
"E-school bags," 42
Ethnic minorities, Internet usage by:
 in Canada, 127–129, 133
 in Namibia, 207
 in New Zealand, 164, 166, 174, 176–177
 in Taiwan, 37, 39, 44
 See also Digital divide
EuroPACE 2000 consortium, 186
Europe, 67–70. *See also* International Study Circles; Ireland; Turkey; United Kingdom
European Association of Distance Teaching Universities (EADTU), 186
European Distance Education Network (EDEN), 186
European Union (EU), 181, 186
Evaluation and Investigation Program, Australia, 183
Exporting e-learning, 129

Face-to-face teaching, 237
Farrell, C., 182
Farrell, G., 185, 194, 195
FernUniversität, Germany, 78
Fiber optic lines, 207, 219
Financial benefits. *See* Earnings, distance education and
Firat University, Turkey, 116

First Nations School Net, Canada, 133
"First order fingertip effect," 174
First Peoples, in Canada, 127–129
Flat-rate narrowband Internet
  access, 83
Flexner, Abraham, 151–152
Focus on Internet News and Data
  (FIND), 37
Fordist culture, of United States, 147
Foreign educational offerings,
  30–31, 191, 250
Foster, J. B., 7
Fraser, Peter, 165
Free trade in education, 184–185
Funding e-learning:
  in Canada, 142
  in China, 29, 31–32
  in India, 54–55
  in New Zealand, 171–172, 173–174
  in Taiwan, 47–48
  in Turkey, 119–120
  in United Kingdom, 92
  in United States, 154–156
  public, 10–12

G. I. Bill, 1
Gandhe, 64
Gates, Bill, 141
General Agreement on Trade in
  Services (GATS), 185
Geographical isolation, 93
Ghana, 187
Gibbons, A., 228
Giddens, A., 223
Ginsburg, Ruth, Justice, U. S.
  Supreme Court, 153
Global Development Learning
  Network, World Bank, 188
Globalization, 8–10
  as international study circle
    subject, 107
  commodification of education
    and, 185, 258
  cultural sensitivity and, 217–218
  definition of, 223
  International Forum on
    Globalization and, 102
  Turkish distance education and, 123
Globalized learning networks, 190

Global Learning Services Division,
  University of Southern
  Queensland, Australia, 183
Global System for Mobile
  Communication (GSM),
  Namibia, 207
Global University Alliance, 191–193
Gold, Lawrence, 11
Goldsmith, 190
Google.com search engine, 243
Gore, Al, 154, 157
GrassRoots program, Canada,
  133, 138, 141
Great Britain. *See* United Kingdom
Grundtvig Scandinavian folk
  schools, 101
Gubernick, L., 3

Hall, J. W., 3
Hanna, D. E., 189
Hargadon, A., 223
Hargittai, E., 137
Harvard University Extension School,
  United States, 257–258
Hawkridge, D., 185
Head Start program, United States,
  152–153
Herod, A., 102
Hewitt, J., 182–183
Hibernia College, Ireland, 80–82, 85
Higher Education Authority,
  Ireland, 77
High-speed Internet access.
  See Broadband Internet access
Highways and Pathways Report
  (E-learning Advisory Group,
  New Zealand), 171
Hills, J., 6
Hirschkop, K., 7, 10
"Hole-in-the-wall experiment,"
  India, 62–63
Home working, 209
Homogenization of learning, 9.
  See also Cultural sensitivity
Hsin Chu Science Park, Taiwan, 43
Hub-periphery learning
  networks, 190
Hulsmann, T., 95
Hu'nan University, China, 32

ICT Capacity Building @ USP program, Japan, 186
ICT School Census (National Centre for Technology in Education, Ireland), 74
Illiteracy, 53, 55, 58. *See also* Literacy problems
ImpacT 2001: Learning with IT (Minister for Information Technology's Advisory Group, New Zealand), 167
Imperial Oil Corp., 135
India, 52–65
  access in, 59–60
  current education in, 53–54
  digital divide in, 63–65
  funding of education in, 54–55
  infrastructure inadequacies in, 60–63
  IT resources of, 96
  open and distance education in, 55–58
  overview of, 52–53
Indian Education Ministry, 53
Indian Institute of Technology, 57, 60
Indira Gandhi National Open University (IGNOU), India, 52, 57
Individuality, e-learning and, 115
Individualization, of e-learning, 8–10
Industrialization, of e-learning, 17–18, 40–43
Industry Canada, 132, 134–135, 138, 140–142
iNET project, Namibia, 207
Information and communication technology, 41, 82–86
Information Highway Advisory Council (IHAC), Canada, 132–133
Information Society Commission, Ireland, 83
Information superhighway, 6
Information Technology Plan, India, 59
Infrastructure:
  in Africa, 200
  in India, 60–63
  in Namibia, 206–208, 207, 219
  in New Zealand, 174
  in Sub-Saharan Africa, 227
  Virtual Colombo Plan for, 188

Inner Mongolia Autonomous Region, China, 26
Innovation, 8, 67, 72–73
Institute of Information Industry, 37
Institute of Land and Food Resources Global Seminar, University of Melbourne, Australia, 181
Instructional methods, 124
Intellectual property, 185
International Council for Distance Education, 183, 185
International Donor Agencies, 208, 210
International Federation of Chemical, Energy, Mine, and General Workers Unions (ICEM), 102
International Forum on Globalization, 102
Internationalizing curriculum. *See* Australia
International Metalworkers Federation World Council, 105
International Standards Association (ISO), 183
International study circles, 101–114
  background on, 102–103
  on computers and worker education, 111–113
  in practice, 105–111
  theory of, 103–105
International Technology University (ITU), 154
International Telecommunications Union, 96
Internet "literacy," 22–25
"Inverse care law," 92
Investment in education, 10–11, 154–155
Ireland, 71–88
  career advancement in, 258
  information and communications technology in, 82–86
  on-line education issues in, 81–82
  overview of, 71–72
  policy framework in, 72–74
  primary and post-primary on-line education in, 74–77
  university on-line education in, 77–81
Irwin, K., 176
Islamic oral tradition, 124

Isolation, e-learning and, 93, 150
Istanbul Bilgi University, Turkey, 116

Jadavpur University, India, 57
Japanese International Cooperation Agency (JICA), 185–186
Jenson, J., 140
JITAITS ("just in time artificial intelligence tutors"), 99
Job market, 121
Job security, 138, 155
Jones University, United States, 146–147

Kaneko, Motohisa, 250
Kappan Testing Service, 153
Karadeniz Teknik University, Turkey, 116
Karelis, C., 189
KAWM network, New Zealand, 170, 176
Kennedy, John F., 127
Khan, Abdul Waheed (vice chancellor, IGNOU), 56
Kiosks, 63
Knowledge, context-free, 9
Knowledge economy, 35, 42, 140, 165, 177
Knowledge Innovation National Grid (KING), Taiwan, 41
Koocheching First Nations School, Canada, 133
Korea, 96, 192
Kostaszek, Karen, 132
Kura Kaupapa, New Zealand, 166

Language:
  conduit view of, 9
  English, as technology, 109, 190, 258
  in Europe, 69
  in India, 64
  Web-based instruction in, 250
Law degrees, online, 153
"Leading from behind," 235–237
Leadspace project, New Zealand, 170
LearnDirect program, United Kingdom, 91, 94–95
Learning, homogenization of, 9

Learning centers, 94, 118
"Learning in the Europe of Knowledge" conference, 2004, 79
Learning Management Systems, New Zealand, 171
Learning to Change: ICT in Schools (*OECD*), Ireland, 84
LearnLink, Academy for Educational Development, United States, 187
Leaving Certificate Applied (LCA) Programme, Ireland, 76–77
Lewis, B., 140
Liberal-progressive approach to education, 165
Libertarians, 149
LibraryNet program, Canada, 131, 133
Lifelong learning, 48, 79, 153
Literacy problems, 72
Localized learning networks, 190
Low-income populations, Internet usage by, 37. *See also* Disenfranchised populations

Market competition in e-learning, 78, 128, 145, 250, 253
Market for e-learning, 184–185
Market Information Center (MIC), Taiwan, 43
Mason, 190
Massachusetts Institute of Technology (MIT), United States, 61, 181
Massey University, Australia, 167, 261
Matthewson, D., 190
Mayadas, F., 189
McIlroy, A., 174–175
McLennan, Anne, 141
McNay, I., 228
Media Lab Asia, 61
Memorization, in learning, 124
Meritocracy, 1, 152–155
MERLOT project, United States, 181, 243–244, 255
Microsoft Corp., 44, 135, 141, 219
Middle East Technical University, Turkey, 116
Migrant Workers in the Global Economy international study circle, 108

"Minimally invasive education," India, 63
Minister for Information Technology's Advisory Group, New Zealand, 167
Ministry of Basic Education, Sport and Culture, Namibia, 218
Ministry of Communications and Information Technology, India, 62
Ministry of Education, New Zealand, 167–168
Ministry of Education (MOE), of People's Republic of China, 22–23, 28–29
Ministry of Information and Broadcasting, Directorate Audiovisual and Communications Commission, Namibia, 211
Ministry of Regional, Local Government and Housing Sub-National Structures, Namibia, 216
Minority peoples. *See* Ethnic minorities, Internet usage by
Mintzberg, H., 190
Mitra, Sugata (National Indian Institute of Technology, India), 62–63
Mixed open distance learning model, 78
M-learning, 99
Mobile devices, 42, 99, 207
Mobile Telecommunication Corporation (MTC), Namibia, 207
Modern Distance Education (MED) project, China, 31
Mohammad (vice chancellor, Ambedkar Open University), India, 60
Moll, M., 141
Monticello University, United States, 147
Moran, L., 193
Motivation to access, 95
Mugridge, I., 193
Multimedia, 35, 78, 119, 135, 195
Murphy, K. L., 124

Namibia, 205–221
  access in, 214–218
  constraints in, 219
  democracy in, 212–214
  development in, 208–210
  education in, 210–212
  infrastructure in, 206–208
Namibia College of Open Learning, 216–217
Namibian Broadcasting Corporation, 213
National Alliance for the Fundamental Right to Education, India, 55
National Association of State Universities and Land-Grant Colleges, United States, 257
National Center for High-Performance Computing, Taiwan, 41
National Centre for Technology in Education, Ireland, 74, 76, 85
National Conference on Educational Technology, 153
National Council for Curriculum and Assessment (NCCA), Ireland, 261
National Democratic Institute for International Affairs (NDI), Namibia, 212
National Digital Archives Program (NDAP), Taiwan, 41, 49
National e-learning Technology Plan, Ministry of Economy and Industry, Taiwan, 41
National Institute for Adult Continuing Education (NIACE), United Kingdom, 93
National Institute of Multimedia Education (NIME), Japan, 250, 255
National Open School (NOS), India, 55
National Policy on Education (NPE), India, 55
National Public Radio, 151
National Qualifications Framework, Ireland, 79
National Science and Technology Program, Taiwan, 41
National Secondary Tertiary Curriculum Alignment Project, New Zealand, 171
National Tong Hwa University, Taiwan, 49

National University of Ireland (NUI), Cork, 261
Nehova, Kandi, 213
Nelkin, Dorothy, 157
Nepotism, 152
NetVarsity, India, 60
Network of Innovative Schools, Canada, 135–136
Network Science Park for e-learning, Taiwan, 42–43
Network to Savings program, Canada, 133
New York University, United States, 5
New Zealand, 161–178
    compulsory education in, 167–172
    distance education since 2000 in, 172–173
    distance education through 1999 in, 166–167
    educational context in, 164–166
    infrastructure in, 174–175
    Internet affordability in, 173–174
    Māori distance education in, 164, 176–177
New Zealand Census of Population and Dwellings, 173
New Zealand Ministry of Education, 165
New Zealand Overseas Development Agency, 186
NextEd Limited, Hong Kong, 191
Nielsen Ratings, 242
Niger, 96
Noble, D. F., 2, 229, 230, 258
Non-government organizations (NGOs), 54
Non-profit organizations (NPOs), 54
Nova Southeastern University, 5
Nzongola-Ntalaja, Georges, 201

Office of International Partnerships, Canada, 132, 135, 142
Olsen, A., 179
One-way technologies, 118
On-the-job training, 46–47
Open access:
    future of, 258
    in China, 28–29
    in United States, 155–156
    international, 195
    issues of, 2–8
    to education, 231–232
Open and Distance Learning Association of Australia (ODLAA), 262
OpenCourseWare programs, MIT, United States, 181
Open distance learning model, 78
Open Polytechnic of New Zealand, 166
OpenUniversiteit, Netherlands, 78
Open University model, 78
Oral tradition, 124
Ottawa, Naoki, 250
Outsourcing, 96
Overcoming Social Exclusion through Online Learning project, United Kingdom, 93
Ozkul, A. E., 120–122

Pan-global open learning systems, 195
Panos organization, 61
Paraguay, 187
Peeples, J., 140
Pennsylvania State University, United States, 5, 257, 262–263, 265
"People's Network" centers, United Kingdom, 94
Perinbam, Lewis, 56
Perkins, D. N., 174
Perraton, H., 182
Perry, Walter, 231
Peters, O., 235, 237
Picot Report of 1988, New Zealand, 165
Policies, public, 10–12, 154
Political instability, 200
Populations, disenfranchised. See Disenfranchised populations
Post-primary on-line education, 74–77
Poverty, 53–54, 214. See also Disenfranchised populations
Power, gap in, 6–7
PowerPoint presentation software, Microsoft Corp., 248–249
Primary on-line education, 74–77
Privatization, 141, 154–155

Problem-based curriculum, in
    e-learning, 246–247
Profits, 18
Programme for International Student
    Assessment (PISA), 72
Project PROBE, New Zealand,
    168, 173–174
Prometric testing organization, 250
"Proxy democracy," 109
Psychological access, 95
Public Network E-Learning
    System, Taiwan, 49
Public policies, 10–12, 154
Pupil-computer ratios, 74
Purchasing power of currencies, 192

Quality control of distance
    education, 147, 185
Quality standards, Framework
    and Guidelines project,
    New Zealand, 172
Quesada, Marlon, 104

Radio, 21, 213–214
Rails to Trails Program,
    United States, 155
Rands Afrikaans University, South
    Africa (RAU), 211
Reich, Robert, 151
Rensselaer Polytechnic Institute
    (RPI), United States, 246
*Report on the Internet Usage of the
    Population in Taiwan, The,* 37
Retention of e-learning, 67, 96–99
Rhetoric of shared experience,
    103–104
Riley, R. W., 153
Risk-sharing, 192, 200
Robertson, H., 9
Rose, E., 136
Rote memorization, in learning, 124
Rural/remote populations:
    in China, 23, 25–27
    in India, 52
    in Ireland, 70, 76
    in Namibia, 205, 207, 210, 218
    in Sub-Saharan Africa, 225
    in Turkey, 118, 124
    school shortages in, 24

Sakarya University, Turkey, 116
Sallis Report of 1990,
    New Zealand, 167
SAT testing organization, 250
Scandinavian folk schools, 101
Scarcity, of educational opportunity, 3
Scholarship Reconsidered (Boyer), 80
Schoolnet. *See* Canada's Schoolnet
SCHOOLNET project, Namibia, 207
Schools, 24, 26, 141. *See also*
    Canada's Schoolnet
Schools Integration Project (SIP),
    National Centre for Technology
    in Education, Ireland, 76, 85
Schools IT 2000 (Department of
    Education and Science),
    Ireland, 74
Schools Online (SOL), India, 63
Schultz, Charles, 161
Science Canada, 132
Sclove, R., 149
Shanghai Jiaotong University, 26
Shared experience, rhetoric of, 103–104
Simon, J., 165, 172
Simpson, C., 93
Singapore, 192
Six-Year National Development Plan,
    Challenge 2008, Taiwan, 36–37
SkillNet.ca program, Canada, 133
Sloan Consortium, 148
Social equity, from e-learning,
    2, 18, 28, 36, 46. *See also*
    Disenfranchised populations;
    Rural/remote populations
Social exclusion, 67, 69, 92–93
"Social justice," 91
Social obstacles, 120–122
Social practice discourse (Bruce), 73
Socioeconomic status, 124
Software industry, 59
South Africa, 205, 219, 258
Southern African Development
    Community (SADC) Protocol on
    Transport, Communication and
    Meteorology, 209–210
South Pacific, 187
Spronk, B., 190
Staffing, of distance education
    programs, 27

Startech-Learning Together:
   video-conferencing, Ireland, 76
Streaming media, 36
Streamlining bureaucracy, 147
Student Selection and Placement
   Center (SSPC), Turkey, 120
Studio Physics, 246
Study circles. *See* International
   study circles
Sub-Saharan Africa, 222–240
   access in, 230–233
   distance education in, 230–234
   e-learning changes to universities
      in, 226–230
   higher education crisis in, 224–226
   "leading from behind" in, 235–237
Sustainability, 61, 189
Sutton, R., 223
Sweden, 96, 128
Swift, Jonathan, 89
Synchronous online education, 176

Taiwan, 35–51
   demand for e-learning in, 45–47
   digital gap in, 37–40, 47–48
   e-learning availability in, 45–47
   e-learning beneficiaries in, 43–45
   e-learning industry in, 40–43
   government activity in, 48–49
   overview of, 35–37
Taiwan Advanced Research
   and Education Network
   (TWAREN), 41
Taiwan Digital Archives (TDA), 41
Taiwan National Science Council
   (NSC), 35
Taxes on Internet use, 154
Teachers' use of Internet. *See* Educators,
   Internet use by
"Teaching machines," 90
Teaching Skill's Initiative (National
   Centre for Technology in
   Education), Ireland, 74
Te Ako Hikohika Wānanga project,
   New Zealand, 172
Technikon South Africa (TSA), 211
Technological determinism, 128
Technological imperative, 136
Technology-mediated learning systems,
   231–232

Te Kete Ipurangi website,
   New Zealand, 168
Telecom Namibia, 207
Television, 21, 64, 118. *See also*
   Educational television
Tertiary online initiatives, New Zealand,
   170–171
Te Whare Wananga Awanuiarangi
   education provider,
   New Zealand, 176
Thaman, K. A., 190
Thomson Learning Corp., 192–193,
   242, 251
Tibet University, 26
Todai, Inc., Japan, 250
TOEFL testing organization, 250
Tokyo University, Japan, 250
*Toward a Unified E-Learning
   Strategy* (UK), 91
Training:
   in Canada, 138
   in Namibia, 216, 219
   in United States, 128, 145, 154
Transnational corporations, 103
Transnationals Information Exchange
   (TIE), 102
Traveling Peoples, 70
Treaty of Waitangi, New Zealand,
   164–166, 176
"Trickle down" polices, 154
Trow, Martin, 100
Turkey, distance education in, 115–126
   affordability of, 119–120
   cultural sensitivity and, 123–124
   social obstacles to, 120–122
   time and location of, 117–118
Turkish Council of Higher Education
   (TCHE), 115–116, 119
Turkish Radio and Television
   (TRT) channels, 118
Turkish Republic of Northern
   Cyprus, 117
*2002 Investigation of the Digital
   Divide in Taiwan Areas, The*
   (Yuan Ze University), 39

U. K. Department for International
   Development, 185
U. K. Open University (UKOU),
   91, 93, 184, 229, 231–232, 264

U. S. Congressional Budget Office, 155
U. S. Department of Education,
 153, 257
U. S. Supreme Court, 153
Uludag University, Turkey, 262
Underprivileged populations.
 See Disenfranchised populations;
 Rural/remote populations
UNDP, 185
UNED, Spain, 78
UNESCO, 185, 209, 225
UNext, Inc., 193, 250
Unions, 102, 138. *See also*
 International study circles
United Kingdom, 89–100
 access to e-learning in, 93–96
 distance learning financial
  benefits in, 93
 retention in, 67, 96–99
 social exclusion in, 92–93
 "widening participation" agenda
  of, 91–92
 See also U. K. Open University
  (UKOU)
United National Development Program
 (UNDP), 55
United Nations Working Group on
 Informatics, 208
United States, 145–159
 Academy for Educational
  Development of, 187
 access in, 96
 Articulated Instructional Media
  (AIM) project, University of
  Wisconsin, of, 232
 digital divide in, 127
 meritocracy myth in, 152–155
 MERLOT project of, 181
 open access in, 155–156
 open higher education system in,
  146–150
 vocational higher education system
  in, 151–152
 vocational nature, of on-line/
  distance education in, 128
 See also Weatherstation project
United States Agency for International
 Development (USAID), 185, 208
United Steelworkers of America
 (USWA), 102

Universitas21 Global, 192–193, 251
Universitate Aberta, Portugal, 78
Universities in the digital age (Brown
 and Duguid), 229
University College Cork, Ireland, 80
University of California at Los Angeles,
 United States, 5
University of Maryland, United
 States, 5
University of Melbourne, Australia,
 181, 192
University of Namibia, 212, 263
University of Pennsylvania, United
 States, 242
University of Phoenix, United States, 5
University of Plymouth's Social
 Research and Regeneration Unit,
 United Kingdom, 263
University of South Africa (UNISA),
 211, 235
University of Southern Queensland,
 Australia, 183
University of Texas, Austin, United
 States, 262
University of Wisconsin,
 United States, 232
University on-line education, 77–81
"Upskilling," 92
Urban underclass, 127
Useem, A., 222
*Use of Information Technology in
 Schools* (Education Review
 Office), New Zealand, 167
USPNet, 186
USQNet, University of Southern
 Queensland, Australia, 183

Vajpayee, Atal Behar (prime minister,
 India), 59, 61–62
Value-neutral tools, computers as, 8
Van Dusen, G. C., 5
Videoconferencing:
 in Australia, 182, 186
 in Ireland, 76
 in Japan, 186
 in New Zealand, 176, 186
 in Turkey, 118
Video games, 35–36
Vidyakash project, India, 57
Virtual capitalism, 8

Virtual Colombo Plan, Australia, 188
Virtual Inequity (Dotterweich), 47
Virtual learning, international, 194–195, 233–234
Virtual Learning Environments (VLEs), Ireland, 78
Vocational nature, of on-line/distance education:
  as primary benefit, 5
  in China, 27–28
  in Ireland, 77
  in United States, 128, 146, 151–152, 157
  See also International study circles

Walden University, 5
Wangusa, T., 199
Warshauer, M., 137
Waterman, P., 113
Weatherstation project, 202, 241–256
  campus protocol for, 242–243
  e-learning boom and bust and, 251–252
  e-learning conditions and, 252–254
  international, 254–256
  tracking web learning and, 243–249
Web-based education. *See* Distance education
WebCT course management tool, 248
Wedemeyer, Charles, 232
Whare Kura, New Zealand, 166

Whare Wānanga, New Zealand, 166, 176
Wide area networks (WANs), 79
"Widening participation" agenda, United Kingdom, 91–92
Wilson, Jack, 246
Winner, L., 6, 11
Wireless Application Protocol (WAP), 94, 99
Wireless Internet access, 195, 207
Withdrawal rates, from online courses, 97–98
Women, in Africa, 218
Women in the Global Food Industry international study circle, 110
Woodley, A., 93
Workloads, of educators, 138
World Bank, 185, 188
World Trade Organization (WTO), 185

Xi'an Jiaotong University, China, 26

Yeats, W. B., 67
Yu, Wei (vice minister, Ministry of Education, China), 23–24
Yuan, Fujie, 250
Yuan Ze University, Taiwan, 39

Zhipeng, Liu (associate director of Higher Education, MOE, China), 31
Zi'ang, Chen, 17

ABOUT THE EDITOR

Alison A. Carr-Chellman is Associate Professor of Education at Pennyslvania State University, where she is in charge of the Instructional Systems program in the Department of Learning and Performance Systems. She taught elementary school and worked in business and industry prior to joining the academy as a faculty member. Her research interests include critiques of distance education and e-learning, systems theory and thinking, educational systems design, critical systems, and user-design. She received bachelor's and master's degrees in education from Syracuse University, and she earned her doctorate at Indiana University–Bloomington, where she studied instructional systems technology with an emphasis in educational systems design.

ABOUT THE CONTRIBUTORS

Bill Anderson is a Senior Lecturer at Massey University in New Zealand. His teaching interests lie in the areas of distance education and teacher education, with a specific focus on the use of information technologies in education. His research interests lie in the area of online education. Current projects include inquiry into interaction and control in computer-mediated communication and investigation of the impact of distance-delivered teacher education programs on subsequent teaching practice.

Paul Conway is a College Lecturer in the Education Department in the National University of Ireland (NUI), Cork. He has been a Visiting Scholar each summer since 2000 in the Department of Counseling, Educational Psychology and Special Education (CEPSE) at Michigan State University, where he teaches in the master's program in educational technology. He previously served as Assistant Professor of Educational Psychology and Human Development at Cleveland State University. He is currently coeditor of *Irish Educational Studies*. His research interests include ICT policy in education, teacher learning, and learning theories.

Diane Dechief is a master of arts candidate at Concordia University in Montreal. She has worked in the fields of IT training and language training for newcomers to Canada. Her thesis research focuses on the social impacts of online access to information, particularly among recent immigrants.

Sarah FitzPatrick is Deputy Chief Executive of the National Council for Curriculum and Assessment (NCCA) in Ireland. She has taught in primary, post-primary, and third-level settings in Ireland and in the United States. She has also worked with a nonprofit educational organization providing in-career professional development support to teachers using ICT. Her current work involves re-envisioning curriculum and assessment in the digital age/knowledge society and developing appropriate supports for teachers and students.

Husra Gursoy is a doctoral candidate in the Instructional Systems Program at Pennsylvania State University. She earned a bachelor of science degree in mathematics from Uludag University, Turkey, and a master's degree in instructional systems technology from Indiana University, where she held a full academic scholarship from the Turkish Ministry of Education. Her research interests lie in instructional design of constructivist learning environments, problem-based learning, and educational systemic design.

Jia Qi Jiang is a doctoral student in the quantitative methods research program in the Department of Educational Psychology at the University of Texas at Austin. She previously taught public school for a number of years in Taiwan, where she integrated multimedia and technology in teaching of English as a second language in K-12 levels. Her passion for the gap of educational accessibility and computer literacy through information technology grew out of this teaching experience. Her research interests include evaluation and measurement in education, educational technology, and distance education.

Colin Latchem has more than 30 years of experience encouraging and supporting educational development in higher education. He has worked in the United Kingdom and Australian higher education systems and served as president of the Open and Distance Learning Association of Australia (ODLAA). Since retiring in 1997 from a professorial level position as head of the Teaching Learning Group at Curtin University of Technology in Australia, he has been involved in open and distance education research and consultancy in China, Hong Kong, Brunei Darussalam, Philippines, Japan, the South Pacific, the West Indies, the United Kingdom, Canada, and the United States. He has written extensively on open and distance education, and one of his books, *Leadership for 21st Century Learning* (with Donald Hanna), received the 2002 Charles Wedemeyer Award for the best book of the year on distance education in the United States.

Wayne Mackintosh is Associate Professor and director of the Centre for Flexible and Distance Learning at the University of Auckland. Prior to his current position, he spent eleven years working at the University of South Africa, an open learning and distance education institution and one of the mega-universities of the world. He is actively involved in the theory and practice of open distance learning and has participated in a range of international consultancies and projects, including work for the Commonwealth of Learning, the International Monetary Fund, UNESCO, and the World Bank. He is a member of the editorial board of *Open Learning* and publishes regularly in the field of flexible and distance learning. His current research interests focus on strategy innovation and organizational transformation associated with establishing new pedagogy now possible through contemporary advances in digital communication technologies.

William F. Massy is Professor Emeritus of Education and Business Administration at Stanford University and president of the Jackson Hole Higher Education Group, Inc. In the 1970s and 1980s, he held senior administrative positions at Stanford University, where he pioneered the use of financial management and planning tools that have become standards in higher education. After founding the Stanford Institute for Higher Education Research (SIHER) in 1988, his research focused on institutional strategy, faculty roles and responsibilities, resource allocation processes, and universities as systems, including the development of a full-scale computer simulation of university behavior released by the Alfred P. Sloan Foundation in the fall of 2000 under the title *Virtual U*. His current research concerns academic quality, productivity, and quality assurance; technology utilization in teaching; resource allocation processes; and universities as economic entities.

Ben Salt is a Research Fellow at the University of Plymouth's Social Research and Regeneration Unit in the United Kingdom. He completed his doctorate in adult education at the University of Georgia and is a recipient of the American Association for Adult and Continuing Education Okes Award for Outstanding Research. His research interests include neoliberal globalization, spacial praxis, popular education, and the impact of publicly funded education initiatives.

Leslie Regan Shade is Associate Professor in the Department of Communication Studies at Concordia University, Montreal. Her research and teaching interests focus on the social, political, and ethical dimensions of ICTs.

Priya Sharma is Assistant Professor of Instructional Systems at Pennsylvania State University. Prior to this appointment, she worked in corporate multimedia training design and development in India and the United States for more than 5 years. Her research interests include appropriate uses of technology for learning environment design and the enabling roles of technology in contributing to self-organized learning.

R. Kavena Shalyefu is a Lecturer at the Department of Adult and Nonformal Education at the University of Namibia and is a doctoral candidate in education at the University of Massachusetts. She holds a bachelor of pedagogics degree from the University of Fort Hare, a bachelor's of education (postgraduate) degree from the University of South Africa (UNISA), a master's degree in education in adult and nonformal education from the University of Massachusetts. She is especially interested in improving teaching and learning, the design of effective and efficient instructional learning environments, and program planning and evaluation.

Ormond Simpson is Senior Lecturer in Institutional Research at the Institute of Educational Technology at the United Kingdom's Open University. He has worked in distance learning for more than 25 years, primarily in the area of student support, and previously taught in Africa and the United States. He is the author of books in this field: *Supporting Students in Online, Open, and Distance Learning* (2002) and *Student Retention in Online, Open, and Distance Learning* (2003).

Robert Zemsky is chair of the Learning Alliance for Higher Education at the University of Pennsylvania, which is a major experiment in bringing just-in-time strategic expertise to college and university presidents. He was founding director of the University of Pennsylvania's Institute for Research on Higher Education. The research for which he is best known has centered on how colleges and universities, in a world increasingly dominated by market forces, can be both mission-centered and market-smart. His writings have regularly appeared in *Policy Perspectives* and in a series of pioneering articles and analyses in *Change*. In 1998, *Change* named him as one of higher education's top 40 leaders for his role as an agenda-setter.

Ke Zhang is Assistant Professor of Instructional Technology in the Department of Educational Psychology and Leadership at Texas Technology University in Lubbock, Texas. Her research specialities are computer supported collaborative learning/work; problem solving; online collaborative learning; cognitive and meta-cognitive strategies for (online) collaborative problem solving; media behaviors in online learning environments; courseware design, development, and evaluation; courseware copyright; and social impacts of collaborative technologies.